Praise for *Becoming a Face of Grace*

Ed Khouri is a sensitive and caring guide who has walked alongside many people finding their way through a tangled web of performing, pleasing, pain avoiding, and pleasure-seeking. He has written a must-read primer for anyone seeking a more authentic life enjoying the *truly* free gift of grace—personally and for others. Expect to be surprised!"

— *Jean LaCour, Ph.D., founder of ICARE,*
Int'l Center for Addiction and Recovery Education

I continue to appreciate Ed Khouri's ability to write compellingly and simplify complex topics. Ed does not disappoint in this inspiring and remarkable work, *Becoming A Face of Grace*. Here is your chance to dive into the deep waters of Scripture and brain science and practice to become a face of grace! Everyone needs a face of grace in their life, and Ed tells us how to be that face of grace for others. Read this book, practice the steps, and buy copies to give people. You will not be disappointed as many good things grow from using this insightful book!

— *Chris Coursey, president of THRIVEtoday*
and author of The Joy Switch

My dear friend Ed Khouri has been exploring the depths of grace for as long as I've known him, and that is a very long time. In Becoming a Face of Grace, Ed masterfully balances a working knowledge of Scripture and neuroscience in a practical and easily applicable way. He balances understanding both why this is important and how to make it so in your life. This life-changing changing book will be more like life transforming as you take his advice and take his daily prescription.

— Andy Reese, engineer, college teacher, author, speaker, and president of Freedom Prayer (www.freedomprayer.org)

Ed Khouri wonderfully weaves together biblical knowledge, personal experience, and scientific research in this passionate, multifaceted book. Not a spiritual do-it-yourself book, *Becoming a Face of Grace* is a heart-to-heart talk written in a spirit of humble prayer. It will prompt your spirit to reside confidently in the Spirit of God. I trust that as you read, you will thirst after transformative discipleship and experience a breakthrough encounter with our Lord and Savior Jesus Christ.

— Dr. Ehab El Kharrat, founder and director of Freedom Drugs and HIV Programme, Egypt, and former president of ISAAC (International Substance Abuse & Addiction Coalition) Elder of Kasr El Dobarah Evangelical Church, Cairo, Egypt

Christians think they know what grace is because, of course, the term is used all the time in Christian circles. However, Ed Khouri has a different focus. He invites us to actually and intentionally become "a face of grace," to discover that God is pursuing an ongoing, intentional relationship with us. *Becoming a Face of Grace* provides a road map through the complexity of relationships and their inevitable challenges. Each chapter is personal and practical, including a study guide that ensures we learn with our heads *and* hearts. Daily affirmations help us speak truths of God over our lives. I know now, for example, that I am God's favourite! Scripture and Scripture reflection also are at the heart of the writing. *Becoming a Face of Grace* will strengthen the weak and weaken the strong. It is a wonderful resource for individual or group use.

— **Dr. Reuben Rose,** *director of Boloco Deep Creek House of Prayer, Australia*

It is a glorious thing for me to be taught by one of my former students. I consider it a privilege to endorse Ed Khouri's latest book, *Becoming a Face of Grace*. Defining the grace of God in relational terms, Ed leads the reader into a personal relationship with God's own face of grace, Jesus. He skillfully sets the stage for a life-transforming experience for all who seek to grow in God's amazing grace. Sharing insights gained along his journey, Ed has become a shining face of grace to his readers.

— *John C. Glenn,* *founder and pastor of Alpha Ministries, Inc.*

Becoming a Face of Grace is much more than information. It is about listening to the voice of God. It affirms who we are in Christ. It helps us remember the people who have been a part of our transformation into the fulness of Christ. A man who has experienced weakness but was transformed into God's strength, Ed is a face of grace to many around the world, including me.

— *Robbie Goss,* LMFT, LMHC

Seldom do I read a book where I know the writer. Ed Khouri is a man I respect and admire immensely. *Becoming a Face of Grace* is not just a book Ed wrote but a written account of his desire to become. *Becoming the Face of Grace* provides a genuine process for all Christians who want to reflect the love of God.

— *Gary L Cobb, founder and executive director of Broken Shackle Ranch, Inc. and Mighty Man Ministry, Inc.*

If you have not understood the power of grace given to believers by God, *Becoming a Face of Grace* is a must read. Not only does Ed offer relatable examples in each chapter, but he masterfully provides questions to take the reader into deeper applications, providing a memorable way to understand and receive God's gift of grace. I especially enjoyed learning how neuroscience confirms the importance of God's Word in our mind, soul, and body. I look forward to using this as a group study resource.

— *Kristine Stroupe, personal ministries pastor at Grace Center, Franklin, TN*

You simply can't read *Becoming a Face of Grace* without being impacted and changed at a very fundamental level—at least that was my experience. It challenged and deepened my understanding of grace. That is no small thing, considering the crucial role grace plays in everything related to the kingdom of heaven. It breathed fresh life into my understanding of relationships and God's commitment to them. It gave me permission to be human, then pulled the covers off of several relational stumbling blocks that have chronically plagued my life. And it provided encouragement and practical steps toward becoming a face of grace as a husband, father, grandfather, friend, and pastor. Thank you, Ed Khouri!

— *Steve Watson, lead pastor, New Life Church, Taylorsville, NC*

Becoming a Face of Grace is full of wisdom. Research shows mothers begin the process of attaching to their infants as early as conception, and infants recognize their parents' voices even before they are born. Feeding time reinforces this bond as they lovingly gaze into their infant's eyes. In *Becoming a Face of Grace,* we learn to receive the kingdom of God like little children. Relational time with Jesus transforms and matures us, making us capable of discipling others. Ed Khouri skillfully describes how we become who we love through careful discussion of the Scriptures, storytelling, and current brain science. If you want to build a culture of life, read this book, engage with the activities, and become a "face of grace"!

*— **Sharon J. MacKinnon,** PhD, associate research scholar at Charlotte Lozier Institute*

Becoming a Face of Grace is an excitingly readable and refreshing book that encapsulates Ed's passion, experiences, and practical insight—interacting to warm the mind, heart, soul, and spirit within us. It will inspire you to visualize possibilities and do concrete actions. Ed encourages us to work out the grace of God—personified, now and for the rest of our lives! How exciting indeed!

*— **Pax Tan,** Lutheran and Baptist pastor Former Senior Director in Malaysian CARE with Prison, Drugs and AIDS work. Vice-president, International Substance Abuse & Addictions Coalition (ISAAC)*

Imagine the transformation in our world if all seekers of goodness, beauty, and truth tapped into the living water of grace each day! In *Becoming a Face of Grace* Ed Khouri offers profound wisdom and a compassionate, practical path to opening our hearts to God's grace in all our relationships! This book is a wonderful companion for living a life of grace upon grace.

— *Marijane R. Michalowicz, Parish lay minister, volunteer and associate of the Sisters of St Joseph*

Becoming a Face of Grace is set upon the foundation of a more thorough definition of the word *grace*. Commonly described as "unmerited favor" in theological circles, Khouri presents a much more precise explanation. Demonstrating how grace is relational to its core, he explores what a deeply relational Christian life and discipleship might look like. I recommend reading this book and doing the exercises at the end of each chapter with a group. You and your group will come away changed.

— *Michel Hendricks, coauthor of* The Other Half of Church *and director of consulting at Life Model Works*

If you want to understand how beautiful grace is, dive into this book and allow the Holy Spirit to transform your perspective. Ed Khouri takes you on a journey that will captivate your mind and heart and cause you to grow closer to Jesus Christ and His Grace!

— **Keegan Mason,** *founder of Freedom Fighters of Georgia Regeneration Program*

Becoming a Face of Grace is such an important book. Ed Khouri's relational and accessible style unpacks what God says to us through the Bible about grace-filled attachments to Him and other people. The format encourages contemplation and action in response to the truths presented. The combination of theology, neuroscience, and practical wisdom makes this a fascinating and profoundly challenging read. The potential impact and application of this teaching are far-reaching. I have already shared insights I gained through reading it with clients and addiction treatment staff, as well as my children.

— **Treflyn Lloyd-Roberts,** *chief executive, Yeldall Christian Centres and general secretary, International Substance Abuse & Addiction Coalition*

In *Becoming a Face of Grace* my colleague Ed Khouri offers an ancient yet compelling idea: grace is relational and experienced relationally. It can be seen and felt in God's face and the faces of people around us. For too long, grace has been viewed as God's best idea, an intellectual concept, or worse, a transaction. How do you live out grace in order to experience transformation into the image of Jesus Christ? This book gives a practical road map. Ed's book is both thoroughly biblical and informed by the latest science about how the human brain actually works. I highly recommend this book!

— *Ray Woolridge, brigadier general-retired, US Army, and executive director, Life Model Works*

Becoming a Face of Grace is a gem. Ed Khouri has done a wonderful job of reminding us that grace means we are God's favorite—a unique delight to Him. Filled with helpful insights and practical tools, this book helps readers learn to hear the Shepherd's voice and live in the freedom of a grace-based life. It is easy to read and full of wisdom. You will be glad you took the time to let Ed guide you on a deeper walk into God's gracious presence.

— *Dr. Marcus Warner, author and president of Deeper Walk International*

becoming a
face
of
grace

becoming a
face
of
grace

NAVIGATING LASTING
RELATIONSHIP WITH GOD
AND OTHERS

Ed Khouri

becoming a
face
of
grace

The views and opinions expressed in this book are those of the author and do not necessarily reflect the official policy or position of Illumify Media Global.

Published by
Illumify Media Global
www.IllumifyMedia.com
"We bring your book to life!"

Library of Congress Control Number: 2021906727

Paperback ISBN: 978-1-947360-90-7
eBook ISBN: 978-1-949021-34-9

Typeset by Art Innovations (http://artinnovations.in/)
Cover design by Bethany C. Moore

Printed in the United States of America

Dedication

To my wife, Maritza,
who joyfully believes in me and unselfishly encourages me to write.
Her heart is as much a part of this book as mine.

Contents

Acknowledgments

It is tempting to believe that because an author's name appears on the cover of a book, they deserve all the credit for its creation. Nothing could be further from the truth. None of us—authors included—live in a relational vacuum. Without the love, support, inspiration, tolerance, understanding, and encouragement from a team, very little written is worth reading. Here are just a few I must acknowledge.

My friend, Jim Wilder, is a huge encourager and closer than a brother. Before beginning, I talked through this book's content with him at great length, and then sent him copies of the work for feedback. Thank you, Jim, for realizing the importance of this work and helping to support the project.

Thank you to the leadership team and the Life Group leaders at New Life Church of Taylorsville, who encouraged me to reframe my thinking. I'm also very grateful to all the folks in our Equipping Hearts Training Class who took the time to read various chapters, listen to me teach, and give me helpful feedback.

To develop this manuscript, I worked with Amy Pierson. Several thousand years ago, King Solomon, a wise man and author, observed, "Of making many books there is no end, and much study wearies the body" (Ecclesiastes 12:12). I wholeheartedly agree and am deeply grateful for Amy's help. Left to my own devices, I quickly get so lost in so much detail that writing can become an unreadable, endless, exhausting task.

Working from my notes, outlines, recordings, and countless video conferences, she and I crafted the work you are now holding. Her assistance with manuscript preparation and concrete suggestions for writing a more engaging, compelling book has been invaluable. I am greatly indebted to her creativity and joyful enthusiasm for this project. It has been a true delight and genuine honor to work with her.

Foreword

Grace?! Really? Is there anything we still need to know about grace?

For most Christians, grace is an idea like electricity. We know about electricity. We understand what electricity can do. Yet, if we need more electricity or something goes wrong in the wiring, we are gripped by an uneasy or anxious feeling of uncertainty. Suddenly, we notice that the idea we thought we understood is a reality we're not so sure that we do. In the same way, we know that grace powers the kingdom of God all the way from salvation through daily life into eternity, but how does that power flow through us? The answer will transform your spiritual life.

When we embody grace and our bodies actually respond to it, we bring and build joy! And others respond to it as well. So, ask yourself:

- What has my experience of grace looked like?
- Do the people in my life experience me as the walking presence of God's grace in their lives? For example, do they experience God's grace through me at least once a week?
- Do I know how to recognize its absence and authentically add grace to a situation when it's needed?

If the answers to these questions escape you, your power may be off.

The number of people in your world who are down, defensive, discouraged, distant, drained, or damaged indicates the great need we have for those who love Jesus to be conduits of such grace. You and I can practice adding grace to their circumstances. In practical ways, we can help one another develop the ability to express it as well. This could and should begin in the real world of our families and small group communities. But how?

In this book, Ed Khouri provides effective, hands-on ideas for expressing grace in our lives. Built upon thorough explanations and practical examples, these pages help move individuals, small groups, and churches into the active power and flow of grace. Every chapter includes a "Making It Stick" activity designed to change the way you live. Grace should not be something you do from time to time. Instead, grace can form who you are and how you live. In reading, not only will you gain a solid biblical understanding of grace in action, but you will learn how grace through you can power the flow of God's kingdom on Earth! You can become a face of Grace!

Becoming a Face of Grace is the book you didn't know you have been waiting for all your Christian life. Gather your friends (or church small group) together and watch the power of the Spirit begin to shine brighter as you become faces of grace together.

— **Dr. Jim Wilder,**
Life Model Works

Introduction

May the grace of the Lord Jesus Christ, and the love of God, and the fellowship of the Holy Spirit be with you all.

—2 CORINTHIANS 13:14

So forget any ideas you've got about lost cities, exotic travel, and digging up the world. We do not follow maps to buried treasure, and X never, ever marks the spot.

—INDIANA JONES

D o you like to travel? I hope so because we are about to take a trip. Keep reading, and we will journey into unknown territories—for many, these are unforged territories of grace. Together we will soar over mountaintop experiences and skirt valleys of shame, searching for new spiritual horizons. As we travel, I hope you notice a change in your inner landscape. I sure have. Over my forty years of teaching and training people how to make better grace-based connections with God and others, I've seen thousands experience the reward of moving toward these foreign shores. But lest you miss it, please notice: I have been *teaching* and *training* people because most of us are not aware of how vital the guidance of God's relational grace is for our ongoing spiritual transformation. Even if you *think* you know where we are heading, you may be surprised by some of the directions we take. So, pack up your nav system and let's go!

LOST ON A DESERT ISLAND

If you were a moviegoer back in 2000, you might remember the Academy Award–winning movie, *Cast Away*,[1] starring Tom Hanks. Hanks's character, Chuck Noland, was an efficiency expert and executive for FedEx. He was a likable, caring guy, but this globetrotting coach of express shipping had lost his relational way somewhere along the route. A workaholic, Chuck's concerns were clearly dictated by the clock (specifically, *beating* it!), and his personal life had suffered as a result. Chuck quickly discovered his suffering was all relative, however, when the plane he was traveling on crashed in a storm off the coast of Malaysia. Somehow, he survived the disaster and—along with some FedEx cargo—washed ashore on a remote island. Thus, he began his four-year ordeal—a battle of survival against hopeless despair and thwarted problem-solving as he attempted to make his way home.

While Chuck had no plan to vacation when his plane went down, it didn't take long for him to recognize that his sanity required companionship. So, he created a friend from a piece of cargo: enter Wilson, the volleyball. Painting a face on his leathery friend, Chuck made a confidant and comrade for himself. Suddenly, thanks to Wilson's presence, Chuck was no longer "alone."

So, let's board here: you and I may not have experienced the catastrophic upheaval of a plane crash, but relationally we will each find ourselves stranded at one time or another. As I hope we quickly learn together, this is a pain that we are not built to bear alone. The ache of relational frustrations can leave the best of us longing for life on a private, tropical island—one where bad things are kept at bay and annoying people aren't allowed onshore. Yet we know better: in our bones, you and I know that we are built for community. Without it, our illusions of a pleasant island vacation rapidly devolve into something more like a shipwreck.

Because people are not as compliant as a volleyball like Wilson, relationships are notoriously complicated. For a variety of reasons, most are a tad messy and unpredictable. As a result, programs that rely upon a formula, strict curriculum, and the study of essential aspects of the Christian faith are easy enough to develop but can never fully contain the sea of relational life. Spiritual growth requires much more than programs. It requires a relationship with God and with others.

What does this have to do with grace, you ask? As you and I will explore, grace, understood for all its fullness, is nothing if not relational. It's rarely experienced when combing the dusty shelves of theological libraries compiled over centuries by post-Reformation scholars. In its most profound form, grace is a relational truth you and I experience (or don't) in the context of our face-to-face interactions with others. That's why learning to find grace reflected in other people's faces and becoming a face of grace to those around us are some of the main themes of this book. Expressed face-to-face, grace defines the relationship we have with God, as well as the relationship we have with others. If grace is more than a theological vocabulary word, you and I must get off the island of our individualistic, Western mentality. To get back home, we will need a GPS—one guided by grace-based attachment. But more about that later . . .

If it sounds like I'm rocking the boat a bit, you are right. Again, if you and I expect to get off the island on which we are spiritually stranded and see our lives (not to mention the world) transformed, then our journey will require a new kind of vessel—one built on a different frame.

BECOMING A FACE OF GRACE

ADRIFT IN FAMILIARITY

At the beginning of his classic, *Divine Conspiracy: Rediscovering Our Hidden Life in God*, Dallas Willard explains, "My hope is to gain a fresh hearing for Jesus, especially among those who believe they already understand him. In his case, quite frankly, presumed familiarity has led to unfamiliarity, unfamiliarity has led to contempt, and contempt has led to profound ignorance."[2]

Much like "presumed familiarity" with Jesus has supplanted His place in many of our lives, grace seems at times to have lost its rightful place in our hearts. We seem to have lost the goodness and honesty of its relational framework. Maybe it is a sheer lack of understanding or, perhaps, purely a *mis*understanding. Whatever the case, the definition of grace is incomplete in the minds of too many. That is to say, a good number of sincere followers of Jesus have unintentionally been operating under a functional—but reduced—theology that centers on grace as it relates to salvation. While this is important, coming at grace this way effectively limits the practical power and application of it in our everyday lives with God. This limited understanding of grace dumbs down life with Him—effectively sucking all the rich marrow from our spiritual bones. Ideas of a with-God life are lost. In the words of Indiana Jones played by Harrison Ford, "We do not follow maps to buried treasure, and *X* never, ever marks the spot."[3]

RECALCULATING DISCIPLESHIP

Recently I listened to a presentation by Greg Hawkins, the executive pastor of Oak Hills Church in San Antonio.[4] Presenting data from a long-term, fifteen-year study of over two thousand churches in the United States, he relayed findings that I can only describe as heartbreaking. Research numbers indicate that programs across our country are failing to help those who profess Jesus actually learn to be His followers. Before this, many ministry leaders (including me, at one time) have erroneously assumed that if we create new and innovative programs and generate attendance, we will produce disciples whose lives are in the process of being transformed. Sincerely, most of us just want to help our people "do the next right thing."

In light of our current cultural climate, it may not be so surprising that Hawkins's data suggests attending the average discipleship class does not make disciples—any more than sitting in McDonald's turns people into hamburgers. The numbers indicate that churches and church programs are failing to make disciples. According to the data, we seem to be creating a generation of "self-centered" Christians who are more interested in asking, "What's in this for me?" than they are in learning to become like the One they claim to follow. Anyone who takes Jesus' command to make disciples should be alarmed!

Hawkins's presentation offered two rays of hope. The data suggested that two critical factors are present in the lives of those who are growing as followers of Jesus. First, discipleship must be relational. Second, disciples must engage with Scripture. In other words, spiritual growth is profoundly rooted in relationships both with God and with each other.

That's why I'm writing this book. If you and I take Jesus' command to "make disciples" seriously, we are going to need grace! Each of us needs a fresh understanding of what makes relationships work in the body of Christ—in all of life, for that matter. Jesus has summed up how Christianity works quite simply: He has asked us to love Him unconditionally and love others deeply as well (Luke 10:27). As Jesus demonstrated, life is completely and totally relational. All. The. Time.

RETURNING TO JESUS' ROUTE

Yes! Life *is* relational! It is the grace-based route that Jesus mapped out for us—and it is time we return grace to a priority. That is why you and I will explore both grace and fear as alternative foundations for life. Both can make relationships "sticky"—attaching us to God and other people. One accomplishes it in a good way, and the other, well, not so much. Throughout this book, relational stickiness is what I'll be referring to when I mention "attachment."

Grace is the glue of healthy, life-giving connections with God and with others. It is foundational to the creation of deep and enduring attachments that help us grow increasingly secure in love. Naturally, we become like the ones we love the most. To become a disciple isn't *something* you and I drift into. It is *Someone* we attach to. Our personal attachments to Jesus and others have a more powerful effect on our behavior than any church program we can join or biblical information we can gather. Because of that, we will look closely at how the people (including God) or things to whom we're most closely attached change how we see ourselves and others.

Fear also makes relationships sticky, but instead of forming healthy connections with God and others, it gums them up. When we operate out of fear, our identity and behavior get "stuck"—miring us in compromise and false religion. Trying to break patterns of unhealthy, toxic, fear-based relationships can feel a lot like running through a swamp at night in waist-deep mud. When we're out there in the dark, sensing laser-red alligator eyes trained on our every move, it's easy to get paralyzed. How will we ever make it out? While fear will keep us fixed in the hopelessness of codependency and all forms of addiction, grace has much to teach us.

Remember the new framework of grace that we are building? Because grace-based attachment is so foundational for healthy relationships, it is designed by God to serve as our GPS for every aspect of our "new life." Even at times when you and I find ourselves in the unexplored wilderness where satellite GPS and maps fail, we can count on our attachments with God and His community of grace will guide us safely home.

So, mark your current spiritual location. I hope you will allow these pages to draw you toward the robust, relational sites that lie ahead—life-giving experiences you may otherwise have missed. These places of grace are the kind of life and community for which we long and to which we're meant to belong.

How to Use This Book

Before it was possible to navigate the globe with my cell phone's GPS, I had a travel ritual before every trip. It involved the purchase of a crisp new road map and a lot of research. For hours, I would pour over my route to find the best restaurants, hotels, and attractions along the way to my destination. I didn't want to miss a thing.

I'm the same way with books. Before I turn more than a few pages in, I flip ahead to see how chapters are organized, where the author may be taking me, and I estimate the kind of commitment reading the book will require. Because that's how I'm wired, let me provide you with a "road map" for what lies ahead in these pages.

First, each chapter will contain what you would expect: I will share information that I hope will equip and encourage you toward vibrant new experiences in your life with God.

At the end of every chapter, you will find a section called Making It Stick. More than just for drill, these pieces have been designed to expand your understanding through practice and personal application. Each Making It Stick section includes the following elements:

A Face of Grace. Grace is not an abstract theological concept—it is a relational reality that can be shared when people interact, face-to-face, in an ongoing relationship. Each "A Face of Grace" section tells the story of my relationship with people who demonstrated grace toward me. Something in their faces told me that I was special to them. Here, I offer stories about people who shared grace with me before I even understood what it was. Eventually, I learned to see myself through their eyes. Looking back on them now, those faces of grace changed my life—my relationships, identity, and behavior—making it much easier for me to receive God's grace later in my life. As you read stories about the faces of grace in my life, I hope it will help you remember and recognize those important people God has placed in your own life. And as you do, my prayer is that *your* face will increasingly reflect that same grace to others you meet along the way. To do this is to become like Jesus.

The Intersection of Grace, Scripture, and Neuroscience. Advances in neuroscience confirm what Scripture teaches: we are designed for relationships rooted in grace. This section will identify common problems many of us thought we had to live with, which grace has much to say about. Here, we will apply our brains to explore the solution grace provides—body, mind, spirit, and relationship! I'm thrilled to share some of the ever-expanding neurological research findings (and a bit of the theology surrounding it) in order to offer insight and inform a solution. These will enhance what you and I already understand about biblical truth.

Daily Affirmation. Every chapter includes a Daily Affirmation portion. Perhaps you are familiar with the concept. For our purposes, each affirmation is not about our sin-related guilt or innocence on a topic. As we recite it, we will acknowledge a biblical truth that relates to our identity; each is designed to affirm and help us recognize how key truths in Scripture apply to us.

Whether you are studying this book alone or with a group, I encourage you to speak each Daily Affirmation out loud as a personal, daily practice. Doing this will affirm and reinforce the specific truth of God in your life. It stakes a claim, so to speak—declaring with your words that in *this* way you belong to God. You may find it helpful to copy each Daily Affirmation on a note card so you will see it as you go about your day. If you are part of a group study, repeat the entire Daily Affirmations list out loud together each time you meet. The one about your current reading will correspond to the chapter you have just read. (For a complete list of all Daily Affirmations, see Appendix A at the back of the book.)

Scripture Reflection. If you want to grow to be more like Christ, you must engage with Scripture. Research indicates that it is nonnegotiable—spiritual maturity just can't happen otherwise. With that in mind, every chapter contains a passage of Scripture to encourage your prayerful interaction with God. You will need a journal or notebook for this, as well as for recording your responses to the Reflection/Discussion Questions. Specific instructions are included in each chapter. A couple of things to keep in mind as you listen to the Lord:

1. Thoughts and impressions that you and I journal do not carry the authority of Scripture.

2. To help discern what God might want you to know, I encourage you to share insights from both your Scripture Reflection and Reflection/Discussion Questions with at least one other trusted, grace-filled friend.

3. If you need help distinguishing what God's thoughts may be, see the list provided in the article "Is the Shepherd Speaking?" located in Appendix B.

Reflection/Discussion Questions. Both types of questions are designed to help you go deeper to apply the chapter's themes and your Scripture Reflection exercise in your life. Items in this section can also help you prayerfully reflect on your life and your connection with Jesus in order to ask Him for help. Expect the Faces of Grace that surround you to become more recognizable as you learn to see others this way. Take the time to let your Daily Affirmation sink in. Record your answers and insights in the same journal or notebook you are using for Scripture Reflection. If you are studying this book with a group, share your answers with other members next time you are together, or seek out a close friend for a conversation about what God is showing you. Sharing this practice will help demonstrate the transformative power of spiritual friendship.

Homework. Unlike schoolwork, these homework assignments are created to be refreshing. Each is set up to help you continue to apply the week's lesson, engage with God, prepare for the next chapter, pay attention, and pray for others—especially those around you who need God's grace.

JOURNEYING WITH FRIENDS

While I've written this book for individual and group use, I hope that you will read through this book together with friends. You will be amazed at the way grace grows when it is shared with others! If you use this book as part of a group study, follow the instructions on each page. Here are some helpful group guidelines.

- Allow at least 60–90 minutes for each group meeting. The larger the group, the more time it will take for everyone to share their Scripture Reflections, ask for feedback, and answer the Reflection/Discussion Questions. You want to create a calm, relaxed learning environment. Naturally, people don't grow or apply information when they feel rushed. If you find yourselves pressed for time, break the Making It Stick exercises into two sessions—covering only half of the material each time you meet. In the first week, each group member should complete and share their Scripture Reflection before asking the group for feedback.

For the second week, share answers to the Reflection/ Discussion Questions with one another.

- Read the Daily Affirmation aloud to begin each group time. As you do, be sure to change each "I" statement into a "we" statement. For example, "I am a person who is being transformed by grace" becomes, "We are a people who are being transformed by grace."

- Before you gather next, read the chapter text, A Face of Grace, and The Intersection of Grace, Scripture, and Neuroscience on your own. Begin your Daily Affirmation practice as described above. When you meet with your group, you will recite the Daily Affirmation, complete and share your Scripture Reflection, and review answers to the Reflection/Discussion Questions together. Complete the Homework on your own.

- Allow 10–15 minutes for everyone to begin the Scripture Reflection. It is best if everyone has a notebook or journal to record their insights. While everyone can remain in the same room, they should do the reflection individually. Dialogue silently with Jesus about the Scripture. Do not share your insights with anyone until the time is complete. You will have time to share your reflection during the group discussion, which comes next.

- Begin discussing the questions, allowing volunteers to take turns sharing their Scripture Reflection. Follow the questions as written. Allow 45–60 minutes for this discussion.

- When listening as a group member shares their Scripture Reflection, do so supportively. This is not the time for uninvited criticism. As you listen, use the guidelines provided in "Is the Shepherd Speaking?" (see Appendix B) to help you discern God's voice.

When sharing your Scripture Reflection, you are free to ask your group for feedback to help you get better at recognizing the Shepherd's voice. You start the feedback process by asking your group to help you recognize if what you've written reflects interaction with God. Here is the suggested process for groups to follow:

1. Remember: your goal is to help each other better recognize when Jesus is interacting with you.

2. Use "Is the Shepherd Speaking?" in Appendix B to guide and limit your feedback. Be supportive and encouraging. This is a learning opportunity for the person sharing and the rest of the group giving feedback. As you listen, observe and compare what has been shared with the characteristics on the list in the article, pointing out any consistencies or inconsistencies. For example, does what has been shared produce a sense of deep peace within you? Does it resonate with the character and nature of God as revealed in Scripture? Is it biblical? Is it consistent with the characteristics listed in chapter 3 of James? Does it grow—or damage—relationships?

3. Never offer criticism, unsolicited advice, or opinions. Your goal is to help each other engage with God more deeply with confidence.

4. Do not use this exercise as an opportunity to "speak for God" into the life of another person. Our goal is to help *them* better connect with *Him*.

Now that you have your road map, let our journey begin!

1 So You Think You Know Grace?

God loves you unconditionally, as you are and not as you should be, because nobody is as they should be.

—BRENNAN MANNING

Indeed, I have been crucified with Christ. My ego is no longer central. It is no longer important that I appear righteous before you or have your good opinion, and I am no longer driven to impress God. Christ lives in me. The life you see me living is not "mine," but it is lived by faith in the Son of God, who loved me and gave himself for me.

—GALATIANS 2:20

For people who follow Jesus—actually, even for those who don't—grace is foundational for everything. Specifically, for those who call themselves Christian, grace is the launch point for each and every faith journey. It is how God loves, gives to, and guides us. Since I assure you, God is not some stingy, celestial miser, let's table the notion that He designed His grace so you and I "get what we don't deserve." While it holds some truth, that way of thinking about it underrates the extravagance of His intention. Just so we are on the same page from page 1, let's begin by defining the term that inspired this book.

GRAPPLING WITH GRACE

Grace. You may be familiar with one standard meaning assigned to the word. Whether as children in Sunday school or sometime after that, many have heard *grace* explained as God's "unmerited favor." The phrase "unmerited favor" accurately conveys that we have done absolutely nothing—good or bad—to deserve grace. In addition to being extraordinarily generous, God's offer here is Truth we can return to again and again. But still, this definition strikes me as a bit one-sided. Frankly, it is a little oversimplified. In wilder imaginations, it seems to diminish grace to something like a game show prize. Without earning it, each contestant can take what's behind "Door Number One," accept their personal reward of salvation, and, someday, receive an all-expenses-paid trip to heaven where they'll get the keys to their brand-new, custom-built mansion. (The crowd goes wild!) With this the game is over, and life for the contestant continues as usual. At one point, I think I remember being a contestant member. But then I learned that there is much more to the prize of God's grace than a shining moment of salvation. It was something I needed to discover for myself—and so do you.

I grew up in Maryland, the first adopted son in a loving Catholic family. On one side there was my dad, Ed. He was kind, compassionate, and loving, but he had a tough time sharing this part of his heart with us. From his upbringing and work as a scientist, he gripped rigid and outrageously high standards for everyone in our family. Presuming that I should be a lawyer or be on my way to law or medical school, Dad was all about my academic achievement—anything else just wasn't that important. Needless to say, Dad didn't do anger or negative emotion very well. On the other side there was my mom, Barbara. She was nurturing, compassionate, and loving. Most of the relational skills I carried into adulthood came from her. Watching her care for our elderly, sick relatives set an example that remains deeply embedded in my heart today. However, to help keep peace in our house at home, Mom tried very hard to ensure that none of us rocked the boat because when Dad was mad, no one was happy. Mom, like me, was afraid of upsetting Dad. Mom and Dad were effective at keeping both tension and secrets hidden.

To me, Ed and Barbara were good, well-meaning parents, and I was a pretty good son; I did well in school, had friends, was an altar boy, played guitar at the folk mass, worked at the church rectory, and on most fronts was doing fine. As long as I can remember, I had an awareness of God—it was an unwavering sense that He was out there and that He really loved me. I never questioned it for a second. God's existence wasn't a problem for me.

Lying just below the surface of my immature faith, however, a program of performance, approval, and expectation continued to run. God was out there, somewhere, and—since my household ran on these dynamics—this was the subtle undercurrent of my understanding of Him. Accepting Jesus' unmerited favor was my proverbial "fire insurance." Heaven forbid that I make God mad.

The nun that taught my school religion class in second grade underscored more of the same anxiety. Undoubtedly with a motive to scare us into the kingdom, she would tell my classmates and me terrifying true stories about various "divine punishments" that had befallen children who had dared to disobey their parents. My takeaway: clearly, God was out there, and He was to be feared! Unconsciously, I figured that this harsh heavenly judge looked at me, my choices, and behaviors with the same cold and critical eye. I understood the dispensation I had in His heavenly eyes, but that's where my religion ended. And at least in part, that is why I distinctly remember thinking, "If this is what religion is all about, I need a drink." It wasn't long after—in my midteenage years—that I made the conscious decision to cut the moral moorings of my upbringing; I drifted into a life of drinking, sex, and drugs. At this point in my story, I obviously hadn't engaged with the fullness of grace.

Another lesson I remember learning from my school days: teachers frown on circular reasoning. As is true for most of us, I'm guessing you've probably encountered a bit in your experience. In the case of unmerited grace, circular reasoning may look like this:

Q: What is grace?
A: Unmerited favor from God.
Q: What is unmerited favor from God?
A: Grace.

See what just happened there? It sounds true. Said in the right tone, it even seems to have authority. But sadly, this description of grace is chasing its tail, not getting anywhere. Anyone who accepts this kind of incomplete, pat answer is either 1) perhaps already in agreement with the answer, 2) possibly too easily satisfied, or 3) probably not thinking deeply enough about the personal implications of grace for their everyday life.

Even as a kid, I was confident that I needed grace, and I was sure that I hadn't done anything to merit God's favor. Because I *knew* I didn't measure up, I was afraid of Him and just happy to stay out of lightning-bolt range. But as I got older, my limited definition of divine grace didn't seem to answer any of the hard or meaningful questions that life often presents. To fully receive the gift of grace in our lives, we need to ask and pursue answers to the questions our souls are asking. For far too long, many have been satisfied with less—and it shows.

What *is* helpful about grace in its definition as "unmerited favor"? It clarifies that we each receive God's grace without having to work for it. As such, we can each be grateful for the fact that grace doesn't hinge on us. Romans 5:8 highlights the idea: "But God demonstrates his own love for us in this: While we were still sinners, Christ died for us." We don't have to agree with the idea—it is just reality, kind of like gravity. And thankfully, neither gravity nor grace has to make complete sense, intellectually. In fact, I'm pretty sure that it is not even possible. Grace just *is*.

YOU ARE GOD'S FAVORITE

Charis is the Greek word for grace. In addition to expressing the idea that we have God's undeserved favor, *charis* translates to mean, relationally and practically, that you and I are special and favorite to God without having to earn it. In other words, we are God's favorite. Without doing a thing, we are so special to God that He is glad to be with us. Before we ever exhibit any change or do anything, grace is an ongoing invitation to live in response to the Lord's divine delight in you and in me.

Charis (grace) takes wings to make what is already amazing an actuality. We can't tape wings on a worm and expect it to flutter off. The same is true about grace. One day we are living our earthbound caterpillar lives among dirt and leaves. The next—as charis begins its excellent work—we, His special and favorite, are spun into the cocoon of God's unmerited favor. Then, with our cooperative effort and in His timing, our trustworthy Friend affects any necessary change in our spirit from the inside out.

God already sees us—and those around us—as He gloriously created us to be. In community, God is transforming each of us within a kaleidoscope of butterflies—beautiful winged beings ready to fly together, embodying His purpose and vision. This is a process.

Sometimes the process can feel like a struggle much akin to our fight to get out of the chrysalis. Yet ultimately, this struggle is the means to our survival—the way to a new way of life. Collaboratively, our place as His favorite compels us closer to the One who loves us most. Like monarchs to Mexico in season, we migrate where we are created to go, always led to know God's heart more deeply. Just like nectar from a flower, grace-based relationship with God and others attracts, connects, and feeds us.

So what exactly do we *do* with "special and favorite"? In Western cultures, we hear this in a very egocentric way. That is, if I am God's favorite, then you are not. I was reminded of that fact recently when I watched the movie *Incredibles 2*. If you saw it, you may remember this scene early on in the film: driving with her boys one day, Mom (aka Elastigirl) exhorts her son, Dash, about the unique gifts everyone possesses. Clearly, the middle child doesn't like what he's hearing. Tenderly unrelenting, his mom says, "Everyone is special, Dash." To which the mini superhero quickly sasses back: "That's just another way of saying no one is."[1] This storyboards the very thing I'm talking about: too many of us think that if *everyone* is special, then *nobody* is special! But God's relational grace is not a competition won by a select few. There is no spiritual one-upmanship here. We are each incredibly special to God!

The amazing thing about God's relational grace is that His love and care *never* diminish. Because of His infinite, unlimited capacity, we are each God's favorite all at the same time. In actuality, our status as His favorite multiplies, allowing amazing things to happen "when two or three are gathered together" (Matthew 18:20 NKJV). Just take a minute to let your soul soak that in. If you catch the idea that you are God's favorite, then that means He can't wait for time with you. He is so excited about you! Out of delight, His attention is always rapt with you! Far exceeding a one-time salvation moment, grace offers us all a new way to live. Way beyond ego, those who discover this relational means for life with God soon realize their opportunity—in essence, we are meant to live this life in joyful response to shared love.

God's unlimited capacity of grace may just sweep you off of your feet! Think of it: before we came into a relationship with Jesus—and ever since—the full scope of His grace has been at work. Without this in play, we would never have found Him. God and His grace are proactive like that (1 Corinthians 15:10). His initiative of grace draws us to Him, spurring us on with a hunger to know Him more deeply, moving us gently into things like Scripture reflection, prayer, solitude with Jesus, and celebrations with His friends. He may invite us to share our thoughts with Him in a journal. In all these ways, we learn to recognize His voice in our lives and find our own in Him. We live with the awareness that this relationship is the only one that will satisfy.

Encountered on this relational level, God's grace continues its work, inspiring our hearts to become more like His, even when that transformation is hard. Down deep, the notion that we are living as His special and favorite person empowers our heart, soul, and spirit to align with His ways. Experiencing life as God's favorite gently draws us into a deep connection with Him that heady ideas about grace simply can't accomplish. As we become like Jesus on the inside, grace will overflow as we interact with the world and begin to see others around us as special and favorite too. This overflow of grace streams from the cross and resurrection to flood our lives.

A RELATIONAL CONCEPT

By now you get the point: the signature of grace is relationship. But author John Barclay further expands upon this, offering us a brilliant look at the historical and cultural roots of grace in his book *Paul and the Gift*.[2] The apostle Paul didn't invent that word, as it turns out. Hundreds of years before his writings, the Greeks referenced the word. Then it filtered its way into Roman culture. For our purposes, its meaning and social context are incredibly important.

According to Barclay, genuine grace was always *experienced in a relationship*, and it was always *an invitation to relationship*. Remember the distinction here: today many are familiar with the idea that accepting God's gift of grace leads to salvation; through no ability or virtue of your own, as it goes, you get saved and then you're in. *Bam! One and done! Life is good!*—but is it?

In Paul's day a gift meant much more. Back then, if I wanted to have a relationship with someone, I sent them a gift—a grace. Big or little, the gift demonstrated my purpose of entering into an ongoing relationship with that individual. If that person received my gift, it meant that he or she intentionally agreed to enter into the relationship *with me*, the gift giver. Accepting it means, "Yes! I want a relationship with you too!"

Grace means the God of the universe is pursuing an ongoing, intentional relationship with you. *Boom! There it is!* Barclay feels the historical context of the word makes all the difference. I'm with him. We didn't choose God. He thought of us first, and He sent us something (the life of Jesus) as a gift—a grace—to draw us back home. And while it was God who gave us the gift, it was not just to keep us out of hell after we die. If that were His only motive, it would not be consistent with the fullness we have discovered. In its complete expression, grace is the undeserved gift of Jesus dying to say, "I want to have a relationship with you. I've taken care of the sin, iniquity, and transgression that kept you from relating to me. Nothing stands between us any longer. Will you accept?"

A BASIS FOR OVERCOMING

What does this mean on a practical level? Jesus says that the cross, the resurrection, and a relationship with Him combine as the basis for overcoming sin, iniquity, and transgression—the three things in life that we can't fix for ourselves. And the process of addressing each is different. Some take longer to deal with than others. Over the course of our days, what's sure is that these three things tend to dog us in life like an angry hound on a postal carrier. Because of His grace, Jesus makes it possible for us to connect with Him despite our problems and shortcomings. But still we long for more—maybe because it seems to be true or perhaps we mistakenly think we could do better. The Holy Spirit is likely to make us aware of the issues that hinder us in our relationship with Jesus. Remember: Philippians 2:13 tells us that "it is God who works in you to will and to act in order to fulfill his good purpose." It doesn't happen all at once. Sanctification is a lifelong process. Little by little, as we (His favorite ones) continue to engage with Him, Jesus will be sure to let us know the specific areas of our lives in which He wants to bring us freedom. How we respond is up to us.

- **Sin** – Sin is simply missing the mark of God's commands for living. It is an old archery term that describes what happened when an archer's arrow failed to hit the intended target and thus missed the mark. Quite simply, in any given situation where you or I violate God's standard— *boom!*—we have blown it. Our energies fail, and you and I *fall short* or aim in the wrong direction. It happens to the best of us. For example, let's look at patience. If I determine that I want to be patient, I am aiming at a good target. When I get home to find my wife's cat has "done his business" in my shoes and I completely lose it, I will quickly realize that I missed the mark of forbearance that I was shooting for. However understandable, my reaction— losing my patience—is sin. According to Scripture, what helps you and me address sin in our lives is confession (1 John 1:9).

- **Transgression** – A transgression is a behavior or attitude that you and I know the Lord has specifically identified as an area we need to change, yet we intentionally ignore it. Such is a deliberate, flat-out rebellion of God's desire for our life. Persistent violations can change our character over time. Again, using patience as my example, if I know God wants me to work on impatience in my life and yet disobediently refuse to deal with it, then I have entered into transgression. Specifically, imagine that God has inspired an idea to help me deal with my habit of impatience toward my wife. During my commute home after work, He has asked me to spend a few minutes dwelling on the things I appreciate about my her before I walk in the door. My heart has also been led to confess the issue to some friends so they can pray for me. If I choose to confess my transgression to these friends and repent—go the opposite way I've been going on any given matter of conviction—all is well. However, if I disregard the conviction and direction, I refuse to repent and obey what God has asked me to do about it. Active repentance and confession help you and me to overcome transgression.

- **Iniquity** – Iniquity describes the things in our lives that have grown crooked or perverse. It may result from habituated transgression or a warping developed in reaction to things that have been done to us. Whatever the case, iniquity affects our personality on a foundational level. It rightly describes when these insidious issues set up home in our character. At the core, iniquity in our lives goes way beyond matters of sin (missing the mark) and transgression (rebellion). It has become a deeply seated and negative part of who we are. It's often so deep we are not aware of it, although its effects show up in the form of character defects—things we don't like and don't want. As our final illustration, using patience as an example again: I may never have witnessed what patience looked like if I grew up in a family where rage was the norm. When occasions called for patience, what I probably saw regularly modeled were responses of rage and blame. This standard would have twisted my character—rewiring me to a regular manner of angry impatience. Like those around me growing up, I might have become an easily offended person whom those around me were careful not to "set off." Consistently walking in Christ-centered, grace-based community can help us overcome the iniquity we may discover in our lives. It takes time, ongoing engagement with Jesus, and the help of others, as well as affirmation and repentance.

Instead of breezing by this, you and I would do well to pause and consider any areas that may be disconnecting interfering with the relationship we long for with Jesus. Knowing well that each and every one of our problems can and will deform our souls, the Holy Spirit is likely to make us aware of the issues that hinder our heavenly relationship with Jesus.

Not all have heard of Orcs, but it was a term coined by J. R. R. Tolkien. Throughout his fantasy writings, *The Silmarillion*, *The Hobbit*, and *the Lord of the Rings*, the Orcs refer to the henchmen of his villainous characters. Orcs served the Dark Lord and everything evil in Tolkien's Middle Earth. They despised all that was good and corrupted all they touched. According to Tolkien's' mythology, Orcs were not part of the original creation. Instead, Orcs descended from Elves (the good guys) who had the misfortune of being captured, enslaved, tortured, and tormented by the Dark Lord. In fact, all of the evil characters in Tolkien's books devolved from those once created beautiful and good in the beginning. Iniquity twists innocence until it is often unrecognizable.

Evil is pernicious this way. Satan loves to twist and distort good character. If we are honest with ourselves, we also know that we can act in ways that don't resemble God's being. Yet in His wisdom God knew these things would always be a barrier. The cross takes care of every evil. The grace of the One who hung there deals with all of our junk. You see, God is much more interested in our relationship with Him—and restoring all relationships—than He is in any of the problems or hang-ups that we have. Jesus' life, death, and resurrection prove it.

Once for all, the cross and God's grace have dealt with our problems—our sins, iniquities, and transgressions. As John writes, if we confess our sins (and iniquities and transgressions), He is faithful and just to forgive us our sins (and iniquities and transgressions) and cleanse us from all unrighteousness (again, see 1 John 1:9). Our problem is that we allow our guilt, shame, and sense of unworthiness to keep us from holding tightly to the One who loves us and helps us overcome. God's grace in relationship draws us to experience His forgiveness and cleansing despite our imperfections.

Grace is the God-given gift of intended, unearned relationship with Him as His special and favorite son or daughter. That is what we receive upon our salvation. Through this relationship, we can look forward to the adventure of a lifelong, transformational process known as sanctification. Following Him, we experience the grace of our new life as it takes off. God kindly draws us into this ongoing quest through the following:

- personal salvation (Ephesians 2:8–9)
- personal growth (2 Peter 1:5–9)

- personal discipleship (Titus 2:11–14)
- personal mending, equipping, and perfecting (1 Peter 5:10)

Driven by the wind of the Holy Spirit, grace-based character formation into the image of Jesus flows this way. Expect it. Inevitably, grace is proactively at work to form and shape our character in everyday life; if it's not, then it won't be real anywhere else. Relationships are like that. Like any friendship, it will require intentionality on our part, but remember, Jesus promised us an easy yoke. When you and I begin to consider His grace in the context of our everyday life, it doesn't take long to realize that what He is offering us is something more light, practical, and empowering to our life with God than we may have ever imagined. Like Paul, give up your old ways for His best. When you and I embrace our place as the Lord's special and favorite, the journey can truly begin.

> Indeed, I have been crucified with Christ. My ego is no longer central. It is no longer important that I appear righteous before you or have your good opinion, and I am no longer driven to impress God. Christ lives in me. The life you see me living is not "mine," but it is lived by faith in the Son of God, who loved me and gave himself for me. I am not going to go back on that.

> Is it not clear to you that to go back to that old rule-keeping, peer-pleasing religion would be an abandonment of everything personal and free in my relationship with God? I refuse to do that, to repudiate God's grace. If a living relationship with God could come by rule-keeping, then Christ died unnecessarily. (Galatians 2:20–21 MSG)

Take relationship out of the definition, and it changes everything. Without it, grace becomes a theological ideal of no relevance to everyday life. But with relationship in place? Now we are talking about grace-based discipleship—a relational reality of life alongside Jesus that promises an eternally fulfilling adventure. Holding hands with our gracious God, we forge ahead, reconciled and empowered.

MAKING IT STICK

A FACE OF GRACE: MOM

Before I began to understand how special I am to God, I struggled hard and wandered far. It took me many years to comprehend that I am indeed God's favorite! Now I can look back over the years and remember the faces of those who saw me through His eyes. Though the message didn't sink in at the time, these faces of grace gave me a foundation for life that prepared me for the day when I was able to respond to God's grace more fully. I'll bet there are faces of grace in your life too.

Without a doubt the first face of grace that comes to mind is my mom. I was adopted at six months old and transplanted to a new family and location. Though I don't remember that transition at all, some of my earliest memories and photos capture my mom's joyful, smiling face—clearly, she was glad to see me. Her face lit up when she saw me, and it told me all I needed to know; she loved, welcomed, and cherished me. Regularly, grace beamed from her face when she looked my way. I knew I was special and favorite.

I saw grace in my mom's countenance as she loved my dad and brother too. And I saw it when she visited and cared for her very elderly and unwell Aunt Helen. Due to a debilitating stroke, mom's aunt was bedridden and experienced great difficulty communicating. The impersonal and intimidating Washington Home for the Incurables confined her life to a small room. Its unwelcoming name and the general unpleasantness of her aunt's circumstances couldn't keep Mom away—her Aunt Helen was special to her.

Mom's brothers were special to her as well. Every Sunday they shared dinner with us, and Mom's grace toward them would shine. One of those brothers was an alcoholic—unpredictable and often mean when he drank. Despite her brother's problems, Mom never stopped loving him and doing her best to include him.

Now, don't get me wrong. No parent is perfect—not Mom and not me—but no matter how angry she could get, her grace toward us was never in question. I always knew that I was special and favorite. I vividly remember when we'd laugh and pretend to "box" with each other when I was much younger. I'll never forget one day when I was in high school: during one of our playful sparring matches, I didn't pull my punch in time and accidentally whacked Mom in the jaw. After a stunned moment of silence, we both burst out laughing! Today at ninety, her sense of humor and smile when I walk in the room reminds me of God's amazing grace toward me. If my mom can see me like this, imagine how much more God sees me as a joy, delight, and His favorite. My first ever face of grace still speaks deeply of these things to me.

THE INTERSECTION OF GRACE, SCRIPTURE, AND NEUROSCIENCE: YOUR BRAIN ON GRACE

In this section you'll discover how neuroscience intersects with grace and Scripture. The reality of God's grace offers solutions and benefits to all aspects of who we are made to be—body, mind, spirit, and relationship!

"These things I have spoken to you, that My joy may remain in you, and that your joy may be full" (John 15–11 NKJV).

Many of us have come to view grace as a mysterious spiritual force in our lives. We see it as something God gives us that is mystically good for our spiritual life but has no direct physical impact on our brain, thinking, or body. Nothing could be further from the truth. Grace actually has a direct, physical effect on our brain's neurochemistry and development. Far more than just something good for us spiritually, grace transforms everything about how our brain works and how our relationships form.

Grace changes the brain through the power of joy. Neuroscience has much to say about the importance of joy in our lives too. The New Testament makes clear the relationship between grace and joy because grace and joy are two forms of the same Greek word. Grace means that we are special and favorite, and joy means that someone is glad to be with me. Joy is our high-energy response to being special and favorite to someone. Where you and I find grace, we always find joy. They always travel together.

When others see me as their favorite, their eyes light up, their face welcomes me, and their body language invites me to come closer. Their grace expresses itself through joy, and coming face-to-face with these special people immediately changes my neurochemistry. In response to such grace-driven joy, within forty milliseconds (faster than conscious thought), my brain recognizes that look. Immediately, a neurotransmitter called dopamine floods my brain and instantly stimulates my brain's reward pleasure center. This chemical change is an exquisite delight to my brain, and before I'm consciously aware of what's happening, I am feeling a great deal of joy. My joyful response causes *my* face to smile, which in turn stimulates the release of dopamine in the other person's brain. Before long, we are sharing between us ever-increasing amounts of grace, joy, and dopamine. Back and forth it goes in six complete cycles per second. We're in the middle of our own private dopamine party, and it's happening so fast we're not even mindful of it. We're sharing life-changing, brain-altering faces of grace together.

The joy that comes from being special and favorite to someone—especially early in life—helps our brains learn to regulate dopamine effectively. God designed grace-filled relationships to be the most significant source of joy in our lives. When grace is plentiful, our brain learns to prefer grace-filled relationships with others over other sources of dopamine such as sugar, carbs, entertainment, excitement, performance, success, and addictions. In high-grace environments, our brain develops resiliency, which allows us to recover more quickly when things go wrong in life. A foundation of grace also helps us recover from trauma and makes us more resistant to addictions. Likewise, we become faces of grace to others as we interact with them. Our brain learns to amplify—and multiply—the grace we receive. Dopamine released in the context of grace-filled relationships makes this possible.

Dopamine-fueled interactions powered by grace have another critical function. They are the basis for bonding with God and with others. The strongest bonds we share are those rooted firmly in repeated, grace-filled, dopamine-triggering interactions. Grace, fueled by dopamine, is the basis for the strongest relational bonds possible. These long-term, grace-based relational bonds help us develop secure, healthy attachments with God and others. Grace is the basis for secure bonds that last a lifetime. The more you and I share and experience grace together with God and others, the more we'll be able to establish grace-based relationships with others in the future. When grace-filled relationships are the greatest joy in life, the artificial high that addictions bring loses its pull. Grace is not just something "nice." It is essential for a healthy brain and life-giving relationships now and in the future.

Many of us feel like we just don't "fit in." We compare ourselves to others and frequently end up feeling that we don't measure up. We compare ourselves to Scripture and feel condemned. Buried in shame, we promise ourselves we'll "try harder," attend church more often, listen to only Christian music or TV, or avoid specific habits. We think our behavior changes will make us a better fit for God and others. With renewed determination, we boldly sally forth to change and soon find ourselves worn out, discouraged, and not looking much different than when we began.

The reason we're so frustrated is that we need a grace-based, relational solution to our problem. My brain and spirit need grace-based connections with God and others to change behaviors—not more attempts to try harder. If grace is missing, my attachments with God and His people are too weak to govern my behavior. Either my brain's dopamine-based bonds are too weak, or they are nonexistent. We end up like the Pharisees who wanted life but wouldn't come to Jesus for it.

It's important to realize that my subconscious brain works a lot like a very speedy calculator. Faster than conscious thought, it computes solutions based on which response leads to the highest dopamine reward levels. When my attachment with God is weak, there isn't much of a pleasurable dopamine-based bond to govern my behavior. According to God's design for my brain, attempts to "try to do things right" without first growing a stronger grace-based attachment with God and with His people are doomed to fail. They simply bypass the bonds I have in my brain and decide which behaviors will bring me the most pleasure— or relief. Then, confronted by my failures, I feel more ashamed, more distant from God, more alienated, and certainly not like God's favorite.

According to Scripture, grace precedes change. According to my brain, grace precedes change. Both recognize that repeated experiences of being someone's favorite are prerequisites for change. Grace is needed to change the dopamine equation and grow stronger bonds with God and His people.

<u>EXERCISES</u>

DAILY AFFIRMATION 1: I AM A PERSON WHO IS BEING TRANSFORMED BY GRACE.

This is your daily affirmation. Read it aloud as an affirmation of God's work in your life each day while you are working with this chapter. If you are part of a group study, repeat this out loud together each time you meet. (For a complete list of Daily Affirmations, see Appendix A at the back of the book.)

SCRIPTURE REFLECTION: EPHESIANS 2:1-9

1. Pray and ask Jesus to guide you as you reflect on this passage of Scripture.

2. Take a moment to remember something you appreciate, or a time you have felt deeply connected to God. Reflect on that moment and remember how you felt.

3. Read the following passage of Scripture slowly. As you read, pay attention to any words or phrases that seem to stand out. Then stop and ask Jesus what He wants you to know about the word or phrase. After you ask, consider any thoughts, feelings, impressions, pictures, memories, or other scriptures that come to mind. Write these in your journal.

EPHESIANS 2:1-9 (NKJV)

And you He made alive, who were dead in trespasses and
sins, in which you once walked according to the course of
this world, according to the prince of the power of the air,
the spirit who now works in the sons of disobedience, among
whom also we all once conducted ourselves in the lusts of
our flesh, fulfilling the desires of the flesh and of the mind,
and were by nature children of wrath, just as the others. But
God, who is rich in mercy, because of His great love with
which He loved us, even when we were dead in trespasses,
made us alive together with Christ (by grace you have been
saved), and raised us up together, and made us sit together
in the heavenly places in Christ Jesus, that in the ages to
come He might show the exceeding riches of His grace in
His kindness toward us in Christ Jesus. For by grace you
have been saved through faith, and that not of yourselves;
it is the gift of God, not of works, lest anyone should
boast.

4. After you've finished journaling your observations, pray over
    them. Ask Jesus to show you if there is anything more that He
    may want you to know about what you've written. Enter these
    in your journal.

5. If you have the time, continue by rereading the passage of
    Scripture, journaling, and interacting with Jesus.

6. After you have finished journaling, read through what you've
    written. Think about what you have learned from this Scripture
    that applies to your life right now. Is there a theme or key lesson

that it speaks to your heart? Or is God calling you to action or further reflection perhaps?

7. Which of your impressions, if any, might be thoughts God shared with you? Remember, thoughts and impressions we journal do not carry the authority of Scripture. It's always a good idea to share your thoughts and impressions with others you trust to help discern what God might want you to know. (If you need help distinguishing what God's thoughts may be, see "Is the Shepherd Speaking?" provided in Appendix B.)

REFLECTION/DISCUSSION QUESTIONS

These questions will help you apply this chapter's themes and your Scripture Reflection exercise in your life. They can also help you prayerfully reflect on your life and your connection with Jesus and ask Him for help. Set aside time during the week to reflect on these questions and write the answers in your journal. If you are studying this book with a group, share your answers with other group members next time you meet.

1. Who is the first face of grace you can remember in your own life? How did you know that you were their "favorite"? How did you feel when you were around them? If you can't remember a face of grace, is there anyone in your life now who sees you through the eyes of grace?

2. Do you remember a time in life when you were not "alive in Christ?" What is the difference between your life then and your life now?

3. Where is God's grace at work to make you more "alive" now in your daily life?

4. Are there areas in your life that are not "fully alive"? Where do you need God's grace the most right now? If these areas were more alive, how do you think your life would be different? Be specific.

5. How does being "alive in Christ" affect your relationships in positive ways—especially those who are the closest to you? Please give some examples.

6. How do the areas you described in question 4 affect relationships with others negatively—especially those closest to you? Please give some examples.

7. If you are in a group, how would you like them to pray for you?

HOMEWORK

Homework helps you continue to apply this week's lesson, engage with God, and prepare for the next chapter.

1. Go "grace watching" this week. Can you find a face of grace anywhere around you? This person might be interacting with you or with someone else. How does watching another face of grace affect you, and how do you feel?

2. Continue reflecting on Ephesians 2:1–9 and journal your observations. Is there someone with whom you can share your insights—or who is willing to reflect on the Scripture with you?

2 *A Relational God*

Know that the L*ORD*, *He is God; It is He who has made
us, and not we ourselves; We are His people and the sheep
of His pasture.*

—PSALM 100:3 NKJV

*Earth's crammed with heaven,
And every common bush afire with God,
But only he who sees, takes off his shoes;
The rest sit round it and pluck blackberries.*

—ELIZABETH BARRETT BROWNING

Design thinking is not new in the world of human-centered innovation. First introduced in the 1960s, the term has evolved to become today's corporate shorthand for "beginning with the end in mind" when developing new literature, art, music, science, engineering, and business. Theoretically, all well-created things should work toward the same.

For example, when Apple created the iPod, it wasn't just to add another MP3 system to the marketplace. Their design thinking aimed to change the way music was delivered to listeners and fans the world over. The iPod wasn't the end they had in mind. Their geniuses created the structure behind it, which essentially heralded the popular dawn of downloadable music, the iTunes Store, the App Store, the launch of uncountable indie music careers, and more. Rising public acceptance was also the death knell for many record and video rental businesses. Today, their technological vision is a standard on most cell phones. They saw into the future, changing the way the music world goes round.

GOD'S RELATIONAL DESIGN

God sees the end He has in mind for us too—all the way around, we are designed for eternal relationship. After all that we are discovering about the nature of grace, there is no other conclusion we can come to. We are *that* special. The basis of our design? The imago Dei—that is, the image of God. According to Genesis 1:26 (csb), "Then God said, 'Let us make man in our image, according to our likeness.'"

Father, Son, and Holy Spirit, the Three-in-One, is our model of holistic well-being. The Eternal "Us." They model what we all long for. As individuals and as a community, They are always demonstrating the healthy, interdependent traits of

Love	Encouragement
Humility	Creativity
Honesty	Mercy
Integrity	Faith
Honor	Life
Building up	Ministry
Hope	Comfort
Affirmation	Righteousness

These are our design specifications too. We are Trinity-designed for Trinity life—the same characteristics are part of our DNA. As you look on the list above, pause to reflect: Do these same heart attitudes mark your relationships with God and others? Does your innermost being align with what these qualities? God designed us, Jesus sacrificed for us, the Holy Spirit is at work in us to refine us—heart, soul, mind, and strength. It is a group effort.

Each member of the Trinity speaks to our social nature. Returning to Genesis 1:26, the Scripture begins, "Let *us* make man in our image" (italics mine). When God said this, He was being relational. He is the Creator, but He wants to share life. The characteristics of the Trinity point to God's intention that we enjoy relationships with Him and with other people as well. In those first seven days of creation, imagine the Trinity arguing over who gets to make the next animal:

> FATHER: So, I was thinking . . . we need something in this area over here. [*gesturing to His newly planted jungles on the island of Borneo*] What do you think?
>
> HOLY SPIRIT (aggravated): It's *MY* turn! Jesus just created giraffes, and look at how ridiculous they came out! My idea is waaaay more creative!
>
> JESUS (jealously demanding): Hey, back off! The giraffe is awesome! Children will be laughing for years. I'm going to have to live on Earth at some point, so *I* should get to make these decisions. *I* get to create the thing.
>
> FATHER (pleadingly, as He hurries to whip up His design): Come on, guys. Why can't you just get along? I'll just do it Myself!
>
> (*A cloud of smoke explodes and clears. A pair of proboscis monkeys appear—dazed— in all their ridiculous glory.)

JESUS AND HOLY SPIRIT (recoiling, visibly exasperated, as they point to the monkey's enormous nose): Whose image did you create him in?

Get the picture? Nobody could imagine the Trinity acting this way. They are a model of a mature and caring relational community. Sure, They laugh and enjoy one another, but not at anyone's expense. No tantrums. No put-downs. No rush to get Their own way. Selfish, prideful posturing, competitive and immature attitudes simply aren't in Their collective makeup. These kinds of shenanigans would simply never happen! The Three-in-One is better than that!

Created in Their image, you and I are better too. Think of it this way: when a car operates according to the manufacturer's design, it works. You wouldn't purposely put diesel fuel in a vehicle that requires unleaded gas, would you? It's not that you *can't* do it, it's just that if you do, it will ruin your car. Similarly, people who try to live without grace-based connections to God and others are unlikely to get far.

PLEASED WITH HIS WORK

When He formed Adam and Eve, God provided a human model of what life *could* have been for us all. "Then God saw everything that He had made, and indeed it was very good," the Bible says (Genesis 1:31). God has always liked His workmanship! From the beginning, He delighted in and enjoyed every aspect of this happy couple, and the Lord is pleased with how He created you and me too. But from the inside out, they were His original favorites. Their regular walks in the garden were a pleasure all around. I mean, what's not to like about Paradise and its Creator?

If you've ever had the experience of being separated from someone you dearly love, you have a glimpse of why, in this life, we often can feel like something is missing. We may not be able to put our finger on just what it is, but something *is* missing. God knew it wasn't good for us to be alone—separated from Him or each other. We were designed by God to live naked and unashamed (Genesis 2:25). Keeping with that Holy intention, when we live according to our created nature, there is no need to hide. Healthy relationship continues to move us forward in reciprocal, interactive ways.

Andrei Rublev's icon, The Holy Trinity[1]

In Orthodox Christian communities, icons have been used for centuries to paint, quite literally, pictures of profound theological truths. Admittedly, some strike me as very dispassionate—almost aloof. Some faith communities resist iconography completely. Whether this classic art form is your style or not, there is much that we can learn from what is represented by one work in particular—that is, Andrei Rublev's icon, *The Holy Trinity*. The fresco was painted for Trinity Cathedral just north of Moscow. Visually it depicts three figures, meant to represent the Father, Son, and Holy Spirit. Profound gesture, symbolism, and color richly represent the nature of Their triune interrelationship. Gathered around a cup of sacrifice ever respectful, attentive, humble, and ready to share nourishment, the three leave space at the table for each of us. Their deep connection holds an invitation. Should you and I choose to join the party, our reception is sure to be warm.

Indeed, this *is* very good!

Though God's grace may be given at a moment in time, it moves forward in reciprocal, interactive ways. And by it, we are transformed. Spending time with someone we love changes us. As love and trust deepen, deference does as well. This is sanctification in action. Essentially, it is a self-forgetfulness in favor of Other-centeredness. Ahead of our interests, we place the one we are smitten with. And the Trinity is smitten with you and with me. Captivated by Their creation, every intention They have and act upon is for our good. Their group effort in our hearts will see it come to pass—that is, if we don't decide to make our own way.

The more time Adam and Eve spent with God, it seems the less they would have doubted His extraordinary intentions, but for whatever reason (and thanks to some belly-crawling lowlife), their doubt led them to pluck eternal life off the tree.

And so it goes. Instead, enjoying our relationship with God as His special and favorite conforms our hearts to the Trinitarian mold. This transformation marks a continuing, relational process of sanctification— one that changes us from the inside out. Not left to our own devices, we are companioned all the way.

RELATIONAL APPRENTICES

Life God's way is a relational sport. Played well, it volleys back and forth between the Trinity and us, between us and others. Discipleship is the name given to the grace training we undergo; it implies that we are intentional about processes of learning, self-discipline, and life application as they are led by God. But too many of us have lost our way around the spiritual court. It appears we are missing the vital point of true discipleship almost entirely.

Matthew 28's description of the Great Commission gets the ball in the air for all who follow Jesus. "Go and make disciples," it begins. But making converts is not the same as making disciples. Perhaps the problem is again due to our Christian lingo. At least in part, I think many have misunderstood the assignment. That's why I prefer the term *apprentice*. All over the world, apprenticeship has been a means of on-the-job training for thousands of years—and never is this training separate from a relationship.

I encountered the distinction a few years ago on a visit to the Frontier Culture Museum in Staunton, Virginia. If you ever get a chance to visit this marvelous living history museum, period-costumed interpreters will help guide you through both the Old World and American sections. These "colonists" reenact stories of early immigrants and their American descendants, demonstrating how our life in the United States today has been dramatically shaped by the past. On my visit, I made friends with the local blacksmith.

"How would someone become a blacksmith back then?" I asked. He explained how, typically when the apprentice was around twelve years old, a commitment was made to enter into an apprenticeship. You'd go live with the blacksmith and his family. The family would take you in and provide everything you needed—food, board, etc. For the bulk of the first year, you would do a lot of chores for the blacksmith, like sweeping the floor, gathering coal, and tending the fire. You didn't read a book about it; you did whatever he told you to do. As time went on, the blacksmith could tell when you were ready for more responsibility. Both the blacksmith and the apprentice expected to work closely together as new skills were taught and correction, big or small, was required. In this way, the blacksmith passed on the values, ethics, and safety of his trade to the apprentice as a way of being in the world and doing the job well.

Living alongside the blacksmith and his family would eventually rub off. As his apprentice, you would adopt his ways and the means of becoming more and more like the blacksmith.

Whatever our nine-to-five may be, aren't we all, as followers of Jesus 24/7, also apprentices then? Closely connecting with Jesus and others, we will learn to live as He did. Somewhere in that process of abiding with Him day and night, we will begin to assume His character and values, training to do things the way He teaches us. Respect for Him will gradually establish itself as our experiences grow into our unique callings. Isn't the goal to become increasingly more like Jesus? We get to know the Master because we live with him. As apprentices, you and I can't have a relationship with Him just because we have read a book about His way of life. While I may admire the man, that is like saying I am like Winston Churchill just because I read one of his memoirs.

It's not a one-off deal. Ongoing apprenticeship is crucial because it forms a relational connection between Jesus and us, His followers. Whatever language you choose, apprenticeship or discipleship, it is a picture of the same process. It's less "knowing about" and more "knowing for yourself." The experience engages our whole heart through the process of relating and refining in love. In his spiritual formation classic, *Divine Conspiracy*, Dallas Willard sums it up this way: "[To] be someone's apprentice, there is one absolutely essential condition. I must be with that person. . . . And provision has been made for us to be with Jesus, as one person to another, in our daily life. But it is also necessary that we have a practical . . . understanding of this arrangement in order to carry on our side of the apprenticeship relation."[2]

The alternative is life under self-imposed religious legalism. This is the crux of it: "I don't want to know the blacksmith . . . just tell me what to do." That was the way the religious leaders of Jesus' day wanted it. For some reason, they were more comfortable trying to follow the letter of their 613 Jewish laws than to believe their Messiah was standing before them, arms open wide. They were God's chosen people, for heaven's sake, and they'd been waiting for Jesus their entire lives! How could that have happened?

Yet isn't that how many people experience religious life today? When you and I leave relational grace out of the equation, functioning only out of one-sided fears and theological debates, we can't help but quickly trip into legalism. Before long we are "doing the God thing" without God. Driven by fear, we opt for control, and control numbs us to the value of relationships—especially our relationship with God. It doesn't take long for us to notice that something significant is broken, incomplete, or malfunctioning. Abiding apprenticeship under Jesus protects us from religion's common dysfunctions.

Those who have the responsibility to teach apprentices are called journeymen. Isn't that fitting? We are all on this journey together. No matter our maturity level, there is an ebb and flow to what we learn alongside one another. Eventually, you may begin teaching others, but you never outgrow the Master. And the Master will never outgrow His desire for an abiding relationship with you and me, His most special and favorite ones. In the beginning, this was the design He had in mind.

MAKING IT STICK

A FACE OF GRACE: UNCLE BILL

Uncle Bill was my mom's youngest brother. He was also my godfather and an important face of grace in my life for many years before I could see myself from God's perspective.

A lifelong bachelor, Uncle Bill never had children of his own and never learned to drive. Working for the State Department, he spent months overseas in nations that were not particularly friendly to the United States. I used to joke with my uncle about him being a spy—which of course he denied and I interpreted as confirmation that he was, in fact, a secret agent!

Most Sunday afternoons Uncle Bill came to our house for dinner. We loved watching football games together. I loved sitting next to him on the couch. While watching the game, we'd do things like thumb wrestle or compete to see whose grip was stronger. Fun all around, he was the only relative who seemed to enjoy playing catch with me, throwing a football, or just talking about sports. Because my dad did not grow up in the United States, he found most U.S. sports perplexing. But not Uncle Bill; he seemed to know intuitively when I needed to toss the ball around and other things like that, which my dad didn't understand were so important to me. Uncle Bill always treated me like I was special, and I knew I was a favorite of his.

If I were in trouble, Uncle Bill was someone I knew I could call. He would often take my brother and me on adventures, like when we traveled to New York on a train to meet my parents who were returning from a trip, or when he took us to downtown Washington, D.C., to show us around. We trusted him so much that we even let him take us to his favorite barber, Nick. When I walked out in shock with a buzz haircut, I could see Uncle Bill's eye's twinkling. He was old-school about things like that, but he loved me and wanted the best. Even though he died many years ago, he is a face of grace that still brings a smile to my face and warmth to my heart.

THE INTERSECTION OF GRACE, SCRIPTURE, AND NEUROSCIENCE: FAMILY MATTERS

In this section you'll discover how neuroscience intersects with grace and Scripture. The reality of God's grace offers solutions and benefits to all aspects of who we are made to be—body, mind, spirit, and relationship!

God created human beings;
he created them godlike,
Reflecting God's nature.
He created them male and female.
(Genesis 1:27 MSG)

God's relational design for our lives is reflected in the way He created the human brain. The more I study it, the more I recognize His fingerprints and how Scripture describes the kinds of things that make our brain work well. Sadly, in my years of ministry I've met many Christians who feel other believers are just too difficult to get close to or trust. Not knowing better, they've decided to try to connect with God privately in nature or away from people.

We are built for relationship! God's relational design is clearly evident in the way our brain develops—and the things it needs to develop well. When we are born, our brain is much like a hard drive on a computer. It has massive potential but lacks formatting to regulate essential neurotransmitters, develop and form relationships, and handle fear and other negative emotions. You and I are not born with an identity. Our brain's identity center only develops in direct response to our interactions with parents and primary caregivers early in life. As such, it's outrageously foolish to dismiss relationships as "fluff" or "nice things to have." God designed grace-filled relationships to provide the central organizing experiences and the primary vehicle by which we learn to experience and respond to all of life.

Trinitarian relationships are particularly important to the brain too. While life-giving, one-on-one relationships are vital; we need the simultaneous, grace-filled relational input from two people for our identity to become stable and complete. Neuroscientists call these types of bonds "family bonds" or "three-way bonds." The grace and joy shared in the context of a three-way family bond help our brain answer the question, "Who am I?"—making our own identity stable and strong. Imagine! A Trinitarian God designed our brain to need a *three-way* bond so that we can understand who we are. The more we experience grace in the context of those family bonds, the more stable and resilient our identity. The Trinity designed us for Trinitarian life!

As we can see from God's design for our brain, He created us with the need to connect deeply with Him—and with others—in grace. While it feels good to tell ourselves that "all I need is Jesus," both our brain and Scripture contradict this oft-repeated saying. Even though we may connect deeply with God when we're alone or find His peace in the beauty of nature, Jesus never intended us to live alone with Him. We need others to develop the kind of strong family in which grace flows freely among us as we engage with God together.

Perhaps this is why Scripture says, "And let us consider how we may spur one another on toward love and good deeds, not giving up meeting together, as some are in the habit of doing, but encouraging one another—and all the more as you see the Day approaching" (Hebrews 10:24–25). We are born needing God's grace, expressed lavishly by Him and shared extravagantly with each other, to live according to God's Trinitarian design for life.

You can begin growing grace-filled connections with others in your Becoming a Face of Grace study group. You can connect with God's love and infinite grace by engaging with Him through your Scripture

Reflection when your group meets and during the week when you are at home. When you share your Scripture Reflection, you will be amazed to discover how God speaks to each member as His favorite. Likewise, your weekly "Face of Grace" story will help you identify with how God expresses His grace uniquely to you and others. These grace-charged environments will help you connect with the riches of God in His people, and support your brain as it begins to develop the kind of family bonds you will share in eternity. Over time, as your face increasingly and consistently reflects grace, people at church are likely to see you as someone they would like to get to know. God, who created the beauty of nature that you enjoy, is committed to helping you find the kind of connections with others He knows you need.

<u>EXERCISES</u>

DAILY AFFIRMATION 2: I AM BECOMING LIKE JESUS BECAUSE I AM HIS APPRENTICE (DISCIPLE).

This is your daily affirmation. Read it aloud as an affirmation of God's work in your life each day while you are working with this chapter. If you are part of a group study, repeat this out loud together each time you meet. (For a complete list of Daily Affirmations, see Appendix A at the back of the book.)

SCRIPTURE REFLECTION: EPHESIANS 3:14-21

1. Pray and ask Jesus to guide you as you reflect on this passage of Scripture.

2. Take a moment to remember a time you have felt deeply connected to God. Reflect on that moment and remember how you felt.

3. Read the following passage of Scripture slowly. As you read, pay attention to any words or phrases that seem to stand out. Then stop and ask Jesus what He wants you to know about the word or phrase. After you ask, consider any thoughts, feelings, impressions, pictures, memories, or other scriptures that come to mind. Write these in your journal.

EPHESIANS 3:14-21 (NKJV)

For this reason I bow my knees to the Father of our Lord Jesus Christ, from whom the whole family in heaven and earth is named, that He would grant you, according to the riches of His glory, to be strengthened with might through His Spirit in the inner man, that Christ may dwell in your hearts through faith; that you, being rooted and grounded in love, may be able to comprehend with all the saints what is the width and length and depth and height—to know the love of Christ which passes knowledge; that you may be filled with all the fullness of God.

Now to Him who is able to do exceedingly abundantly above all that we ask or think, according to the power that works in us, to Him be glory in the church by Christ Jesus to all generations, forever and ever. Amen.

4. After you've finished journaling your observations, pray over them. Ask Jesus to show you if there is anything more that He may want you to know about what you've written. Enter these in your journal.

5. If you have the time, continue by rereading the passage of Scripture, journaling, and interacting with Jesus.

6. After you have finished journaling, read through what you've written. Think about what you have learned from this Scripture that applies to your life right now. Is there a theme or key lesson that it speaks to your heart? Or is God calling you to action or further reflection perhaps?

7. Which of your impressions, if any, might be thoughts God shared with you? Remember, thoughts and impressions we journal do

not carry the authority of Scripture. It's always a good idea to share your thoughts and impressions with others you trust to help discern what God might want you to know. (If you need help distinguishing what God's thoughts may be, see "Is the Shepherd Speaking?" provided in Appendix B.)

REFLECTION/DISCUSSION QUESTIONS

These questions will help you apply this chapter's themes and your Scripture Reflection exercise in your life. They can also help you prayerfully reflect on your life and your connection with Jesus and ask Him for help. Set aside time during the week to reflect on these questions and write the answers in your journal. If you are studying this book with a group, share your answers with other group members next time you meet.

1. Who was the face of grace you saw this week? How did they communicate "special and favorite" to you or someone else? How did you feel when you experienced this grace?

2. Are there other people who you see through eyes of grace? How do you express grace to them? How do you feel while you are interacting with them? Be specific.

3. What do you think it would be like if you experienced the depths of God's love more consistently? What would it be like if you could share His love more consistently with others? How would you like to do that? Where would you like to begin? Be specific.

4. Are there times when you feel like God's favorite? When? What is happening?

5. Are there times you don't feel like God's favorite? When? What is happening?

6. Read through the list of healthy, interdependent characteristics of Trinitarian life in this chapter again. Do you see any of these dynamics in your relationships? Are there specific relationships in which you would like to see them increase?

7. Becoming an apprentice of Jesus requires spending time sharing daily life with Him. How are you spending time with Him? What are you doing? Where do you see progress? Are there areas of life in which you'd like to see more improvement?

8. If you are in a group, how would you like them to pray for you?

HOMEWORK

Homework helps you continue to apply this week's lesson, engage with God, and prepare for the next chapter.

1. Go "grace watching" again this week. Can you find a face of grace anywhere around you? This person might be interacting with you or with someone else. How does watching another face of grace affect you, and how do you feel?

2. Continue reflecting on Ephesians 3:14–21 and journal your observations. Is there someone with whom you can share your insights—or who is willing to reflect on the Scripture with you?

3. Write out a prayer asking God to help you experience more of His Trinitarian life in your relationships. What would you like Him to do? What characteristics of His life would you like to develop in your relationships?

3 *The Bad Breakup*

There is but one good; that is God. Everything else is good when it looks to Him and bad when it turns from Him.

—C. S. LEWIS

So when the woman saw that the tree was good for food, that it was pleasant to the eyes, and a tree desirable to make one wise, she took of its fruit and ate. She also gave to her husband with her, and he ate. Then the eyes of both of them were opened, and they knew that they were naked, and they sewed fig leaves together and made themselves coverings. And they heard the sound of the LORD God walking in the garden in the cool of the day, and Adam and his wife hid themselves from the presence of the LORD God among the trees of the garden.

—GENESIS 3:6–8 NKJV

Have you ever weathered a bad breakup? Most of us have. Grief, regret, pain, shame. What makes it even worse is when you're on the receiving end and someone breaks up with you. Often, it can cause you to wonder, *Am I really that special?* But what about when you decide to be the heartbreaker? In our culture of soap operas, reality TV, social media, online dating, and hookups, it's hard to believe that others are special and favorite. That is especially true when the notion driving us is that someone is out there who could make our lives better by being _____ (insert smarter, better looking, funnier, or richer, to name a few) than the one we are with. Telling ourselves we can do better and be more fulfilled with someone else, we break hearts. There. That's when it happens. Broken hearts and betrayal replace special and favorite.

If in the perfect environment Eve and Adam betrayed God, why in our broken world wouldn't you and I? Essentially, Adam and Eve were God's heartbreakers. Even though they were clearly His most special ones, they broke up with Him. Can you imagine?

Up to this point in world history, God's grace had been the glue that had joyfully held their relationship with Him and one another together. They were stuck on each other. Despite the knowledge of being God's favorite, His obvious pleasure in them, the companionship they shared in the Garden, and God's provision for their every need, Eve and Adam cheated on Him. They questioned the relationship, found a new method to make themselves feel more special and favorite, and chose their own way. In short, they betrayed Him, and with that, "Genuine love was reduced to self-love, and the result was egocentricity and estrangement from our deepest self, God, and others."1 What had once been the perfect relationship became broken and incomplete; the design malfunctioned, and their connection to the designer died. Bottom line: the "perfect couple" questioned God's freely given grace and, by doing so, moved on to a life of bondage. Considering the heights of their existence, what could possibly entice them to break their connection this way?

REALLY?

If we look at what happened in Scripture along with our original design specifications, you and I can begin to make some biblically educated guesses. The nature of the temptation went something like this: "Are you *really* that special and favorite to God? He's holding out on you. He's holding you back from being all you can be. Listen to me and eat this fruit. It will make you even more special and favorite than you already are." In Genesis 3, the tempter slithered onto the scene and called God's grace into question. It is still his favorite strategy today.

The Hebrew translation implies that Adam was probably next to her; apparently, she did not have to search for him in order to share what she harvested. He went right along with the fruit-eating fandango. That being the case, I have a good question I'm saving for Adam: *Why didn't you say anything?!* After all, God directly told him not to eat from the tree! Was Eve such a complete knockout that Adam decided he'd rather suffer consequences and stick with her? Beautiful mate or not, if Adam truly trusted God, there would have been no room for doubt—eating its fruit was a horribly bad idea, and at the core, God had said it was forbidden! Yet both were snagged by the nature of the temptation. Tricked into believing she could become *more* special and favorite, Eve ate. Adam, who knew better, deliberately chose the fruit, his wife, and her opinion over God. Believing that by taking matters into their own hands they could become more—more than God's most special and favorite—they broke God's heart and broke paradise.

As for what happened next . . .

Then the eyes of both of them were opened, and they knew that they were naked; and they sewed fig leaves together and made themselves coverings.

And they heard the sound of the LORD God walking in the garden in the cool of the day, and Adam and his wife hid themselves from the presence of the LORD God among the trees of the garden.

Then the LORD God called to Adam and said to him, "Where are you?"

So he said, "I heard Your voice in the garden, and I was afraid because I was naked, and I hid myself."

And He said, "Who told you that you were naked? Have you eaten from the tree of which I commanded you that you should not eat?" (Genesis 3:7–11 NKJV)

THE GREAT COVER-UP

Before this point, there is no fear recorded in the Bible. Their solution: "Quick! Let's hide!" So began the first attempted cover-up in history. Previously naked and unashamed, they began a panicked attempt to invent clothes. The two sewed fig leaves together and hid in the trees to cover up parts they thought less presentable. (Perhaps this was the first attempt at camo wear?) Now, I know a little about fig leaves. Growing up, my dad had a fig tree in our backyard. The leaves' undersides are rough, sticky, and full of fuzz. As they dry out, the leaves become prickly and sharp. Not optimal clothing material, to say the least. The Word says Adam and Eve fashioned a *chagawr*—a belted girdle-like apron—out of them. Sound comfy? Nope, probably not. It would have taken many leaves somehow strung together and secured with . . . a vine? Picture them: scrambling around frantically gathering leaves, rushing to jerry-rig a covering for the nakedness of their shame before their Father showed up. If the invention of itchy, prickly underwear was their best idea, they were in serious trouble. It would almost be comical if it weren't such an epic tragedy. Literally, it was anything "butt."

Next we discover that Adam and Eve perpetuated their cover-up by deciding to hide from God. Were they so stricken with shame, guilt, fear, or so intellectually diminished that hiding behind a tree from their Creator seemed like a good idea? Did they imagine that God would be fooled by a strategy that sounds a lot like, "There's nothing to see here . . . just move along"? Denial begins its long and inglorious history behind a tree in the garden. Adam and Eve's response to God only makes the situation worse.

> Then the man said, "The woman whom You gave to be with me, she gave me of the tree, and I ate."
>
> And the LORD God said to the woman, "What is this you have done?"
>
> The woman said, "The serpent deceived me, and I ate." (Genesis 3:12–13 NKJV)

Exposed, Adam did what we all do at one time or another—he pointed the finger. By pointing the finger at others and pretending he was innocent, denial increased and blaming was born. Soul mates be damned. As quite factually the first man in history to cast blame, it doesn't seem that Adam even blinked before pointing the finger at both God and Eve for the whole debacle. He blamed God for making the woman and took zero responsibility for his own actions. Then he blamed Eve for handing him a helping. *Seriously, Adam?!* Equally brilliant, Eve demonstrated that there was plenty of blame to go around, identifying the lowlife serpent who set her up as the cause of all their woes. Throughout the entire account of the Fall, neither stepped up to take responsibility.

IN THE AFTERMATH

At this point let's pause for a minute and consider some other significant consequences. If you're like me, it's easy to look at God (especially in Old Testament accounts) as someone who likes demonstrating His wrath, enjoys a routine smiting, and readily hurls casual thunderbolts at those who make mistakes. But nothing could be further from the truth. The relational dynamics in the aftermath of the Fall—including fear, shame, cover-ups, hiding, denial, and blame—are a grief to the heart of God. They are not punitive but, rather, the natural and relational results of Adam and Eve's behavior.

God warned Adam and Eve ahead of time that they would surely die if they ate the forbidden fruit. Think about it like this: if I attempt to defy gravity by stepping off the roof of a tall building, God isn't punishing me by allowing me to hit the ground. Instead, my foolish decision naturally meets the invisible law of gravity. An invisible natural law called gravity is the reason. It's not a punishment. It is simply a natural consequence. In the same way, Adam and Eve couldn't imagine what relational death would look like until they hit the ground. Fruits of the Fall are always found in relationships that lack grace or when we attempt to earn our way into "special and favorite." As Adam and Eve's story continues, we now discover new and painful results of the Fall.

To the woman He said:
"I will greatly multiply your sorrow and your conception;
In pain you shall bring forth children;
Your desire shall be for your husband,
And he shall rule over you."

Then to Adam He said, "Because you have heeded the voice of your wife, and have eaten from the tree of which I commanded you, saying, 'You shall not eat of it':

"Cursed is the ground for your sake;
In toil you shall eat of it all the days of your life.
Both thorns and thistles it shall bring forth for you,
And you shall eat the herb of the field.
In the sweat of your face you shall eat bread
Till you return to the ground,
for out of it you were taken;
For dust you are,
And to dust you shall return." (Genesis 3:16–19 NKJV)

There were—and still are—enduring, real, and immediate consequences for their actions. Adam and Eve paid the price in areas initially designed for our most profound reward and fulfillment.

EVE: SORROW AND CONTROL

Eve's first consequence was that having and raising children would bring her great sorrow instead of God's original intention that it bring tremendous joy. Anyone who has raised kids can attest: as wonderful as it can be, there is also a lot of pain involved—physical, mental, and emotional pain. Now, it became difficult for our first parents to pass the life of God on to children of the next generation, and the next, and so on. The very next story in the Bible illustrates it: one sibling kills another (Genesis 4:1–16). At the moment she took her first bite of forbidden fruit, something went haywire. Even today, we wring our hands and lament, "I don't know what to do with this next generation!" But it hasn't been any different since the Fall.

The second consequence: Eve's desire would always be for her husband, Adam, and he would rule over her. Once again, we must look at the Hebrew for a better understanding of the word *desire*. By definition, the word picture here is "to reach forward and grab ahold in order to control." In the aftermath of the Fall, God plainly tells Eve that she would now actively seek to hold and control her husband. We find the same word (and word picture) in Genesis 4:7 just before Cain kills Abel. God warns Cain, "If you do not do what is right, sin is crouching at your door; it desires to have you." The kind of desire Eve would feel for Adam was both powerful and controlling.

How would Adam respond to Eve's attempts to control him? God said he would "rule" over her. Up until this point, Adam had been commissioned by God to rule over plants, the animals, the beasts of the field, and the birds of the air. Eve was not part of his domain! But now? Adam would actively assert his rulership over his wife. From this point forward, family dynamics would be marked by the terrible urge for husbands and wives to rule and control each other. I probably don't need to point this out, but this kind of desire paired with these dynamics makes for one big emotional mess. I don't think I've ever counseled a couple in which one or both partners weren't busy trying to control the other.

Now, let's consider Adam's personal consequences.

ADAM: ANGER AND FRUSTRATION

From the original language, there is a graphic word picture behind the phrase "by the sweat of [Adam's] brow" (Genesis 3:19). The picture is of a face that is sweaty, red, and angry. Why would Adam be sweaty, red-faced, and angry? Food that once grew beautifully and easily wouldn't grow that way anymore. From this time forward, the ground was cursed. Instead of eating from the trees God planted in the garden, Adam would now have to work hard to grow his own food. Mixed with any good seed that Adam and his descendants would plant, thorns and thistles would spring up, making it one big hassle to farm and make a living. The things that Adam didn't plant—the things he didn't count on—would just spring up, uninvited. This wasn't fun. It still isn't fun. Thorns and thistles hurt, entangle, and are certainly not life-giving food. All of this would make Adam red-faced, angry, and frustrated at how hard work and life had become. Essentially, God said to Adam, "Going forward, as you try to take care of yourself and your family, it is not going to work the way I originally intended. You just made it about one thousand times more difficult for yourself. Oh, and by the way, someday after all of this frustration, you're going to die."

LIFE AFTER THE FALL IN THE TWENTY-FIRST CENTURY

To this day the Fall and its aftermath explain how our relationships become broken, incomplete, malfunction, and die. Its tragic toll on our lives can take the following forms:

- Pursuing things that we think will make us more special and favorite to God—but can't
- Coveting new things, information and experiences—instead of relationship with God
- Shame, cover-ups, and hiding
- Fear
- Separation from God and each other
- Controlling relationships
- Difficulty passing-on healthy relationships to children and the next generation
- Denial and blaming
- Anger
- Sorrow
- Death
- Addictions

The toll of this last one—addictions—is something that should give us pause. Whenever someone asks me where addictions first occur in the Bible, I send them to this passage. First book, third chapter. After the Fall, Adam and Eve used trees that were "pleasing to the eye and good for food" to hide from God and each other (Genesis 3:6). They used the things God created for their pleasure to cover their distress, deal with relational conflict, and manage their upsetting emotions. They used a tasty fruit to make themselves feel more special and favorite. Adam and Eve hid in stuff that wasn't good for them and were lured into things that weren't good for them and could never bring life. False and momentary satisfaction will never replace grace. In our age the pursuit and misuse of pleasure have resulted in an epic flood of addictions and death.

The presence of addiction and all the other relationship killers we've previously looked at are clear indicators that we've missed God's grace. Too often, in an effort to get right, we even make these grace substitutes part of our "religion," but any substitute for grace is doomed to multiply the relational consequences of the Fall in our lives. By holding on to these behaviors, we practice, behave, and view the world imperfectly again—to our detriment. Whether consciously or unconsciously, each variety is our attempt to make a better way than God's. A. W. Tozer penned the words that capture the point in his book *The Pursuit of God*: "The shallowness of our inner experience, the hollowness of our worship, and that servile imitation of the world which marks our promotional methods all testify that we in this day, know God only imperfectly, and the peace of God scarcely at all. If we would find God amid all the religious externals, we must first determine to find Him, and then proceed in the way of simplicity."[2]

When I roll around in my mind what Adam and Eve forfeited at the Fall, I often speculate about how they must have felt. Surely, a sinking horror and overwhelming regret must have overtaken them as they came to terms with the consequences of their decision to betray the Father. (Frankly, I'm almost surprised that having such an intense spiritual connection ripped from their souls didn't instantly kill them.)

Without a doubt the realization was a brutal blow akin to having every bit of wind knocked indefinitely out of their perfect lungs.

I liken my imaginings to what I witnessed years ago during a counseling session. "Sara" came to my office to process the betrayal she had inflicted on her twenty-year marriage. After cheating on her husband with his cousin, she sat before me with head in her hands. Sara's grief was visceral—especially with the realization that her husband knew and her relationship with him was now irretrievably broken. Her grief spontaneously poured itself out in deep, guttural moans of pain as she pulled at her hair—and suddenly yanked some out entirely.

As we talked, Sara remained inconsolable. She recognized the magnitude of the damage forced on the people she loved and the scope of all she had lost. Working through her sin was agonizing for her, made worse as she wrestled with the reality that there was no one else to blame. The experience required every ounce of compassion I could muster. Honestly, the image still tears at my heart when I think of her. What must the weight of their cosmic betrayal have been like for Adam and Eve? More importantly, how did God respond? As always, He responded with outrageous grace and love!

HELP IS ON THE WAY

In the same breath, God cursed the serpent and delivered His prophetic promise of redemption for all humankind. In effect, God's response: help is on the way! This promise hinted that a Messiah was en route to restore the hope of unbroken fellowship and, by grace, to put right what the serpent had made wrong with His dear people: "Because you have done this, cursed are you above all livestock and all wild animals! You will crawl on your belly and you will eat dust all the days of your life. And I will put enmity between you and the woman, and between your offspring and hers; he will crush your head, and you will strike his heel" (Genesis 3:14–15).

Though they jilted Him, God was undeterred in His love for them. Because Adam and Eve were still His special and favorite children, God was determined to restore them. Remaining steadfast, He fashioned coverings for them so they no longer had to feel so naked, ashamed, and vulnerable. God's grace covered the weaknesses of His beloved. In an age in which the press, social media, cynics, critics, and religious people take great delight in finding and exposing others' weaknesses, this is an important lesson. Adam and Eve's weaknesses and failures were evident and exposed. God's grace was—and is—more interested in covering than embarrassing, in restoring than rejecting, and in practically healing than scolding. That's because God's grace simply places a higher value on restoring relationships than on blaming, scolding, and publicly "outing" those who fail. Our culture's negative tendency to love scandal and feel self-righteously somehow morally superior to those caught is prima facie evidence that grace is missing. God's heart is always grace-filled restoration and forgiveness. Even when God exposes sin as the gift of repentance is rejected—or when actively predatory behavior threatens His children—God's heart is grace. We find this cry of God's heart in His promise of a coming Messiah that would defeat the enemy and offer the possibility of grace-filled fellowship to a fallen world.

Though Adam and Eve quickly discovered living outside the garden was much harder, God continued to pursue them—to commune with them—just as He does with each of us. For you and me, this glimpse of divine grace should clear up any question of who God is and who we are to Him. Colossal failures do not change God or His grace for us. We are special and favorite to God because that's who He is—and not because we perform well.

Grace is essential because it keeps us on course, restoring us to relationship with God and helping us stay strongly attached to Him. Left to our own devices, we amplify the relational dynamics of the Fall and find ourselves far off course. It's kind of like what pilots and ship captains call the 1 in 60 Rule. One degree off on a flight plan may not seem like much, but for a journey to the moon, I'd miss it by almost 4,200 miles (more than twice the moon's diameter). We either hit the target or we don't. Operating apart from grace, our natural state will always be a little (and sometimes a lot) off—without God's guidance, it's just our tendency. Bad things don't have to happen for us to go there. It's our default since the Fall.

God's design, desire, and intentions have never changed for us. It has nothing to do with religion and everything to do with restoring our relationship with Him. God's grace draws us toward relationship, a restoration of what we lost in the Fall. Sharing that grace in relationships with each other opens the door to the kind of life-giving relationship that God intended for you and me all along. His grace is what makes all things new in you and in me. When you and I experience grace as a response to God-given desire for relationship, we can put our bad breakup behind us and move eternally ahead in our with-God life.

MAKING IT STICK

A FACE OF GRACE: AUNT MAE

One of my favorite childhood photos shows my Aunt Mae holding me as a baby. Very soon after I was adopted, my dad took the photo in our yard at home. The look on my aunt's face says it all: love, care, smiles. Her whole face lit up as she looked at me, radiating with amazing grace. She had a strong French accent, and when she spoke to me, her words sounded like a song. I was captivated. She was a face of grace way before I understood grace!

Aunt Mae and her husband, Uncle Pete, lived in New Jersey, right by New York City. At least once or twice a year, we'd make the drive to see the two of them. Each time, for days before our trip, my excitement would build. They made it clear to me that they saw me as a very special person. Long before we got there, the cooking at Aunt Mae's house would begin so that by the time we arrived, their home was filled with the promise of our favorite foods. Even now, it still makes my mouth water! Knowing that I loved sleeping in one particular downstairs bedroom, she always made sure it was ready. On holidays or other special occasions, Aunt Mae invited other relatives and family friends from miles around to celebrate and share a meal. All of us were treated like royalty. She made sure.

As I grew, I began to understand how hard Aunt Mae and Uncle Pete worked running their commercial art studio. My favorite room downstairs was next to her office, and I often awoke at night to find her bookkeeping well after two a.m. Somehow she managed to radiate grace to me despite her long hours. One summer I had the joyous opportunity to stay at her house and work at the studio while my parents stayed home. I loved my time with her—and all the traveling adventures our families shared. Today I still feel calm, warm, joyous, and loved whenever I think of her or look at that fantastic photo her face of grace.

THE INTERSECTION OF GRACE, SCRIPTURE, AND NEUROSCIENCE: BROKEN ATTACHMENT

In this section you'll discover how neuroscience intersects with grace and Scripture. The reality of God's grace offers solutions and benefits to all aspects of who we are made to be—body, mind, spirit, and relationship!

> "Then the eyes of both of them were opened, and they knew that they were naked; and they sewed fig leaves together and made themselves coverings" (Genesis 3:7 NKJV).

Have you ever thought the losses you suffered in life may be too big to get over? If this problem is familiar to you, you are definitely not alone. Lost, broken, damaged, and distant relationships with people we love are a sad consequence of the fall of Adam and Eve. To make it worse, the closer we feel to someone, the more it hurts if the relationship breaks down. The kind of losses we can't seem to get over only occur when we've cared deeply for another person. To help us understand why these losses cut so deeply, let's look at the subject of attachment and see what happens in our brain when we form close relationships with others.

Attachments—the kind of long-term relationships we develop with others that endure over time—are the central organizing principle for our brain. When we are born, each of us has billions of neurons in our developing brain, which fill us with incredible potential. Connections with other people guide the trillions of necessary interactions between those neurons. Specifically, grace-based joyful attachments with others optimize these connections as we grow—teaching us how to interpret and respond to input from others and learn things like how to recognize a smiling face, feelings of hunger, and when it is safe to cross the street, etc.

When we are attaching with others, brain scans show high activity levels deep in the subconscious regions of the right hemisphere. This is our attachment center location, and it is where the foundation for the brain's emotional and relational control forms. When attachments are strong and full of grace, the upper regions of the control center develop more optimally. Grace-based attachments tend to lead to healthy behaviors.

When my attachments with others are grace-filled, my brain strongly prefers connecting with those people instead of others. It's not that others are unimportant. My brain simply favors those with whom I share a grace-based bond instead of others. To some degree, this was my experience. But what happens when grace is missing?

A lack of grace-based, joyful attachments leaves the attachment center in acute pain, known as "attachment pain." We experience this deep, subcortical pain when we feel alone or don't feel like we belong. Even though we are rarely aware of it, this pain is so deep that we can't consciously control it. We can only recognize it indirectly when we learn to notice its symptoms.

Attachment pain also occurs when the strong bonds we share with others fade, become strained, or rupture entirely. These losses are a shock to the brain because the attachment it relied upon is no longer available. The pain feels intolerable because it occurs at the very foundation of our emotional and relational regulatory system. It cuts deeply. Often, the pain we can't seem to overcome is rooted in our attachment center. We might even bury it so deeply that it's hard for us to notice, although we may observe its symptoms. Strong cravings often serve as clues—a constant hankering for high-sugar, high-carb comfort foods like muffins, donuts, ice cream, candy, chips, snacks, and other sugary treats helps point out that attachment pain is active in our life.

I suspect that Adam and Eve experienced attachment pain suddenly in the immediate aftermath of the Fall. As described in Genesis

3, their behaviors are symptoms of attachment pain, reflecting broken attachments. On its own the brain has no mechanism for resolving attachment pain. In my experience and that of others who work with those wounded in this area, the only one able to fill the empty places in the brain's attachment center is God. Engaging with Him through activities such as the Scripture Reflection steps below helps us experience His relational grace personally. These interactions allow the Lord to heal our sense of being alone. His presence begins to fill the relational void to bring healing. God loves to fill those empty places in our lives.

Grace also plays another essential role in recovery from attachment pain. In order to heal, you and I need to connect deeply with a fellowship of grace. We need the steady support of a grace-based community to receive the relational support needed to grieve, heal, and grow. However, our community cannot take our pain away for us, and it can't fill the empty place inside us. Our brain will not allow anyone else to fill the void left from broken attachments. Only God can do that.

Your Becoming a Face of Grace group can help you begin developing the kind of supportive, grace-based attachments needed for healing. By practicing and sharing Scripture Reflection on your own and subsequently with your group, you will experience the kind of direct, personal interactions with Jesus that we all need for healing. In the long run, grace-filled connections with Jesus and my grace-based community are much more satisfying (and less fattening) than donuts!

EXERCISES

DAILY AFFIRMATION 3: MY HEART IS AT HOME WHEN I AM WITH JESUS.

This is your daily affirmation. Read it aloud as an affirmation of God's work in your life each day while you are working with this chapter. If you are part of a group study, repeat this out loud together each time you meet. (For a complete list of Daily Affirmations, see Appendix A at the back of the book.)

SCRIPTURE REFLECTION: PSALM 84:1-12

1. Pray and ask Jesus to guide you as you reflect on this passage of Scripture.

2. Take a moment to remember something you appreciate, or a time you have felt deeply connected to God. Reflect on that moment and remember how you felt.

3. Read the following passage of Scripture slowly. As you read, pay attention to any words or phrases that seem to stand out. Then stop and ask Jesus what He wants you to know about the word or phrase. After you ask, consider any thoughts, feelings, impressions, pictures, memories, or other scriptures that come to mind. Write these in your journal.

    Psalm 84:1–12 (NKJV):
    How lovely is Your tabernacle,
    O LORD of hosts!
    My soul longs, yes, even faints
    For the courts of the LORD;

My heart and my flesh cry out for the living God.
Even the sparrow has found a home,
And the swallow a nest for herself,
Where she may lay her young
Even Your altars, O LORD of hosts,
My King, and my God.
Blessed are those who dwell in Your house;
They will still be praising You. Selah

Blessed is the man whose strength is in You,
Whose heart is set on pilgrimage.
As they pass through the Valley of Baca,
They make it a spring;
The rain also covers it with pools.
They go from strength to strength;
Each one appears before God in Zion.

O LORD God of hosts, hear my prayer;
Give ear, O God of Jacob! Selah
O God, behold our shield,
And look upon the face of Your anointed.

For a day in Your courts is better than a thousand.
I would rather be a doorkeeper in the house of my God
Than dwell in the tents of wickedness.
For the LORD God is a sun and shield;
The LORD will give grace and glory;
No good thing will He withhold
From those who walk uprightly.

O LORD of hosts,
Blessed is the man who trusts in You!

4. After you've finished journaling your observations, pray over them. Ask Jesus to show you if there is anything more that He may want you to know about what you've written. Enter these in your journal.

5. If you have the time, continue by rereading the passage of Scripture, journaling, and interacting with Jesus.

6. After you have finished journaling, read through what you've written. Think about what you have learned from this Scripture that applies to your life right now. Is there a theme or key lesson that it speaks to your heart? Or is God calling you to action or further reflection perhaps?

7. Which of your impressions, if any, might be thoughts God shared with you? Remember, thoughts and impressions we journal do not carry the authority of Scripture. It's always a good idea to share your thoughts and impressions with others you trust to help discern what God might want you to know. (If you need help distinguishing what God's thoughts may be, see "Is the Shepherd Speaking?" provided in Appendix B.)

REFLECTION/DISCUSSION QUESTIONS

These questions will help you apply this chapter's themes and your Scripture Reflection exercise in your life. They can also help you prayerfully reflect on your life and your connection with Jesus and ask Him for help. Set aside time during the week to reflect on these questions and write the answers in your journal. If you are studying this book with a group, share your answers with other group members next time you meet.

1. Who was the face of grace you saw this week? How did they communicate "special and favorite" to you or someone else? How did you feel when you experienced this grace?

2. Do you long for deeper connections with God? What does that longing feel like? What emotions do you feel? What does your body feel like? Be specific.

3. What do you feel like when you experience connecting with God? What changes when you are aware of His presence? What emotions do you feel? What does your body feel like? What response does it elicit? Be specific.

4. Being an apprentice of Jesus means spending time with Him. How do you engage with God to experience His Grace, presence, and leading? What are the practical steps you take? For example, do you have time set aside to pray, journal, read your Bible, and talk with God about life and His Word? What kinds of things work well for you as you try to connect—and what things do not? Be as specific as you can.

5. Pretend you want to tell someone else about the changes in your life since you first started to experience God's grace and presence. What would you say? How would you encourage them to engage with God?

6. If you are in a group, how would you like them to pray for you?

HOMEWORK

Homework helps you continue to apply this week's lesson, engage with God, and prepare for the next chapter.

1. Go "grace watching" this week, as you've done before. Can you find a face of grace anywhere around you? This person might be interacting with you or with someone else. How does watching another face of grace affect you, and how do you feel?

2. Continue reflecting on Psalm 84 and journal your observations. Is there someone with whom you can share your insights—or who is willing to reflect on the Scripture with you?

3. In your journal, take a moment and write a prayer to God, asking Him to help you become increasingly hungry for His grace, love, and presence.

4. As you worked through the exercises for this chapter, perhaps you realized a need to change how you spend time with God. Make a list of possibilities and consider sharing the list with someone you trust.

4 *Grace and Attachment*

Religion can be the enemy of God. It's often what happens when God, like Elvis, has left the building. A list of instructions where there was once conviction; dogma where once people just did it; a congregation led by a man where once they were led by the Holy Spirit. Discipline replacing discipleship . . . It's a mind-blowing concept that the God who created the universe might be looking for company, a real relationship with people, but the thing that keeps me on my knees is the difference between Grace and Karma.

—BONO

If you should be loving me, you will be keeping my precepts.

—JOHN 14:15 CLNT

Breaking news: we are not in the garden anymore.

According to the experts, at any given moment each of our GPS devices is "visible" to at least four satellites, orbiting unseen roughly twenty thousand kilometers overhead. It only takes three to triangulate our location at the speed of light and guide us to our destination. So spiritually, where are you and I heading?

Ever since our ancestors were bounced from the garden's bounty, we have yearned to get back inside its boundaries. More than its fruit, we miss the closeness and connection we once enjoyed during our daily walks with the Master Gardener. We have an unquenchable and often seemingly inexplicable desire—to be special and favorite to someone. What turns do we need to make to find our way back to the kind of connection we are talking about with God? With one another? With our truest selves? Where is the relational garden that grows for us now? We need a GPS to guide us home. Though we may feel lost, we are not lost to God.

God's GPS is always simple. He designed us for grace because the experience of being God's favorite is what makes our attachment to him "sticky." Grace is the glue that forms, shapes, strengthens, and holds our attachment with God together and keeps it healthy. Grace is much more than "something nice," feel-good fluff, or a good idea God had to make us feel better about ourselves. Grace and grace-based attachment with God are our primary guidance system for life. Experiencing God's grace draws us and keeps us longing for more. This innate bond—or the longing for it—is what He knew would make our attachment to Him stick. Grace and grace-based attachments are a GPS that never fails. Following its direction will restore us to the kind of relational reality God intended for us before the Fall.

THE POWER OF GRACE-BASED ATTACHMENTS

God knows that our strongest attachments have the biggest impact on our behavior. This is how grace-based attachments work: at the core, they shape our identity, our personality, our brain, and our nervous system. In God's grand scheme of things, how we attach to Him and others has more influence over the formation of our character than anything else. When it comes to influencing our behavior, our attachments with the people (or things) we love will always trump good information, helpful teaching, or new books about living the Christian life. Who or what we love shapes our lives and behavior more powerfully than anything.

Are you wondering how being special and favorite so powerfully influences behavior? Perhaps you're asking, "How can loving someone the most make a difference in who we become?" Think about the things you liked to do before you met your partner or even your closest friend. Think of the things you do now that you would never have thought of before. Why do you do those things?

Let me illustrate. My wife's name is Maritza. Her mom is Panamanian, and her dad is Puerto Rican. In their cultures, dance is very important. But for me? I'm from Maryland and with no rhythm in my heritage. Dancing isn't my thing. Somehow, the first time I went to visit her in Florida, we ended up in a dance class. When it was over, we signed up for more. Why? Because I was attaching to her, so it became important to me; dancing was significant to her and the people she most loved. My growing connection to her changed how I behaved; what mattered to me shifted out of love.

The One who designed us for grace and love knows that attachment is our GPS. Perhaps this is why Jesus clearly told His apprentices, "If you love me, you will keep my commandments" (John 14:15 ESV). Go back to the Greek with me again. In its proper tense, what the verse actually says is, "If you are loving me, you will be keeping my commandments." It doesn't say, "Prove your love to me by behaving yourself." If you and I are loving and really connected with Him, we readily will do the things He wants us to do—the outflow of grace-based attachment. The guidance system of divine grace is boosted by love.

True spiritual formation freely flows from a vibrant connection to the Father, Son, and Holy Spirit. It is neither forced nor earned. But if we genuinely want to become like Jesus, God does not generally bop us on the head like one of Cinderella's mice-turned-white horses. If we really want to be like Him, it typically requires some effort. We must learn to engage with God to experience His grace.

Because I love Jesus, I want to be where He is and do what He's doing. He emphasized His intention, praying "that all of them may be one, Father, just as you are in me and I am in you. May they also be in us so that the world may believe that you have sent me" (John 17:21). Honestly, we can't get much more attached to Him than that. It is relational—not just positional. We are inseparably joined—happily, we cannot untangle ourselves from the love of the Trinity.

GRACE, ATTACHMENT, AND GUIDANCE

Once we understand the meaning and implications of grace and attachment, it isn't hard to see the potential of their combined influence. Knowing that we are special to someone changes us—it draws us to them like a magnet to steel. And, the more time we spend together, the more like-minded we become. Isn't it obvious? Doesn't that seem essential, in fact?

Recalibrating My GPS

I'm not exactly sure why God's grace and attachment with Him as a primary guidance system for life have become so obscured. Perhaps we tend to choose the easy path of gathering information *about* Jesus over the lifelong journey of actually getting to know Jesus. Many of us are like the children of Israel before Mount Sinai. It's easier to ask Moses (or someone else) to tell us what God wants than it is to meet Him face-to-face. Maybe it's easier for us to gather data about God and use reason and logic to deduce His will than to wait to discover His leading.

I remember the first time I came face-to-face with the idea that God wanted me to learn to be led by Him rather than rely on my "best "thinking" about what He might want. A class at my church taught me about God's heart to lead and interact with His people. The teacher taught us how to write our thoughts and impressions in a journal as part of engaging in prayer or reading Scripture. Part of the process involved learning to go through our journal and identify whether our impressions were more than our own thoughts. Could God actually respond to our prayers?

Until this point, I had diligently practiced what I'd learned from others about living as a Christian. Reading Scripture and keeping a journal about my spiritual growth had been part of my spiritual life for years. My journal was honest, and I was hungry to know God. I learned that the best approach to the Christian life was to study the Bible, journal, reflect, and then make good choices based on my understanding of Scripture. I added more information to the mix from what I learned reading Christian books, listening to sermons, and gleaning wisdom from others. All these things fed my decision-making process for life. Although I didn't recognize it at the time, the GPS for my Christian life depended on gathering the best data I could find to make my own informed decisions. Assuming I had God's tacit approval, I meandered my way through the Christian life, hoping I was getting it right. This arrangement kept me biblically informed—and, admittedly, pretty comfortable.

So, when it was time to do the first exercise in my new class, I found myself suddenly terrified. What terrified me? The shocking possibility that God might actually want to communicate with me more directly left me in a cold sweat. It dawned on me in a flash: my GPS for the Christian life depended on *my* thinking and *my* understanding. *I* made the decisions; *I* was in control. Doing the exercise opened me up to the possibility that God's understanding and God's will might differ from mine. *Gasp!* Suddenly, I realized that trying to connect with God more clearly meant that I could no longer pretend to figure out what

He wanted. To live with integrity, I would need to relinquish control and yield my will to His. The comfortable arrangement I had for living as a follower of Jesus would have to change. I never went back to that class, but what I learned stayed with me, and my hunger to know Jesus continued to grow. Before long, I returned to prayer, reading Scripture, journaling, and pondering the impressions I wrote down. Unsatisfied by my old ways, I wanted to be led by His will. I became an apprentice of Jesus.

Jesus understands the fear and hesitancy in each of us. Perhaps that's why He refers to His followers as sheep and Himself as "the good shepherd" in John 10:11. Maybe some sheep facts will illustrate His point: Sheep are herd animals and tend to stick together. They don't have a particular reputation for their bravery or intellect. They can't run away from danger very fast and have no teeth or claws to defend themselves. Independent, "loner" sheep that wander away and become lost will eventually lie down and begin to bleat loudly. This sounds the dinner bell for any hungry predators within earshot. As a group, sheep tend to overgraze a field and try to return to it—even after it ceases nourishing them. See? Sheep desperately need shepherding. Otherwise, their natural tendencies will kill them. Close attachment to a shepherd is essential for their survival.

As a flock, sheep spend a lot of time with their shepherd; it is his job to know each one, and they know him. Imprinted by his voice at a young age, they come when the shepherd calls, follow where he leads, and will run from any poser attempting to take his place. Because they aren't known for having great eyesight, sheep also rely on their shepherd to direct them on where to go for green pastures, still waters, safe rest, and care when they are hurt. This provides a picture for you and me. Our Good Shepherd connects and cares for us so deeply that He offers us the same direction and life—quite literally, He has laid down His own for us.

Jesus' GPS

Jesus modeled this life of grace-based attachment as His GPS. At His baptism and throughout His ministry, it is clear. Luke records the amazing story: "When all the people were being baptized, Jesus was baptized too. And as he was praying, heaven was opened and the Holy Spirit descended on him in bodily form like a dove. And a voice came from heaven: 'You are my Son, whom I love; with you I am well pleased.' Now Jesus himself was about thirty years old when he began his ministry" (Luke 3:21–23).

In our culture we value the "strong, silent type" who can stand alone against impossible odds. Countless movies portray a hero who walks into a bad situation and—with gritty, steely-eyed determination—single-handedly vanquishes the bad guys. Yet Jesus, the most powerful person in history, never traveled solo. Amazing, right? Grace-based relationship with His Father was His modus operandi. When challenged by the Pharisees at the Pool of Bethesda, He explained His life, ministry, and GPS this way: "Very truly I tell you, the Son can do nothing by himself; he can do only what he sees his Father doing, because whatever the Father does the Son also does. For the Father loves the Son and shows him all he does. Yes, and he will show him even greater works than these, so that you will be amazed" (John 5:19–20).

For Jesus, grace-based attachment to God was primary—the basis for all He said and did. This is the Jesus lifestyle—a God-soaked, minute-by-minute awareness that God is with me, ready to speak and direct my steps. It is how Jesus lived. And this is how grace-based attachment with Him looks. Like Jesus, God intends it to be our primary guidance system for everything we say and do. As we learn to live this way—interacting with God about all the issues of life—we will start to see ourselves and others like Him more and more, rest assured. And as this becomes our way of life, we will find it progressively harder to imagine going back to our old ways. We will quickly begin to recognize that life just doesn't work the same way without this close connection. We need God's guidance system! All this to say: be sure "ewe" are part of a close flock guided by the Good Shepherd!

For All Time

The apostle Paul understood the importance of God's navigation system for Jesus' disciples. In Paul's letter to Titus, his own apprentice, he clarifies the importance of grace and grace-based attachment for all time, and explains the movement necessary to carry us from an understanding of saving grace to the reality of a transformed life: "For the [unmerited] grace of God [which deems us 'special' and 'favorite'] has appeared that offers salvation to all people. It teaches us to say 'No' to ungodliness and worldly passions, and to live self-controlled, upright and godly lives in this present age, while we wait for the blessed hope—the appearing of the glory of our great God and Savior, Jesus Christ, who gave himself for us to redeem us from all wickedness and to purify for himself a people that are his very own, eager to do what is good" (Titus 2:11–14).

This passage is remarkable—both for what Paul says and what he doesn't say. Notice that it is grace *and* an attachment with God rooted in grace that helps us live the Christian life. Experiencing the reality of being God's favorite is the relational guidance system that helps us to follow Jesus. The word for "teaches"—*paideuō*—in this passage also helps us understand Paul's intent. It means "to train or to disciple," the same way that a master craftsman would train an apprentice. As we have already noted, an apprentice learns by participating in a close, personal relationship with his master. According to Paul, apprentices of Jesus need the kind of GPS found only in the context of grace-filled attachment with Jesus.

Also, notice what Paul *doesn't* say about our GPS. He doesn't say that we need to think better, or have more faith, or study harder, or learn to make better choices, or memorize more Scripture, or practice more spiritual disciplines. Although these are all good and helpful practices, they don't activate God's GPS; these cannot replace the power of a grace-filled attachment with God.

A GPS from Hell

Trying to live the Christian life as an apprentice to Jesus without personal attachment with Him will never turn out well. That's because our GPS is calibrated incorrectly without it. Up is down, and right is left. Self-effort replaces grace, and behavior becomes conformity without the internal motivation of love. On the inside—where it matters most—we remain stubborn, self-willed, and in control of our own lives. Instead of soaring as transformed butterflies, we end up living as caterpillars with artificial wings. We crawl and claim to fly. Living this way will land us in the same tribe as the Pharisees; in the words of Jesus, life like this will make us "twice as fit for hell" (Matthew 23:15 ISV). "How terrible it will be for you, scribes and Pharisees, you hypocrites! You devour widows' houses and say long prayers to cover it up. Therefore, you will receive greater condemnation! How terrible it will be for you, scribes and Pharisees, you hypocrites! You travel over land and sea to make a single convert, and when this happens, you make him twice as fit for hell as you are" (Matthew 23:14–15 ISV).

No compassion. No abiding. No relating. Our religion becomes a matter of outward conformity while our hearts are far away from Jesus on the inside. Anytime you and I do "religious things" this way, we become nothing more than human doings—we miss the relationship that is meant to be the center of everything. Calibrated on religious externals, our guidance system primarily helps us maintain outward "Christian" appearances.

Like the Pharisees, some of us are very capable, highly functioning people. We can maintain appearances for a long time—maybe even for life. But resisting God's grace for the sake of appearances is very costly.

This kind of lifestyle is exhausting and keeps any of us who adopt it in constant fear—worrying that at some point our veneer will crack under pressure. So that they don't put too much stress on us, we attempt to control our circumstances and other people. All the while, our hearts are hardening because we consistently resist God's grace.

Could similar motives of self-interest and self-preservation have caused the Pharisees to miss the Messiah when He came? If so, how tragic! After waiting centuries for Jesus and eagerly studying signs of His arrival, instead of recognizing and enthroning Him, they saw to His crucifixion. His grace and the offer of grace-based attachment to Him challenged the façade of their religious pretense. (People can react in pretty terrifying ways when their sacred things are threatened.) In the end, the Jewish leaders and worldly authorities preferred to preserve their façade over a covering, grace-based attachment to Him. When we resist God's grace to maintain our façade, are we any different?

THE GREAT EQUALIZER

The good news? We are not stuck forever! We are never too old—or too far gone—to grow in grace and develop a stronger attachment with Jesus. If you and I pay attention throughout our days, we will notice that God is continuously reaching to connect with us. Whether or not we respond to take hold of the grace He's offering is up to us.

As His apprentices, the ongoing classroom opportunity of life is designed to teach us how to receive grace from the Lord and to share what we have received with others. It can—and will—strengthen our attachments, all the way around. This is our option as long as we live.

Grace is the great equalizer. It doesn't require conformity to Old Testament Law, a PhD in theology, or any other religious designation; Jesus promised that all His sheep would hear His voice—not just the super smart. God's grace doesn't bow to an economic or social position. And there are no ribbons for perfect performance either. Jesus simply told us to listen to His voice and follow Him.

Every day, let grace be your guidance system.

* For more information on attachment styles, read "How Do Attachments Grow?" located in Appendix C.

MAKING IT STICK

A FACE OF GRACE: JIMMY

I started school a year early and was smaller and less mature than many of my classmates. I became an easy target for bullies in no time. My tendency to cry when I felt powerless and helpless to defend myself only made it worse. That stigma stuck with me through all the early years of my schooling.

Then I met an amazing face of grace in fifth grade. His name was Jimmy, and he transferred to our class. Jimmy quickly became a very popular guy. He was good at sports, confident, and secure—all the things I wasn't. I was amazed when he began talking with me in the school cafeteria during lunchtime. He smiled when he saw me and was quick with a joke. Right away, he included me in the fun that seemed to surround him. When he invited me for a sleepover at his house, I was astonished.

I grew to love being at Jimmy's house. His parents were laid-back and fun. Over the years, we played every imaginable sport, got into acorn fights with other neighborhood kids, listened to lots of music, talked about girls, and took turns pushing each other around in the laundry cart his mom kept in their basement. I'll never forget the two of us lying in the snow after a big storm, at first stuck and then stumbling our way out of the tall drift. When we were ready to start high school, Jimmy and I went to summer school to learn the art of debate. Together we joined the debate team in High School and became partners. We both still laugh about the time I got up to speak in our first debate competition; I was so nervous that I knocked over our file boxes full of the carefully researched notes gathered to support our arguments.

Jimmy's face of grace helped me realize that I was much more than I imagined. His kindness helped me grow in confidence and uncover gifts I didn't know I had. I learned to be a better friend. Last year I saw Jimmy at our fortieth grade-school reunion. (Yes, we did have one.) Being with Jimmy, laughing, talking, and reminiscing with other friends reminded me how grateful I am for his enduring friendship. We haven't made it yet, but we are still plotting a trip to the Rock & Roll Hall of Fame together!

THE INTERSECTION OF GRACE, SCRIPTURE, AND NEUROSCIENCE: RELATIONAL WIRING

In this section you'll discover how neuroscience intersects with grace and Scripture. The reality of God's grace offers solutions and benefits to all aspects of who we are made to be—body, mind, spirit, and relationship!

"If you should be loving me, you will be keeping my precepts" (John 14:15 CLNT).

God designed our brains, from the moment you and I were born, to respond uniquely to people (usually Mom, Dad, and other primary caregivers) when they share grace-filled, joyful interactions with us. When these exchanges are consistent, ongoing, and in tune with our needs, our brain's attachment center forms deep, enduring bonds with these special people. Our attachment center can form similar bonds with very close friends, spouses, and children later in life.

Once our attachment center forms bonds with this very select group of people, it expects those relationships to be permanent; nobody else can take their place. Have you ever seen a baby crying for Mommy, refusing comfort from anyone else? That's because the baby's attachment center has created a unique "parking space" for Mommy and will not allow anyone else to fill it. Healthy, grace-filled attachment bonds add color, texture, joy, and beauty to life. These relationships shape our brain's chemistry, structure, and function so radically that we become "wired" for relationship—especially for the people with whom we are most closely attached. This neurological wiring provides a blueprint for our brain's future relationships as well as our behavior. But what if these important, close attachments don't take place?

The ability to form attachment bonds has a profound effect on our behavior and shapes it more powerfully than anything else. When our attachment center forms an attachment with Jesus, we live the reality of His command, "If you are loving me, you will be keeping my commands" (John 14:15, CLNT). Obedience flows from the inside out when we share this kind of attachment with Him. It is simply how God designed our brain.

If we are only casual acquaintances with Jesus, we can't develop a deep, enduring attachment with Him. Acquaintances are content to simply read about the Master or listen to others talk about Him. Because they never actually engage with Him or enjoy the experience being His favorite, their attachment center does not form a deep bond with Him. Apprentices are with their Master—learning, studying, watching, and practicing with Him systematically and with intent. He becomes their primary attachment. Engaging with Him and experiencing His grace allows our attachment center to open to Him directly. We want to learn to engage with Jesus for our brain to find what it really needs: a deep, lasting, grace-filled attachment with Jesus!

EXERCISES

DAILY AFFIRMATION 4: I AM LEARNING TO KNOW MY SHEPHERD AND HEAR HIS VOICE.

This is your daily affirmation. Read it aloud as an affirmation of God's work in your life each day while you are working with this chapter. If you are part of a group study, repeat this out loud together each time you meet. (For a complete list of Daily Affirmations, see Appendix A at the back of the book.)

SCRIPTURE REFLECTION: JOHN 10:7-16

1. Pray and ask Jesus to guide you as you reflect on this passage of Scripture.

2. Take a moment to remember something you appreciate, or a time you have felt deeply connected to God. Reflect on that moment and remember how you felt.

3. Read the following passage of Scripture slowly. As you read, pay attention to any words or phrases that seem to stand out. Then stop and ask Jesus what He wants you to know about the word or phrase. After you ask, consider any thoughts, feelings, impressions, pictures, memories, or other scriptures that come to mind. Write these in your journal.

JOHN 10:7-16

Therefore Jesus said again, "Very truly I tell you, I am the gate for the sheep. All who have come before me are thieves and robbers, but the sheep have not listened to them. I am the gate; whoever enters through me will be saved. They will come in and go out, and find pasture. The thief comes only to steal and kill and destroy; I have come that they may have life and have it to the full.

"I am the good shepherd. The good shepherd lays down his life for the sheep. The hired hand is not the shepherd and does not own the sheep. So when he sees the wolf coming, he abandons the sheep and runs away. Then the wolf attacks the flock and scatters it. The man runs away because he is a hired hand and cares nothing for the sheep.

"I am the good shepherd; I know my sheep and my sheep know me—just as the Father knows me and I know the Father—and I lay down my life for the sheep. I have other sheep that are not of this sheep pen. I must bring them also. They too will listen to my voice, and there shall be one flock and one shepherd.

4. After you've finished journaling your observations, pray over these observations, asking Jesus to show you anything more that He may want you to know about what you've written. Write these in your journal.

5. If you have the time, continue by rereading the passage of Scripture, journaling, and interacting with Jesus.

6. After you have finished journaling, read through what you've written. Think about what you have learned from this Scripture that applies to your life right now. Is there a theme or critical lesson that speaks to your heart? Or is God calling you to action or further reflection perhaps?

7. Which of your impressions, if any, might be thoughts God shared with you? Remember, thoughts and impressions we journal do not carry the authority of Scripture. It's always a good idea to share your thoughts and impressions with others you trust to discern what God might want you to know. (If you need help distinguishing what God's thoughts may be, see "Is the Shepherd Speaking?" provided in Appendix B.)

REFLECTION/DISCUSSION QUESTIONS

These questions will help you apply this chapter's themes and your Scripture Reflection exercise in your life. They can also help you prayerfully reflect on your life and your connection with Jesus and ask Him for help. Set aside time during the week to reflect on these questions and write the answers in your journal. If you are studying this book with a group, share your answers with other group members next time you meet.

1. Who was the face of grace you saw this week? How did they communicate "special and favorite" to you or someone else? How did you feel when you experienced this grace?

2. In what ways are you learning to know your Shepherd and hear His voice? Be specific.

3. Imagine that you were in the crowd that heard Jesus teaching about being a Shepherd to His sheep. In the crowd that day were Jesus' disciples; people who were curious about Him; people who did not like Him; and the Pharisees, who thought he was evil. How do you think these people reacted as they listened to Jesus? Why do you think God wanted them to understand the picture of Jesus as Shepherd and us as His sheep?

4. What is your primary guidance system for life? On a scale of 1 (lowest) to 10 (highest), how much does a grace-based attachment with Jesus help you navigate life? What other guidance systems do you use? How well do they work for you?

5. Make a list of all the guidance systems you used to make decisions yesterday. What influenced you the most? How much did your guidance system rely on your attachment with Jesus? How often did your guidance system rely on other things?

6. If you are in a group, how would you like them to pray for you?

HOMEWORK

Homework helps you continue to apply this week's lesson, engage with God, and prepare for the next chapter.

1. Go "grace watching" again this week. Can you find a face of grace anywhere around you? This person might be interacting with you or with someone else. How does watching another face of grace affect you, and how do you feel?

2. Continue reflecting on John 10:7–16 and journal your observations. Is there someone with whom you can share your

insights—or who is willing to reflect on the Scripture with you?

3. After reading this chapter and completing the exercises, are there any changes you would like to make to your life? How would you like your guidance system to change? Make a list of anything you'd like to be different and ask Jesus to help you. Share your list with someone you trust.

5 *Weakness Required*

It is necessary to understand that it is not sin that humbles most, but grace.

—ANDREW MURRAY

What makes the temptation of power so seemingly irresistible? Maybe it is that power offers an easy substitute for the hard task of love. It seems easier to be God than to love God, easier to control people than to love people, easier to own love than to love life . . . One thing is clear to me: the temptation of power is greatest when intimacy is a threat. Much Christian leadership is exercised by people who do not know how to develop healthy, intimate relationships and have opted for power and control instead.

—HENRY NOUWEN

My grace is sufficient for you, for my power is made perfect in weakness.

—2 CORINTHIANS 12:9

y friend Alan is a wise, God-loving man. He is also a farmer. In the years that we've been friends, Alan has shared a lot of metaphors with me regarding our organic, God-implanted design as humans. One time, he taught me something that I find remarkable, especially when I think about attachment and weakness. He held up a kernel of corn and explained that each time he plants one in the ground, it occurs to him that it contains all the same DNA as a mature ear of corn. Then he asked me, "Since everything it genetically needs is self-contained, what do you think it is that causes it to begin to grow?" I verbally ticked my way down a mental checklist with my friend: Is it water? *No.* How about light? *Uh-uh.* Fertilizer? *Nope.* I think he could tell I was running out of my big-city ideas, so he gave me the answer: "The thing that causes the kernel to begin to grow is warmth!" Buried deep and dark in the dirt, what coaxes this seed to start sending its tender green growth to the surface is warmth. Aren't we kind of the same?

God is the person and presence of this warmth in our lives. Like sunshine over a midwestern cornfield, the grace of God's faithful presence generates warmth in our lives. Emanating from His grace, this warmth draws us to attachment with Him—inviting the seed of our faith to sprout.

Alan continued the lesson. "What else is needed?" he asked. "How do you think the seed breaks through the hard outer shell that protects it?" Seeing the blank look on my face, he went on, "Once warmth calls the seed to life, water softens its hull [the shell] so new growth can emerge from within. Without water, the seed and all of its potential would die." No warmth, no water, no life.

Weakness makes us tender enough to grow. Keeping with Alan's analogy, water represents the issues of life—things like suffering, crisis, and physical or emotional weakness. Whether we like it or not (more often *not*), the hard stuff we go through makes us feel vulnerable. Internally and externally, these issues soften the shell of our façade enough for the life of God to spring from within. It's then—when we find ourselves buried deep in our weaknesses or just hiding who we are from others—that God's warmth breaks through the cold, dead ground to draw you and me out of the dark. The water of weakness softens and tenderizes us, and as it does, our new life gets an *opportunity* to grow and become fruitful. That is, if we let it. Grace has the power to "resurrect" the seed of any soul that once looked dry and dead.

Paul understood. In 2 Corinthians 12:8–10, he shared something instructive about his own painful imperfections that, like water, allowed him to grow: "Three times I pleaded with the Lord to take it away from me. But he said to me, 'My grace is sufficient for you, for my power is made perfect in weakness.' Therefore I will boast all the more gladly about my weaknesses, so that Christ's power may rest on me. That is why, for Christ's sake, I delight in weaknesses, in insults, in hardships, in persecutions, in difficulties. For when I am weak, then I am strong."

In Christ we lack nothing. When struggling with our frailties, it may not feel this way, but you and I do well to remember that vulnerability is what makes us strong. It drives us to Jesus—the power of the Holy Spirit—for connection and strength. Our needs remind us that we are special and favorite and that the God of the universe wants a relationship with each and every one of us.

The soil of need is soft. It is where grace-based attachment with God grows best. In contrast, the hard-baked, rocky soil of perfectionism or religiosity just doesn't plant well; both leave us scattered with nowhere to root. But when we get to the end of our own devices, God warmly and proactively engages with our need by His grace, drawing us more deeply to Himself. Acknowledging his deficiency, Paul affirms, "But by the grace of God I am what I am, and His grace toward me was not in vain; but I labored more abundantly than they all, yet not I, but the grace of God which was with me" (1 Corinthians 15:10). Paul knew he needed the Savior.

So what about you? Do you need the Savior . . . *really*?

CAMOUFLAGING WEAKNESS

Walk through the doors of too many churches in America, and it may make you wonder. Once over the threshold, you will often pick up subtle but immediate undercurrents of "us" and "them" in the crowd of congregants. It's all just camouflage.

Those like "us" are the familiar ones—part of "our group." Everyone else is "them." Church-wise, when you consider the variety of cultures and subcultures represented, there is a potential plethora of such factions. It's only natural. We gravitate toward what is familiar, and sometimes it can create division. The diversity of age, ethnicity, or culture isn't the issue. What creates problems is this: each group is likely to share grace only with those who are like them—part of their group—when someone is one of "us." Anyone outside their circle? Well, um, maybe. Generally speaking, their practical, tangible expressions of grace can be a little stingy for those who are different from them. Either as a member of "us" or on the outside, as one of "them," have you ever had that experience?

Holding tightly to what is familiar, we tend to insulate ourselves from other people and groups we don't understand. Since we don't know how to relate, we opt to keep a polite distance or, worse, look for their faults in order to justify our detachment. *They aren't quite spiritual enough, righteous enough, informed enough, mature enough, together enough*, we tell ourselves. In not so subtle ways, we convey the message. Not enough. Outside the group. When we fall into this behavior, our pride reeks of self-righteousness. By doing so, we alienate ourselves from the grace of God that we—and they—so desperately need.

It's easy to stereotype those who think they have their act together as "winners"—especially if they're part of our group. Winners are strong, slick, fine, and beautiful people. They appear to have all the answers along with plenty of influence.

Though no one will probably come right out and say it, where there are winners, there must also be "losers." These folks are allowed in the door on a marginal basis. Some of them are treated more like problems to be dealt with (or avoided) than as people Jesus loves. If they stick around, they will probably keep their heads down and try to stay out of trouble. For whatever reason—their station in life, the circumstances of their brokenness, or their deep wounding—this group often finds itself kept in isolation (or at least out of the spotlight). But when you think about it honestly, who is more isolated? And who is more aware and desperate for the presence of God?

After years of working with churches and hurting people, I came to a startling revelation: in order to appear strong, people in both groups are desperately afraid of being found out and equally desperate to distance themselves from their weaknesses. Whatever group we find ourselves in, you and I tend to carefully construct masks designed to hide our weaknesses behind a façade of strength.

People who appear strong are afraid their inadequacies and insecurities will be exposed if they interact with the weak. After all, it's hard to relate to someone with whom we have nothing in common, we reason. Our thoughts race even to consider it: *What will I say? What will I do? What if they ask for help or ask me a question I can't answer? What if they ask me to do something and I don't have the time or know-how? Or* (*gasp!*) *what if they want my money? Why can't they just get over their problems? Can't one of the pastors just get them to behave?* Truthfully, it's easier to avoid these uncomfortable questions altogether. It's much easier to hang out with just our peers and social group. So, in many cases, that's what we do.

Not surprisingly, those who are weak, hurting, or struggling in some way have the same interior tussle. They've picked up on the loser vibe they've been labeled with. Their thoughts and questions race through their minds as well: *How do I talk with those people? What do I say? We have nothing in common, and their lives seem so perfect. How do I tell them that my son is in jail or my daughter is using drugs? How do I explain the bruises on my arms and why my husband is not with me? Could they really have it that together?* In the end, if they choose to keep their distance, they may justify their distance like the "winner" crowd does: *They are just a bunch of phonies! They just don't know how to get honest with themselves as I do!*

Both groups huddle in the same church building, subconsciously dodging potential sniper fire, protecting weakness, and fearing exposure. Pride rules. Weaknesses are hidden. Grace is hard to find.

AUTHENTIC STRENGTH

Whether you recognize your need or not, know this: apart from weakness, it's very hard, if not impossible, to receive the message of God's grace. Those who may look "successful" often have a great deal of difficulty growing an attachment with God that is based upon how *He sees them.* Yet it's no easy chore for the rest of us either. Honestly, life is just harder for some than others. I don't know why. Especially in our image-driven culture, those who aren't prosperous, achieving, charismatic, or beautiful are set up to try to hide their frailties. I mean, why wouldn't they?

In bold humility, Peter wrote to remind us what he learned firsthand: "God opposes the proud but shows favor to the humble" (1 Peter 5:5). Let us embrace it! Whatever our position, attachment to God—spirit to Spirit—occurs as you and I come to terms with our weaknesses. If we are not deeply connected and experiencing the grace of attachment with Jesus, we will inevitably try to make our own way and to hide our weaknesses. By doing so, we harden ourselves, thus resisting the warmth of God and others that will help us grow. Truthfully, our struggles don't exclude us. They cultivate our growth.

Whether in the church community or not, as a rule, most of us are taught that we need to "be strong." That usually means one of two things: either 1) we figure out how to be strong, or 2) we hide our weaknesses so that we appear to be strong. Both ways of coping have a built-in resistance. Each one makes it very difficult to respond to a God who says, "You are special and favorite! I want to have a relationship with you."

But this offer is worth the risk! If we understand it is essential to our growth and transformation, why wouldn't we take it? Grace-based vulnerability turns my weakness into the ultimate strength. When I know I'm special and favorite, I can be vulnerable and authentic because I'm not busy trying to gain your approval or feeling pressured to perform to be special and favorite to you. Thankfully, God has settled that question on my behalf—and yours.

When we remove our needs and weaknesses—our weak places—from view, we inadvertently remove the passion that brought us to the cross in the first place.

FINDING PRESENCE IN WEAKNESS

In 1992 I was doing pretty well, growing as a supervising therapist at a large secular treatment program. In the evenings I worked with a variety of Christ-centered support groups and house churches. While working at the treatment program, I accidentally hurt my knee one day. As it turned out, the injury required surgery. Following my operation, I developed an excruciating and disabling disease known today as complex regional pain syndrome. The progressive disease affected my nervous system, causing all physical sensation to register as excruciating pain. What began in my knee slowly advanced, taking over my body from my head down to my feet. Suddenly, my life changed forever. I quickly found myself extremely weak, desperate, and isolated.

Over the next several years, I became unable to work and had to quit graduate school. My family fell apart. Racked with pain, I could barely think or move many days. Over time, the disease hijacked my entire body and my mood. I was depressed and in despair.

I lived alone, and because of my disability, I was often by myself—confined to a wheelchair, companioned by pain all the time. The disease had left me really, really weak. But in this weakness, I discovered something life-changing.

I never thought it was possible, but my weakness ultimately opened the door for me to experience God's grace and attachment with Him as never before. At the weakest place I had ever been, I discovered an awareness of God's presence I had never known before. Most nights (sometimes all night), I would lie awake and in pain. Without fail, God would make His presence known to me then. Despite my agony, I found myself journaling to Him or playing my guitar in worship, all the while knowing that He was right there with me. Through these intimate times, I became increasingly convinced that I was His special and favorite. Experiencing His grace in a new and priceless way, I discovered an unshakable bond. It was a supernatural thing—somewhat bittersweet; I mean, what normal person would want this disease? Yet these times with God were precious to me.

Then one night, I had a vivid dream; in my spirit it seemed so real! I dreamed that I was walking back in time through a tunnel. I was talking to God (or someone representing Him), and He gave me the opportunity to return to a time before I was not sick. It was immediately clear to me that doing so meant I would not have to endure the physical, emotional, or relational pain and losses that I had gone through up to that point. But not to experience the season of suffering that I was in meant losing the incredibly close, grace-based connection that Jesus and I had developed due to my illness.

Was it tempting? I considered it only for a second. Counter to what you'd think, I didn't want to lose even a bit of the experience of God's presence that I now knew. It wasn't worth the trade. Without the disease, I would never have been able to grasp what my soul already knew. It needed God's abiding presence. All of what I'd gained during that time of infirmity is foundational to what I know of God and to who I am today.

Grace was—and is—God's response to weakness . . . not strength. And as much as I'd like to say something else, I found this to be true: suffering opens the door to grace and attachment with Jesus like nothing else. Nobody wants to hear that. It is very antithetical to our culture. But like Paul, I've discovered that it is much better to boast about my weaknesses and what I experienced in that dream. Thankfully, after ten years of pain, the Lord healed me, but my decision to choose weakness and rely on His sufficiency came long before.

DOORWAYS: HUMILITY AND PRIDE

Without a life-altering illness, how can we come to know God's strength in our lives? Echoing Paul, James 4:5–6 (NKJV) affirms where we can begin: "Or do you think that the Scripture says in vain, 'The Spirit who dwells in us yearns jealously'? But He gives more grace. Therefore He says: 'God resists the proud, but gives grace to the humble.'"

If this seems familiar, it is because God makes the same statement twice in the New Testament. Any time He repeats himself twice, it's because He's really serious and wants our attention! There are a couple of key points here: clearly, weakness and humility open doorways to the fullness of grace. But unless you're a Greek scholar, you may not know that the word used here for "proud" is a compound word that translates as one who "over shines." Generally, you and I resist grace when we try to "outshine" God or another person. Way down deep, consciously or unconsciously, we have an alarming desire to shine more brightly than anyone else. We are prideful glory hogs. Phonies. Let's face it, we all want something to make us feel *more* special and *more* favorite than others. Even in those moments, despite our pride and arrogance, each of us is still special and favorite to God.

But truly, amid our weaknesses, we must find our strength in Him. "Finally, my brethren, be strong in the Lord and in the power of His might" (Ephesians 6:10 NKJV). A little more Greek for you: this verb tense—"be strong"—is known as a present-passive imperative. That means that a past action is continuing and impacting us in the present. Just as if He is passing us a ball of His strength to us, He's got a good arm and careful aim. And while this strength does not originate in any of us, He has aimed it our way. The ball is in the air, and it is ours to catch.

Some of us have acted like arrogant wide receivers. We play to the crowd instead of the quarterback. If out of pride we fail to look for God's ball of grace or we act out of our own strength, it will bounce right off. We shut down the play. We entirely miss opportunities for new teaching, discipleship, or grace.

In his book *Humility: The Journey Toward Holiness*, Andrew Murray writes: "Faith and humility are at their root one . . . we can never have more of true faith than we have of true humility. It is possible to have strong intellectual convictions and assurance of the truth while pride is still in the heart, but it makes living faith, which has power with God, impossible."[1] Yet too many of us as Christians want to go straight to strength, avoiding weakness altogether.

Let's face it, nobody likes to feel like a weakling. But we are talking about a posture of humility—not humiliation. Healthy humility says, "We are all in this together." Pride, on the other hand, communicates, "We may all be in this, but I (and my ideas) matter most." People who struggle with pride are easy to spot; they may do any or all of the following:

- be cynical
- enjoy scandal
- need to be right all the time
- tend to judge the behavior of others in order to make themselves feel superior
- predict the "wrong" actions of those around them so that they feel more "right"

God, please forgive me of ALL my PRIDE....

Sometimes proud people are just plain mean—especially when they think their nastiness can be religiously justified, which it can't ever be.

While I may find it easier to spot these characteristics in others, it's probably harder for me to see these in my own life. But if you and I are willing to be brave and take a look, we are sure to find the toxin of pride rooted deeply inside. I say this with assurance: pride is the fruit of the Fall. Pride is never helpful to the body of Christ either; my pride hurts me, and it hurts others. None of us are any different. Attempts to "outshine" God or others, whether consciously or unconsciously, are not what will make us strong. Quite the contrary! Any efforts to steal God's glory will only keep you and me stuck—our hard outer shell will kill our interior life with Him.

Because of God's favor, you and I can assume that no matter how far away we feel, how tough our struggles may be, His grace will pull us back to Him. We can't white-knuckle righteousness, and He knows it. In the words of Romans 5:20, "The law was brought in so that the trespass might increase. But where sin increased, grace increased all the more." Vulnerability points us to grace.

I am not for a moment suggesting that we dwell in our pain, wearing whatever it may be as a badge of honor for all the world to see. But it *is* important to remind ourselves—clearly and often—that it is the weak places in life that "qualify" us for redemption. Not. The. Strong. Places.

FIT TO FOLLOW

When Jesus gave us the mandate to go into all the earth and make disciples, He wasn't expecting them to be all "pretty" and "put-together" folks right out of the gate. He certainly didn't pick His disciples from the ranks of the religiously spotless. By all reports He chose the unlikely and the unlovely as His apprentices, and as His followers as well. In fact, Mark 2:15–17 brilliantly illuminates what I find to be important about whom Jesus chooses. Earlier in the day, Jesus met Levi, the tax collector, and quickly invited himself to dinner.

> Later Jesus and his disciples were at home having supper with a collection of disreputable guests. Unlikely as it seems, more than a few of them had become followers. The religious scholars and Pharisees saw him keeping this kind of company and lit into his disciples: "What kind of example is this, acting cozy with the riffraff?"
>
> Jesus, overhearing, shot back, "Who needs a doctor: the healthy or the sick? I'm here inviting the sin-sick, not the spiritually-fit." (Mark 2:15–17 MSG)

On closer reading, it's easy to see what He's saying: those who think they're spiritually well-off—spiritually fit "winners"—don't understand their need for the Savior. He invested the time He had in those whose sin had rendered them invalid, at least in the eyes of the religiously righteous community.

The spiritually "elite" Jesus was addressing had no awareness of their deep need for a Messiah packaged as Himself. Surprised they were on the guest list, those at the dinner table were having a raucous time together, I would venture to guess.

There were many years in my Christian life that I thought, "If I can just do [BLANK] or stop doing [BLANK], then I will conquer this discipleship thing." In part, I wanted a formula because I sincerely wanted to make myself better suited for the call God had on my life. And I know I'm not the only one. I've met many people over the years who have been frustrated by the same desire for a program to help them succeed at the Christian life (whatever that means). But God never said He wanted us to be successful; He said He wanted us to be *followers*. The Lord has no illusions about who we are and what we are really like deep in our souls. We were born special and favorite to Him—not perfect.

AN INVITATION TO RESTORATION

Still, you and I have a question to answer for ourselves: *Spiritually speaking, do I want to mature?* If so, then each of us must learn to see our imperfections as the advantage that they are: our flaws signal an invitation to grow . . . probably much more than you may have previously realized. Spiritual growth requires a healthy, ongoing consciousness that suffering affords us intimate and robust experiences of God's grace; we must recognize that suffering forges attachment with Him. If we ever get done suffering through weaknesses, then we are dead. Until we are in heaven, all of life is a process of soul restoration to God's original design—an opportunity to let Him come in and renovate our lives with His unshakable, loving grace.

But somehow it seems too many have forgotten that we are all weak in some way, we all have failed. Somewhere along the line, we believed a lie that sounded something like this: *I can't talk with God because He's too holy and I'm not,* or *I can't approach Him until I get a better handle on this problem.* So, we avoid going to God—or even places where His people may catch a glimpse of who we *authentically* are. In truth, this is when God most wants us to come and hang out.

I have a friend named Harry. He's a good guy. A hard-working plumber, he has spent many years working long hours to make ends meet. At times it has been pretty tough. Though he's had a relationship with the Lord for years, Harry has waged a huge war with lust that has manifested in the form of a pornography problem. Every time he thought about getting close to anything spiritual, all he could think of were his unholy failures. Needless to say, the last thing Harry felt was that he was God's special and favorite. His sin only reminded him that he wasn't who he wanted to be. That lie kept him in hiding—far away from the One who intimately cared for him.

Harry's struggle with pornography is no different than any of our secret issues. Many of us have wrestled with this; we want to have our act together if we are going to be around other Christians. But this is a fake performance. Like actors on a stage, we don costumes to mask what is going on inside. Commonly, you and I drift into a couple of behaviors: one is to hide, the other is to pretend. We cover up to avoid admitting we aren't as strong as we think we should be. Either way, we are faking it.

We may be faking it, but God is no poser. God never fakes His intentions toward us. Always and actively, the Lord is drawing us to Himself. He is no stodgy, hands-off grandfather waiting for us to come to him. Involved and relentlessly passionate, He pursues us with an ongoing invitation, making it clear that we are His special and favorite ones.

God doesn't assume we are going to respond to him perfectly. He is crystal clear about us before we are, and because of that, God knows what we need. First Peter 5:10 (NKJV) explains the blessing and purpose of our suffering: "But may the God of all grace, who called us to His eternal glory by Christ Jesus, after you have suffered a while, perfect, establish, strengthen, and settle you."

Read that to yourself a couple of times.

Going in, the Lord expects that we are going to need to be repaired and restored to His design. The word *perfect* means "to mend," as fishermen mend their nets. In Jesus' day, nets were made of linen. They were easily tangled and torn, requiring great care and considerable maintenance. Loading them up, casting them in, pulling them out, and putting them away were all time-consuming steps, but they were each an expected part of the process. Rushing compounded problems; instead, patience was required, and perfecting—the mending the nets to keep them functional—was expected. Peter knew from on-the-job experience that tears in the nets were not an *if* but a *when*.

Like Peter, if you and I learn nothing else as Jesus' apprentices, God's grace must teach us to respond tenderly to our own weaknesses—whatever they may be.[2] God judged our *sin* but deals tenderly with *us*. In no way does God take sin lightly. Seeing things as they truly are, God does not confuse us with it. After all, sin was judged and dealt with fully on the cross. So now, Scripture nails it: "If we confess our sins, He is faithful and just to forgive us our sins and to cleanse us from all unrighteousness" (1 John 1:9 NKJV). A grace-based attachment with Him will transform us from the inside out, and He knows that this kind of attachment is the basis for overcoming weakness.

Today, Harry is back in church. Now, he embraces his place as God's special and favorite. But in order to do that, he first had to receive God's loving grace in the middle of his weakness. Harry needed to need his Savior. And just like him, if you and I cannot recognize our weaknesses, we will miss God's heart to repair what is broken.

The Lord longs to see us restored to His original design. In my years of recovery ministry, I uncovered the common denominator behind what drives people to rehab: it is fear. Whatever it was—jail, losing family, homelessness, death—initially, it was fear that brought almost everyone I worked with through the door for treatment. I found something else to be true as well: fear simply won't change you in any lasting way. Only love will—love firmly rooted in grace-based attachment with God and others. For successful and sustainable recovery, the motivation absolutely has to shift from fear to love. Scripture bears it out: though God's wrath is very real, the Word of God says that it is His loving-kindness that leads us to repentance (Romans 2:4).

Don't fear God when you recognize your faults and malfunctions. Instead, as the Holy Spirit sheds light on your areas of weakness, just be honest and release those things to His care. They are keeping you from connecting with Him. Trying to pretend we are strong is the surest way you and I can allow weakness to creep into the dark places of our lives and flourish like black mold. As much as we may wish we could clean up our own act, God knows that "we are nothing but dust" (Psalm 103:14 NASB)—it's just another part of what He loves about us.

MAKING IT STICK

A FACE OF GRACE: MONSIGNOR LEWIS

I graduated from eighth grade at Holy Cross School in the spring of 1973. At that time I was very involved in the life of my church. I'd served as an altar boy for years and enjoyed playing guitar at our Saturday night "folk mass." Church life, including its priests and nuns, were an integral part of my world.

Monsignor Lewis was the senior pastor of our parish. Just after graduation he offered me a job at the rectory as a receptionist. One week out of each month, I would work from 6:00 to 9:00 p.m., taking phone calls and messages, answering the door, and completing any other tasks the priests requested. I could do homework as I sat at the desk, I could listen to the radio (if I played it softly), and—best of all—I got paid! It wasn't long before Monsignor Lewis became a face of grace to me.

At the rectory my office was right outside his office. That allowed me to watch him interact with parishioners on a regular basis. I never saw him lose patience or become upset, and I still remember him kindly welcoming those who attended his weekly Bible study. While a few of the priests and nuns I encountered were stereotypically stiff-starched, formal, and seemingly thrived on intimidation, Monsignor Lewis was the polar opposite. He always greeted me with a warm smile when I arrived for work, and what was even better was how he always took the time to ask me how I was doing. He genuinely seemed to love His work—and people . . . including me.

When I first began working there, Monsignor Lewis was careful to tell me that his door was always open to me. After a while, I became confident enough to start asking him questions about things that concerned me. One night when he and the other priests were not around, I had to deal with a series of tough phone calls from a woman who was seeking an abortion. From what she said, it was clear that she wanted to be talked out of the decision. My attempts to connect her with numerous clergy members failed. Unbelievably, it seemed like no one was willing to talk to her.

Upset by their lack of compassion, I left a distraught message for Monsignor Lewis before going home. I angrily questioned the integrity of the church as well as priests and nuns who were too busy to talk with the pregnant woman. When I arrived for work the next night, he met me at the door with compassion, invited me into his office, and did his best to help me process what had happened. He understood why I was angry and never condemned me for it. Although I still wasn't happy about how everything unfolded, Monsignor Lewis's kindness and patience helped me see the situation differently. I can still feel his kindness and concern today.

Later, when my relationships with my mom and dad were struggling, he was one of the first people I called. We set up a time to get together, and when I showed up for our meeting, he treated me like one of the many adults I'd watched him greet over the years. Even though I was still a kid, he warmly ushered me into his office, and we proceeded to talk as though we were equals. Never for a moment did I feel like Monsignor Lewis was talking down to me—his understanding, kindness, and wisdom floored me. It was as if I was the most important person in the world. Although I didn't realize it at the time, he represented the smiling face of Jesus to me. Truly, I felt like I was his favorite whenever I was around him. Monsignor Lewis died many years ago, but my memories of him are foundational to who I am today.

THE INTERSECTION OF GRACE, SCRIPTURE, AND NEUROSCIENCE: TUNING-UP ATTUNEMENT

In this section you'll discover how neuroscience intersects with grace and Scripture. The reality of God's grace offers solutions and benefits to all aspects of who we are made to be—body, mind, spirit, and relationship!

"Laugh with your happy friends when they're happy; share tears when they're down" (Romans 12:15 MSG).

All of us are born into weakness. We don't know how to care for ourselves, feed ourselves, find water, regulate our temperature, see clearly, or even go to the bathroom without making an extraordinary mess! We need others who are stronger to "tune into our needs" and take the initiative to care for us and help us learn the thousands of tasks we must perform every day to survive. When others meet our needs—while treating us as special and favorite—we grow stronger physically, emotionally, relationally, and mentally. As they do this, they help each level of our brain's emotional and relational control center function in harmony together. External tuning from others helps set our internal tuning correctly.

The somewhat clinical name for this process is called "attunement." If you or I don't get this from other significant people in our lives, it is very difficult to give it to others we care about. Imagine two-stringed instruments getting ready to play music together, and it's easy to understand. Because I've played guitar and enjoyed music most of my life, I am very sensitive to the sound of an out-of-tune guitar trying to play with a band. It doesn't matter how skilled the player or how fast he or she can shred, if an instrument is out of tune, it sounds like two cats fighting! To play well together, instruments must be externally and internally attuned.

Think of it like tuning a guitar: to do so, I play a note on a piano for a reference tone. The source of this piano note serves as an *external* reference point—helping me tune the guitar string to match it correctly. To play together, other instruments must be tuned to the same piano note.

Internal tuning means that all other strings on *my* guitar are set to play in harmony with the initial string I tuned to the piano note. Both internal and external attunement are needed for instruments to play together. Beautiful music follows!

In the same way, our developing mind needs both external and internal attunement. Initially, our brain requires someone (an external source) to attune to our needs. As we experience repeated interactions with those who see us through eyes of grace and attune to our needs, our brain "tunes itself" to the grace, joy, shalom, and the emotional energy of those caretakers. That external attunement allows each developing level of our emotional and relational control center to "tune up" in response. If these levels are out of tune, our brain's ability to form and repair attachments, maintain a consistent identity, behave consistently, and regulate fear and other negative emotions will suffer. When each level of the control center learns how to "stay tuned" to the others, we are able to play well together in the grand symphony that is life. The greater the external attunement from others, the more each level of the control center is able to communicate and work in harmony with the others.

Much like guitars, rock bands, and orchestras, our brain needs attunement!

EXERCISES

DAILY AFFIRMATION 5: MY WEAKNESSES ARE AN OPPORTUNITY FOR GOD'S GRACE TO GROW MORE DEEPLY IN ME.

This is your daily affirmation. Read it aloud as an affirmation of God's work in your life each day while you are working with this chapter. If you are part of a group study, repeat this out loud together each time you meet. (For a complete list of Daily Affirmations, see Appendix A at the back of the book.)

SCRIPTURE REFLECTION: 2 CORINTHIANS 4:6-18

1. Pray and ask Jesus to guide you as you reflect on this passage of Scripture.

2. Take a moment to remember something you appreciate, or a time you have felt deeply connected to God. Reflect on that moment and remember how you felt.

3. Read the following passage of Scripture slowly. As you read, pay attention to any words or phrases that seem to stand out. Then stop and ask Jesus what He wants you to know about the word or phrase. After you ask, consider any thoughts, feelings, impressions, pictures, memories, or other scriptures that come to mind. Write these in your journal.

2 CORINTHIANS 4:6-18 (NKJV)

For it is the God who commanded light to shine out of darkness, who has shone in our hearts to give the light of the knowledge of the glory of God in the face of Jesus Christ.

But we have this treasure in earthen vessels, that the excellence of the power may be of God and not of us. We are hard-pressed on every side, yet not crushed; we are perplexed, but not in despair; persecuted, but not forsaken; struck down, but not destroyed—always carrying about in the body the dying of the Lord Jesus, that the life of Jesus also may be manifested in our body. For we who live are always delivered to death for Jesus' sake, that the life of Jesus also may be manifested in our mortal flesh. So then death is working in us, but life in you.

And since we have the same spirit of faith, according to what is written, "I believed and therefore I spoke," we also believe and therefore speak, knowing that He who raised up the Lord Jesus will also raise us up with Jesus, and will present us with you. For all things are for your sakes, that grace, having spread through the many, may cause thanksgiving to abound to the glory of God.

Therefore we do not lose heart. Even though our outward man is perishing, yet the inward man is being renewed day by day. For our light affliction, which is but for a moment, is working for us a far more exceeding and eternal weight of glory, while we do not look at the things which are seen, but at the things which are not seen. For the things which are seen are temporary, but the things which are not seen are eternal.

4.   After you've finished journaling your observations, pray over them, asking Jesus to show you anything more that He may want you to know about what you've written. Write these in your journal.

5.   If you have the time, continue by rereading the passage of Scripture, journaling, and interacting with Jesus.

6.   After you have finished journaling, read through what you've written. Think about what you have learned from this Scripture that applies to your life right now. Is there a theme or key lesson that speaks to your heart? Or is God calling you to action or further reflection perhaps?

7.   Which of your impressions, if any, might be thoughts God shared with you? Remember, thoughts and impressions we journal do not carry the authority of Scripture. It's always a good idea to share your thoughts and impressions with others you trust to discern what God might want you to know. (If you need help distinguishing what God's thoughts may be, see "Is the Shepherd Speaking?" provided in Appendix B.)

REFLECTION/DISCUSSION QUESTIONS

These questions will help you apply this chapter's themes and your Scripture Reflection exercise in your life. They can also help you prayerfully reflect on your life and your connection with Jesus and ask Him for help. Set aside time during the week to reflect on these questions and write the answers in your journal. If you are studying this book with a group, share your answers with other group members next time you meet.

1. Who was the face of grace you saw this week? How did they communicate "special and favorite" to you or someone else? How did you feel when you experienced this grace?

2. Are there places in your life right now in which you feel "hard-pressed," "perplexed," "persecuted," or "struck down"? What are those areas? Why do you feel this way? Do you feel alone—or do you feel that someone is with you in your struggle?

3. Have you experienced weakness in an area of life that has grown stronger? What is that area of life? How did it grow stronger? What did you do? What helped you—and what did not help you?

4. What is your view of suffering? Do you believe that suffering is actually an opportunity to grow a deeper, grace-based attachment with Jesus, or do you believe that you can avoid suffering? Do you believe that suffering can be eliminated from your life if you have enough faith—or behave correctly? Why did Paul experience such intense suffering?

5. Are there times in your life when you act in pride and try to "over-shine" another person? Why? How do you know when you are feeling this kind of pride? How does it affect your relationships with others?

6. If you are in a group, how would you like them to pray for you?

HOMEWORK

Homework helps you continue to apply this week's lesson, engage with God, and prepare for the next chapter.

1. Go "grace watching" again this week. Can you find a face of grace anywhere around you? This person might be interacting with you or with someone else. How does watching another face of grace affect you, and how do you feel?

2. Continue reflecting on 2 Corinthians 4:6–18 and journal your observations. Is there someone with whom you can share your insights—or who is willing to reflect on the Scripture with you?

3. If, after reading this chapter and completing these exercises, you discover that there are areas of life in which you are acting prideful and hiding weakness, tell God. Ask Him for help. Ask God to help you bring your weaknesses to Him, and be honest with Him about them.

6 *Grace and Identity*

So from now on we regard no one from a worldly point of view. Though we once regarded Christ in this way, we do so no longer. Therefore, if anyone is in Christ, the new creation has come: The old has gone, the new is here!

—2 CORINTHIANS 5:16–17

Identity theft is a massive problem today. You may remember this story. In 2017 the credit-reporting giant, Equifax, announced a data breach that affected an estimated 148 million Americans setting up a slew of potential problems for those innocents involved.[1] The personal information of these unfortunate victims is now forever "out there," along with haunting possible repercussions—financial, emotional, and chronic. More than half of the U.S. population was affected. Because of the massive breach, many of us can still feel the life drain from our days as we try to clean up the mess. Sadly, as cyber thieves and fraudsters get more and more sophisticated, they put us all in similar danger on a daily basis. Being vigilant about your credit and identity information is essential!

Believe it or not, there is a costlier crime perpetrated against you and me: it's the loss of our biblical identity. So, who are you *really*?

INDIVIDUAL IDENTITY
Grace Finds "Me"

When it comes to your true identity, a complete answer can only be found in the context of relationship. Probably even more than you think.

From the start, our closest relationships—the bonds with our parents and other dear caregivers—are vital in helping us discover who we are. To find our true identity, you and I need answers. We are not born with a preloaded, prefabricated identity. You and I don't know who or what we are at first. We don't know how to connect or form relationships with others. Born into a "post-fall" world, our original, God-given identity is lost. At the deepest level imaginable, we're born needing others to help us find the keys to a grace-filled, healthy identity. What we are searching for is found in the answers to these questions:

- Who am I? (What's my identity?)
- Where do I belong and who am I connected to? (Who is my family?)
- Who loves me and whom do I love?

Because we come by these questions naturally, grace and a grace-filled identity are profound gifts that all parents can give their children. Repeated interactions with them can help us establish both.

Before we have any capacity to care for ourselves, we pick up cues about how Mommy and Daddy are relating to us. The first couple of years of our lives are strongly shaped by the self-concept we receive from them during feedings, changings, times of comforting us when we are crying, playtime, and more. Such times communicate a sense of value to us as infants. From this, our most dependent and needy baby state, identity is born and progressively takes form. The more you and I come to know ourselves through our parents' joyful eyes of grace, the more we begin to see ourselves that way, and in turn, we can see others in the same way as well. By establishing our significance early in life, our parents make it much easier for us to believe and receive the same from God later on.

These special people are the ones we are most attached to, and as we discussed in the last chapter, these attachments drive our behavior. If those I am most attached to regularly remind me of their delight in me—how special I am and how I'm their absolute favorite—I begin to live it out, freely and boldly; I call this sense of self "Grace-full Me." At my truest core, I am full of grace—safe in the heart of God as His special and favorite; this is the identity the Lord desires to enlighten in each of us.

Mirrors reflect light, you know. That is how they work. Just as mirrors reflect light, so our parents are intended to collect God's grace and reflect it to us. They become our mirrors. Quite literally, our brains reflect the fact. Neuroscientists tell us that our identity center is loaded with what they refer to as mirror neurons. More mirror neurons are located there than in any other part of our brain. Direct interaction and modeling are needed for them to do their job. When you see someone yawn and you reflexively yawn in response, that is an example of your mirror neurons in action. Without an external point of reference, there is no reaction.

Our identity is the same. Our mirror neurons need those outside ourselves to help us to discern who we are, in practicality. Sure, we can look in a mirror on our own, but for a clear and complete view of who we are (not just what we look like on the outside), we need the input of others. It is something far beyond skin deep. Through their eyes and input, Grace-full Me comes to know: I am special. I am valued. I am joyfully received. And you are too. We must take in this reality. In all situations and under every circumstance, the consistency of this message is vital.

Like our lungs need air, a child's developing mind needs to know he or she is special in order to form a stable, healthy identity. In all different circumstances, each of us needs to experience this reality in heavy and reliable doses. When this is the world I live in, my dad may be angry and express it to me, while still seeing me through eyes of grace and treating me as someone quite special and favorite to God—and to him. Because of my dad's demonstrated, unconditional love, I can be secure; anger is not a scary, disruptive emotion. That means I'm able to act out of my God-given identity consistently; I'm able to see myself with grace and act like the same graceful person when people are angry and when they're not. Even in the presence of distressing emotions, my identity remains the same. This vital relationship trains me to see someone special, valuable, and delighted in each time I look in the mirror. The more consistently full of joy my important people are as they relate with me, the more stable my sense of identity will become.

FEAR DISTORTS "ME"

Sadly, too many of us grow up without the reassurance such constancy affords. Though we are built to be received as grace-full, a regular routine of negative interactions with those we hold dear packs a punch when it comes to our identity. Do you see the disconnect? These inconsistent, contrary messages you and I have internalized may spring from ongoing mundane exchanges or more traumatic negative interactions with those to whom we are attached. Both have a significant impact on how we see ourselves. Insidiously, each communicates that I am special and favorite—*but only sometimes.*

Let's suppose I have a mom who has a problem expressing anger. When she is angry with me, she often conveys that I'm an incompetent failure or somehow worthless. Sometimes it is inferred. Other times she cruelly aims these messages at me with overt precision. This kind of anger is scary—a thing to be avoided, for sure. When that happens,

I don't know how to act out of my biblical identity around her rage. Because of that, my feelings and behaviors become inconsistent—I have no idea who I am in moments like these. Whether people are angry or not, the problem is how I see myself. When I'm not seen through eyes of grace in all situations and circumstances, Grace-full Me is stunted; I don't have a chance to grow. I don't know who I am.

An unstable parental identity is reflected in the life of a child. If our parents and caregivers don't have a consistent, grace-filled, and stable identity of their own (a sense of their own Grace-full Me), the consequences to us can be vast—causing distortions and damage to our self-concept. When that happens, it is like looking in a funhouse mirror—my image becomes warped and malformed by their own.

Suppose you and I are treated inconsistently or only one parent (not both) delivers consistency. When that happens, we begin acting like somebody who isn't really us—unstable and unsure of who we are. Resorting to things like people pleasing and performance, we may strive to make ourselves "okay" or move toward more destructive ways of numbing our pain. Without a stable identity inside, we get a sense that something is missing or wrong about us; who we are and who we understand ourselves to be may shift depending on the people around us or the situation in which we find ourselves.

A note here to imperfect parents: Before you hang your head in despair, please hear me—no parent models it perfectly. As a good friend of mine likes to say, "The only thing that makes good parents is a very forgiving child." Herein lies genius; it is a treasure trove of wisdom. Because the Fall screwed up relational dynamics for everyone, we are all in need of grace—parent *and* child. That's part of the reason Jesus is such good news. You, every kid ever born, and I need the restart of God's grace. *Each of us needs to meet our own Grace-full Me.* The main idea that I hope you take away is that the more strongly we relate with grace toward our children (and others, for that matter), the easier it will be for them to internalize it. Hearing that, if you feel it is necessary, just ask your child for forgiveness as you remind him or her of how special and favorite they are—to God and to you. And know that you can each now move forward in healthier, redemptive ways.

Most of us don't fully understand the identity we have in light of grace. To know Christ more deeply opens us to the possibility of knowing ourselves more fully. Along these lines, Paul admonishes us to follow his lead and motivation:

> I want to know Christ—yes, to know the power of his resurrection and participation in his sufferings, becoming like him in his death, and so, somehow, attaining to the resurrection from the dead.

> Not that I have already obtained all this, or have already arrived at my goal, but I press on to take hold of that for which Christ Jesus took hold of me. Brothers and sisters, I do not consider myself yet to have taken hold of it. But one thing I do: Forgetting what is behind and straining toward what is ahead, I press on toward the goal to win the prize for which God has called me heavenward in Christ Jesus.

> All of us, then, who are mature should take such a view of things. And if on some point you think differently, that too God will make clear to you. Only let us live up to what we have already attained. (Philippians 3:10–16)

Under all different kinds of circumstances, when you and I keep relationship the main thing and see each other through eyes of grace, we are empowering one another to maintain a stable identity. If we are going to take apprenticeship seriously, God is committed to helping us stay connected and express His life when things are really hard. But Jesus understands.

HOW QUICKLY WE FORGET

Simon, (aka Simon Peter), son of Jonah, is an excellent example. In Matthew 16:15 (NKJV), when Jesus asked him directly, "Who do you say that I am?" Simon gave the game-winning answer in verse 16: "You are the Messiah, the Son of the living God." The next thing you know, Jesus replied, "'I tell you that you are Peter [*Petros*], and on this rock [*petra*] I will build my church, and the gates of Hades will not overcome it. I will give you the keys of the kingdom of heaven; whatever you bind on earth will be bound in heaven, and whatever you loose on earth will be loosed in heaven.' Then he ordered his disciples not to tell anyone that he was the Messiah" (Matthew 16:18–20).

This was a pivotal moment in Jesus' life and ministry—and in Peter's as well. Imagine it! Your Lord, your rabbi, the God-man who picked you out of the Galilean sand to be His fisherman-turned-disciple, calls you out, proclaiming that your right response has made a place for you: "You are Petros," the rock, the foundation of His church. Of special note: in the Greek, Peter (Petros) is a name connoting a small stone or piece of rock. Jesus affirms Peter's identity and then goes on to say, "On this *petra* I will build my church." Literally translated, petra that the church is built upon is "a massive, virtually immovable rock." The ramifications to Peter's identity as it relates to Jesus—his attachment to him—cannot be overstated. This is huge! In effect, Jesus was saying, "Great answer, Peter! You're a chip off the old block! Here are the keys to the kingdom: together we are an immense and enduring force!" Can't you just feel Peter's heart swell with joy? But wait, there's more.

Peter's undying commitment to his Master—probably coupled with his new title and an occasionally brash personality—quickly put him at odds with the Savior's Word. He momentarily forgot himself. As the passage continues, their interaction takes a quick turn:

> From that time on Jesus began to explain to his disciples that he must go to Jerusalem and suffer many things at the hands of the elders, the chief priests and the teachers of the law, and that he must be killed and on the third day be raised to life.

> Peter took him aside and began to rebuke him. "Never, Lord!" he said. "This shall never happen to you!"

> Jesus turned and said to Peter, "Get behind me, Satan! You are a stumbling block to me; you do not have in mind the concerns of God, but merely human concerns."

> Then Jesus said to his disciples, "Whoever wants to be my disciple must deny themselves and take up their cross and follow me." (Matthew 16:21–24)

In the span of just a few verses, we watch as Peter stumbles from his status as "the rock" star of Christ's church to "Satan." Apparently, he completely forgot his God-given identity for a moment.

From time to time, this is us. Every so often, negative circumstances or bad choices we have made can uproot us. It prompts the best of us to forget who we are; we behave very unlike our God-given identities. Sometimes, if we express our self-searching in Christian circles, we may be pointed to Scripture and chided: "C'mon! You need to claim what God says about you." Now, don't get me wrong: it *is* important to know and remember what God has to say—especially as it pertains to our identity. But amid our malfunctions and mistakes, what is entirely unhelpful is to ignore the reality of where we actually are and what we have done to get ourselves here. Doing so is kind of like telling a tree that's been blown over in the wind to get up and start acting like all the other trees in the forest. It's just not that simple.

As you and I pursue and increasingly grow into our God-given identity, we will mature into a way of being that lines up with God's Word. We don't work harder—doing things or otherwise "faking it" to make ourselves okay. We look to Scripture for an indication of our progress.

In the myriad of our personal circumstances, understanding our true, God-given identity is a wise place to begin. But it is just that: a beginning. Both Scripture and personal estimation will only provide us a partial understanding because the head knowledge they offer is not all that we are after.

DANGER: IDENTITY WITHOUT ATTACHMENT

Many years back, I was working in a Christ-based rehab facility. Because of a serious addiction to crack cocaine, a guy named Carl joined our program. His family led a large ministry, and despite their best efforts, Carl's drug habit grew to the point where he was unable to function on his own. But the program confronted him with some challenges he never expected. Like many addicts, Carl had a tough time coming to grips with his addiction, but not for the reasons you may guess: the real problem for him was what the Bible said about him. Confused?

Let me explain: Carl realized he had a problem but thought it was because he had not claimed the identity that Scripture describes for believers. With that idea so deeply planted in his thinking, it was almost impossible for him to admit his faults, allow Jesus to repair the broken places in his life, or discover the *actual roots* of his addiction. If we said "Carl, you have a crack addiction," he would invariably respond, "That's not who I am. I am the righteousness of God in Christ Jesus" (2 Corinthians 5:21). That was the way he replied to virtually every attempt we made to help him recognize the character flaws and wounded places in his life—those very places that helped feed his addiction.

As his treatment went on, he seemed to make very little progress. He had a tough time with accountability and found basic work assignments difficult. While he was in the program, Carl maintained his sobriety and reestablished a relationship with his family. All of them seemed to believe that Carl was finally putting on the true identity Jesus had given him.

I didn't hear anything about Carl for several years after he finished the program. Then I received the tragic news that he had overdosed on drugs while on a mission trip outside the United States. Carl lacked a secure attachment with Jesus that would have enabled him to claim his biblical identity. Such relationship would have empowered him to face his fears, weaknesses, and shortcomings courageously. Addressing these issues with a growing, grace-based attachment to Jesus would have allowed him to begin walking in the reality of his Grace-full Me identity. Instead, Carl tried to assert his God-given identity without the grace-based attachment that would've allowed that identity to take root, grow, and produce fruit.

Have you ever read a description of your God-given identity in the Bible—the way He says He sees you—only to recognize that it doesn't really fit who you are? Like a little child putting on Mom's or Dad's shoes and clomping around the house, we've all got some growing up to do before our spiritual size fits God's Word. We are to set our minds and hearts on these things without illusion, in lockstep with His grace (Colossians 3:1).

When I was about thirty, I was grappling along these lines as a dear mentor, John, helped me work through some major trauma that had occurred earlier in my life. By then I'd been in ministry for a few years and I firmly believed what the Bible said about me—but when I got honest, something wasn't sitting quite right inside my soul.

I was familiar with the book of Romans and had specifically studied everything chapters 6 through 8 had to say about my God-given identity. I had Romans 6:11 (NKJV) memorized, and as far as I understood it up to that time, I was following its instruction to "reckon [myself] to be dead, indeed to sin, but alive to God in Christ Jesus our Lord." Following Romans 8:1, I could recall that because of Jesus, I no longer lived under condemnation. I understood. I had counted the cost. There was no doubt in my mind that all this was true. *Theoretically*, I agreed with these sacred words and all those in between.

Suddenly, it was like a halogen bulb lit up something that I hadn't noticed before. What had previously been pushed off to the side, hidden somewhere in the shadow of my heart, was now in plain sight: the relationship I'd had with God up to this point couldn't support the identity I was proclaiming over myself through Scripture. My weak relational attachment with God was undermining the way I honestly saw myself *in Christ.* Grace-full Me was a stranger! I was still busy trying to perform and people please my way into feeling more special and favorite. Unbeknownst to me, I was attempting to earn the grace that God wanted to share with me freely. Because I didn't understand myself to be God's special and favorite, it didn't matter how many verses I committed to memory or even how accurate I believed them to be.

Coming to grips with the trauma, feeling its pain, and recognizing its impact created an opening in my life for a deeper attachment with God. The reality of my pain, broken identity, and weakness collided head-on with my performance orientation. John's wisdom, the Living Word of God, and the work of the Holy Spirit combined with my pain to help extricate me from darkness into the light of freedom.

Carl and I both experienced very different versions of the same thing: our foundations were off. To walk more fully in our God-given identity, we both needed to experience a deeper attachment with Jesus. That required looking at our own wounded places in the light of Scripture. Otherwise, our attempts to cover these areas with Bible verses and biblical truths were actually preventing our spiritual growth. The same is true for each of us. Abiding attachment with Jesus and an increasing sense of our identity in Him come as we embrace the suffering of our broken places. There we meet Jesus and encounter the joyful truth: we are special and favorite. No. Matter. What.

For sincere followers of Jesus, avoiding our brokenness can be spiritually (and sometimes physically) deadly. Just as Carl and I had done, many people think of suffering as bad or evil—something to be avoided or cast out. Instead, we need to encourage one another to bravely explore the pain of our brokenness as an opportunity to encounter more profound levels of God's grace. If we are willing to go there, you and I will experience deeper attachment to Him and, subsequently, the freedom to live more fully in the truth of who we were created to be.

Because we hadn't embraced our brokenness, Carl and I were both inadvertently bypassing the important point of our suffering and hoping we could lay claim to a biblical identity we had only read about. But it simply can't be done that way. Think of it like this: healthy babies attach to their caregivers out of need and weakness; when the baby has a boo-boo, loving adults provide comfort and help them resolve the pain. A child's dependence results in growing love and trust—ultimately, these help their identity begin to take form. In that way, we are all just big babies. God promises to comfort us, never to leave us or forsake us as we take necessary steps to work through our life's hurts.

Avoidance does not build a solid relational foundation of God's grace in our lives. It undermines it. Whenever we do this, you and I build on sand; anything we construct atop will be unstable. But once the deep groundwork of grace has been laid, our first floor can be framed in: starting with a sill of ongoing attachment with Jesus, the structure of the floor, ceiling joists, and wall studs can be built to last. With careful crafting, this level will support all that comes later. After it is put firmly in place, only then is it time to build the second floor: our identity.

Because our identity is ever growing, our attachment with Jesus must keep pace with its new additions. The more you and I hang out with Him, the more our foot plate will continue to expand—architecting an attachment to Jesus that will be able to support our identity. Otherwise, trying to claim who we are—even if that identity is scripturally based— is like forcing an enormous structure to balance atop a tiny base. If we build this way, our flimsy foundation will be exposed whenever life's stresses occur, sending the structure of our identity sideways. *Jenga!* When a solid foundation of grace-filled attachment with Jesus has been built, stresses may sway us a bit, but we won't topple over.

Carl's topple ended in tragedy. By the grace of God, mine led to transformation.

RESTORING "ME"

Imagine you have a foundation of grace solidly in place. You may even have been blessed to start your spiritual journey understanding that it is a lifelong endeavor to become. You are well on your way. But what far too many of us misconstrue is that *we* have to find, understand, and fix our broken places as a part of the process. Yes, understanding a problem can be useful, but it should never be confused with the solution. Let me reiterate: understanding ≠ solving. In fact, finding new and better ways to explain our dysfunction tends to be depressing. Rather than attempting to solve our own problems, an opportunity exists: we are invited to engage with God and allow Him to fill our broken places. The question is, will we? Growing a grace-based identity means we must connect with God and others who can see us through eyes of grace— often when we don't have the vision for ourselves.

Honestly, when expressed in the context of an actual relationship like this, grace has an opportunity to grow and, consequently, so does our identity. By God's design, we desperately need one another! Apart from community, our Christian identity is nothing more than an idealized theory. Though our culture may insist otherwise, you and I are incapable of creating our own identity. More information (even biblical information), social media posts, online communities, books, TV, movies or music, just can't grow one. Only attaching to Jesus and meaningfully connecting with others will. These are essential to constructing the healthy, God-given identity we long for.

Undeniably, transformation is a core component of new life in Christ and discipleship for each one of us. Scripture tells us that followers of Jesus have already been crucified with Christ so that now, in the present, we have the opportunity to live extraordinary lives, full of grace. Galatians 2:20–21 (NKJV) explains: "I have been crucified with Christ; it is no longer I who live, but Christ lives in me; and the life which I now live in the flesh I live by faith in the Son of God, who loved me and gave Himself for me. I do not set aside the grace of God; for if righteousness comes through the law, then Christ died in vain."

Crucified. Christ took on the work of our righteous reconstruction at Calvary. Of significant note: nowhere in this verse—or anywhere else in the Bible—are you and I empowered to nail one another to self-styled crosses of personal expectation and legalism; these are nothing more than religious deadwood. Recognizing this will help us keep our relationships stronger and more important than any problem that may arise.

Why is this so important? Because God and countless research studies indicate that human identity cannot and will not grow by merely telling someone what they're doing wrong. Think of your own experience. While this kind of input may temporarily modify your behavior, correction outside of grace-based relationship will never lead to a lasting reformation of your character. Like all of us, even if you are making mistakes, you have the unique privilege to grow, transform, and respond in lasting ways when treated as the special and favorite person you are designed to be.

There it is again: out of our weakness, we grow. I believe this is the joy Christ kept His eyes on from the cross (Hebrews 12:2). When we are seen and received as more than the sum of our problems, you and I can be sure that we are on a transformational journey toward Christlikeness.

GROUP IDENTITY

"We": Finding My Herd

Both individuals and groups want to know: how does an identity grow?

We are not meant for life as lone rangers. God designed us to be part of a tribe or, as imagined in the animated movie *Ice Age*, a herd. When Manny the wooly mammoth, Diego the saber-tooth, and Sid the sloth end up battling enemies for the common (and dangerous) cause of returning a baby boy to his human herd, their conversation went something like this:

> **MANNY:** That's what you do in a herd—you look out for each other.
> **DIEGO:** Well, thanks.
> **SID:** *[slight pause]* I don't know about you guys, but we're the weirdest herd I have *ever* seen.[2]

Aren't we all, boys . . . aren't we all.

Despite all our quirks, God is serious about this group identity thing. We don't seem to understand the size and power of the connections that surround us. Most of us haven't begun to tap into what life together would look like, but the unharnessed potential energy of this part of our biblical identity is worth considering. In it, God calls us near as part of the ultimate "we"—His family:

And He came and preached peace to you who were afar off and to those who were near. For through Him we both have access by one Spirit to the Father.

Now, therefore, you are no longer strangers and foreigners, but fellow citizens with the saints and members of the household [relatives, family] of God, having been built on the foundation of the apostles and prophets, Jesus Christ Himself being the chief cornerstone, in whom the whole building, being fitted together, grows into a holy temple in the Lord, in whom you also are being built together for a dwelling place of God in the Spirit. (Ephesians 2:17–22 NKJV)

We all have a place. (Family, herd, team)—whatever you want to call it, God knows we need one. Early in my career, I spent four years as a police officer. During my training days in the academy, this lesson came to life for me; our group identity as a team became more important than me or my comfort.

Eight hours each day for a warm Southern springtime week, we had firearm training at an outdoor shooting range; at the end of the week my fellow officer candidates and I were exhausted. As part of the department's qualifying, we had to complete a timed shooting test that included rapidly reloading our guns. Back then, police officers carried 6-shot revolvers. We each had to fire eighteen rounds in rapid succession for the test, which meant reloading our weapon twice. Because part of our score was based on how quickly we could finish firing, we would just dump the spent brass shell casings on the ground while practicing and testing. Once we were done, we would then have to pick up—or "police our brass." The training instructors called the spent shells "wounded soldiers" and made a huge deal out of making sure that no brass was left on the ground; repeatedly, they warned us not to leave "wounded soldiers" on the battlefield (aka the shooting range).

The range was about a hundred yards long, with what seemed like a hundred-foot-tall berm behind the targets. We were used to running laps around the range and up and down the berm as part of our drills. To simulate the physical stress of actual shooting scenarios we may face once we were on the force, instructors would stress our bodies with these sprints before making us fire rounds at targets. At the end of each of these demanding days, they would diligently check our individual firing areas to ensure that we policed our brass. If we missed even one, the penalty for the offender was to run laps on the berm while carrying a full case of ammunition (roughly thirty-five pounds of it). It was designed as a punishment—and it was!

Late one afternoon, after shooting and exercising all day, we were instructed to police the brass before we could go home. The instructors searched the area and found one blasted shell casing on the ground at a station where a fellow squad member had been firing. Swiftly and certainly, our trainers barked her penalty: "START RUNNING! AND DON'T FORGET THE AMMO!"

We all knew she was in for quite a few laps. Just before she had a chance to begin, our squad spontaneously stepped alongside her. As a team we were one unit. Despite our collective exhaustion and physical pain, we told the instructors that if she had to run, then we would all run with her. At that moment, sharing the discomfort of running with her was more important to us than our personal comfort. Amazed, the instructors took a step back, seeming to warm up just a bit. "This," the senior training officer informed us, "is what we've been waiting for. You have formed a team and care for one another as a team. Because of that, none of you will have to run the berm." *Whew!*

My group identity as part of the training class became so strong that I was willing to suffer for it. In my experience, the vast majority of my teammates in law enforcement felt the same way. For all the negative press out there, most officers are willing to be hurt or killed to protect another, whether officer or civilian, in trouble. Sadly, although there's a lot of talk from the pulpit about laying down one's life for another, I can't say this is the norm for most Christians in our churches these days.

So, ask yourself some key questions:

- Who are your teammates?
- In your life, with whom do you share a mutual sense of caring, concern, and sacrifice?
- Who are those personal people in your everyday life who are so safe that you allow them to see and understand who you really are?
- From God's perspective, what relationships in your life make both you and the other person better?

Your answers to the above probably won't yield a long list. But if it helps you narrow the field, think of it like this: for anyone who makes the cut, you should be able to say that "our" survival is more important than my own; in other words, these are the people you would die for.

SEEN AND HERD

You see, we are all in this together. *We.* Community reflects the nature of the Trinity. You and I don't just connect with God and—*bam*—discover our identity. Grace experienced is grace to be shared, as they say. That being the case, when talking about identity, our focus must be decidedly *we*-centered.

To count ourselves part of Christ's body, we must learn to see ourselves and others as unique parts of a whole. That is how God sees us, after all. Time with Jesus, and with other people attached to Him, helps you and me see the commitment to grow into His likeness through to our spiritual maturity. Both are designed to remind us of who we are and who we are becoming. Let me remind you: you are a valuable, loveable, worthwhile person, capable of bringing Him joy.

Does something inside you soften as you read those words? I hope so. Is there any word on that list that particularly touches you? I guarantee you there is someone in your life who recognizes these things in you. When we experience God's grace through the presence of others, you and I can actually see ourselves more clearly. These relationships and our God-given identity grow best when they are full of interactive grace, love, joy, and peace.

In addition to attachment bonds, another essential part of our spiritual process begins when we are very young. How people interact with us early on affects how we tend to see others. Seeing people the way we have been seen, you and I develop general impressions as to whether people are good or bad, are friendly or unfriendly, like us or don't like us, and so on. It's a sort of mental-emotional "posture" that we take regarding others around us. It is somewhat of a "herding instinct."

As you may predict, this posture is influenced by how well an individual's sense of their God-given identity, their Grace-full Me identity, has been established. If it is strong, then the individual will relate to others in healthy ways. Together, the Grace-full Me identity and the special people who see the individual through eyes of grace form a unique group bond I call "Grace-full We." This special connection affords us a sense of belonging. We come to know this close, grace-based community as "our people," our herd; for most of us, it begins with parents and caregivers and then grows to include friends in the neighborhood playgroup, our Sunday school class, and other groups to which we belong.

When you and I hit puberty, on an unconscious level the drive for a group identity grows to become absolutely enormous. The stress hormone, cortisol, literally dissolves old, underused neuropathways in favor of structuring new ones to make way for peer relationships and pressures (clinically, this process is known as "pruning and parcellation.") Parents, prepare to take a backseat . . . peers rule during this phase. This is the developmental stage when who I am and who my people are get externalized. I form new, meaningful relationships with the larger community. On some levels, this shift makes perfect sense: we need to individuate in order to pursue our grown-up goals of personal interests, career, spouse, and family.

But to be clear, our identities never outgrow the need for close relationship—whatever the source. That's because we do not live in some sort of divine vacuum. God—not Dyson—was responsible for our design scheme. Sorry to report: life just isn't all about you—or about me, either. We are intended to share life together, and Lord knows, for this we need His grace. Even though we've been given a new identity in Christ, sometimes our self-oriented behavior betrays us. In times like these, it is as if we have forgotten the words of Colossians 3:3: our life has been hidden in His, not the other way around.

Too often, I've noticed, my ungraceful face pokes itself out from beneath the covers at key moments in the game of life, my fleshly, untransformed parts exposed. But there is something else that has also caught my attention: praise be to God, I am noticing more often when it happens. Truth be told, I didn't used to. So, while it doesn't excuse the lack of grace in how I may have treated someone, I sense God growing me—making me more alive to Him—at the same time.

AN IDENTITY FAR FROM ORDINARY

In the game for developing our individual identity, the players are me-Jesus-others. Consistent attachment with the Lord continues to reveal the vast implications of grace—how it affects me and how I affect others. It is safe to come out of hiding. Invited by grace, I discover more of who God made me to be. *Olly, Olly, oxen free!* More and more, in my vulnerabilities I recognize the Lord's intention that the grace I have experienced should flow into the connection I have with others; grace connects and grows these connections in us both. Uncovered by it, you and I are free to understand and walk alongside one another as our true selves. Now we can begin to see each other differently—becoming faces of grace for one another.

Paul helped to put it plainly in 2 Corinthians 5:16–19:

> So from now on we regard no one from a worldly point of view. Though we once regarded Christ in this way, we do so no longer. Therefore, if anyone is in Christ, the new creation has come: The old has gone, the new is here! All this is from God, who reconciled us to himself through Christ and gave us the ministry of reconciliation: that God was reconciling the world to himself in Christ, not counting people's sins against them. And he has committed to us the message of reconciliation.

You are a new creation! I am a new creation! Grace makes it possible, and grace can reconcile us all; this is the lens we must look through. Before God can raise us to the robust group identity He has in mind, we must care deeply about Him, these words of His, and we must also care for others—deeply enough to die—even when they do the most unlovely things. In no uncertain terms, you and I are to become like Him, so this is how we need to see—through eyes of grace.

In the words of C. S. Lewis,

> There are no ordinary people. You have never talked to a mere mortal. Nations, cultures, arts, civilisations—these are mortal, and their life is to ours as the life of a gnat. But it is immortals whom we joke with, work with, marry, snub, and exploit—immortal horrors or everlasting splendours. This does not mean that we are to be perpetually solemn. We must play.

But our merriment must be of that kind (and it is, in fact, the merriest kind) which exists between people who have, from the outset, taken each other seriously—no flippancy, no superiority, no presumption. And our charity must be a real and costly love, with deep feeling for the sins in spite of which we love the sinner—no mere tolerance, or indulgence which parodies love as flippancy parodies merriment. Next to the Blessed Sacrament itself, your neighbour is the holiest object presented to your senses. If he is your Christian neighbour, he is holy in almost the same way, for in him also Christ vere latitat—the glorifier and the glorified, Glory Himself, is truly hidden.[3]

Whether we are talking about individuals or groups, in order to grow a grace-based, Christ-centered identity, we must not forget Lewis's words. Only as you and I hold the vision of God's glory in one another will we begin to see ourselves freely take form in our world; it is then we will start connecting with one another around our truest identities.

I've always admired poets and songwriters. Like Lewis, they put themselves out there with a high degree of vulnerability and insight—offering us encouragement, validation, and healing for things we may not have previously been able to put into words. These artists help us see with new eyes and hear with new ears through their exacting lyrical abilities. Their way of being in the world, of observing and recording our shared human condition, is astoundingly brave, uniquely intimate, and tremendously powerful. Releasing His work into the world, God is much like them. Remember?

"For we are His workmanship, created in Christ Jesus for good works, which God prepared beforehand that we would walk in them" (Ephesians 2:10 NKJV). His workmanship, *poiema*, is the word Paul chose to use. This side of heaven, it denotes a masterpiece—an epic rich with literal textures, tastes, and tones that only the Divine can fathom. The word for how God created you and me was drawn from a poem. Let yourself connect with that for a moment. You and I are lyrical—expressing God's heart, beautiful and crafted for purpose in Christ. Do you see that about yourself? When you read the poem of your life, do you like what is on the page of your soul? Who has written on your heart about who you truly are? And do you like what you're reading? I hope so because that is your identity.

If you don't like what's on the page, remember this: the best poems have rhythm and elements that rise and fall, twist and turn—every verse designed to keep things uniquely interesting. The Lord is our divine poet laureate, our Dove Award songsmith. Knowing the end of our days from the beginning, He doesn't wing it either. He is working by design—we are bespoken beings. God's lyrical genius manifests as we cooperate with His grace-filled crafting of our character, relationships, and experiences. All is grace. Walk with others in it, and you will discover the truth of who God says you are. Whatever you do, don't let it be stolen from you.

MAKING IT STICK

A FACE OF GRACE: BRIAN

By the time I arrived at college, I was a mess. I was angry, disillusioned, and fresh off a bad breakup with my first serious girlfriend. I found myself alienated from my parents too. For the first time in my life, I was really on my own. Before long I began seeking refuge in drinking and drugging—the anesthesia they provided seemed like just what I needed. My hair and my anger both continued to grow. I started hanging out and demonstrating with a group called the Revolutionary Student Brigade, a Maoist Communist organization. I attended weekly Marxist study groups and rigorously practiced guitar with serious hopes of auditioning for a rock band. For the most part I stayed numb, angry, and distracted enough to stave off any painful feelings (except for the time I repeatedly punched a case of beer . . . but that's another story). Oddly, despite my antics, I managed to do well academically and was a member of the university's honors program.

During my freshman year, I met Brian in my Honors French 3 class. He became the face of grace that led me back to Jesus. In class, this funny, outgoing senior had a contagious smile, and long hair like mine. I knew that he was a musician who had recently released an album, which of course I thought was very cool. We seemed to have a lot in common. Brian had seen me demonstrating and making speeches on campus. After class one day, when Brian asked me to have lunch with him, I quickly said yes.

Over sandwiches, Brian asked me about my life and listened to me talk about what fueled my anger, my love for being "high," and my fierce ambition to be a musician. He asked excellent questions and seemed genuinely interested in me. At the very end of our lunch, Brian let me know that he was a serious follower of Jesus and a leader and pastor at a small community Bible fellowship. I was astounded that someone like him would be interested in spending time with me—but that's precisely what he wanted. He and I were soon having weekly lunches— talking politics, injustice, music, philosophy, Marxism, and just about everything else. Brian never pushed Jesus on me, and I never felt like I was his "evangelism project." We met regularly throughout the year, and eventually Brian began inviting me to his church. I declined every time.

The following summer, I lived alone and worked long hours at a moving company. Continuing my lifestyle of drinking and drugging, I noticed myself becoming increasingly burned-out and frustrated. As the level of my emotional pain continued to rise, a new thought slowly dawned on me: *Is this the way I want to live for the rest of my life?*

Even though I didn't really understand what it meant, I found myself missing God's presence in my life. Desperate, I called the only person that I knew would understand: Brian. He quickly agreed to meet with me, and he listened as I told him honestly about my life and unhappiness. I also told him I wanted to "do Jesus" but planned to continue getting high. Brian smiled and gently said that God didn't really work that way and that ultimately I would need to choose. There was no condemnation in his statement; I understood that he was just telling me the truth. Once after a late night of partying, I showed up at his church in pretty bad shape; I was so strung out that my hands were shaking. Even then, Brian and everyone there received me with love.

Before long I surrendered my life to Jesus and began to attend church as many times a week as the doors were open. Brian's eyes of grace opened my heart to Jesus and what it meant to follow Him. Introducing me to authors such as C. S. Lewis and Francis Schaeffer, Brian also helped me realize that Christians can ask profound questions, think deeply—and still be God's favorite!

THE INTERSECTION OF GRACE, SCRIPTURE, AND NEUROSCIENCE: THE TEENAGE BRAIN

In this section you'll discover how neuroscience intersects with grace and Scripture. The reality of God's grace offers solutions and benefits to all aspects of who we are made to be—body, mind, spirit, and relationship!

"Train up a child in the way he should go, And when he is old he will not depart from it" (Proverbs 22:6 NKJV)

Until the time we hit puberty, our brain has been developing strong attachments and individual identity. It's been busy helping us answer the essential questions, "Who am I, and how do I like to behave?" Trillions of neural connections in our brain develop to help us do everything, such as wash our face, ride a bicycle, discover if we like chocolate ice cream, or say "Sir" or "Ma'am" when addressing adults. Interconnected neural pathways also help you and me feel and regulate distressing emotions such as anger, sadness, or hopeless despair. These connections lead us to develop new attachments with others and to regulate fear. Brain development during childhood is an amazing, intricate, and incredibly complex process.

But when you and I hit puberty, our brain is ready for something else entirely. Instead of focusing primarily on individual identity, our brain turns its attention to the formation of peer relationships that will help guide us into adulthood. At this developmental point, the brain is readying itself to form the kind of attachments you and I will need to become healthy spouses and parents, as well as good workers, friends, and members of our own unique "herd." When we're healthy, life becomes more about "we" than about "me."

The process of prepping for this transition is known as "pruning and parcellation." Much like a landscaper trimming a tree to allow healthy new growth and fruit, the brain systematically eliminates what it considers excessive, underused neural pathways to make way for new relational growth. This is a time of preprogrammed cell death in which the brain actually dissolves neural pathways that are not well established or used frequently. Just as an arborist avoids trimming back the main branches of a tree, the brain tends to ignore strong neural pathways. For example, the brain is unlikely to eliminate the neural pathways used to brush our teeth. We simply use those pathways too often. However, it is more likely to prune pathways that help us know what to do when we experience strong feelings such as anger, especially if we were never very good at it to begin with. If you or I learned to avoid emotionally hard things instead of developing our capacity to grow, these skills may have been neurologically "trimmed back" during adolescence. The brain uses a powerful hormone called cortisol to eliminate old pathways.

From the outside, adolescents hitting this stage may seem to lack the common sense and good behavior they may have previously had. Internally, the combination of powerful hormones plus pruning and parcellation means that some of the pathways that might have once governed behaviors (including good, kind, considerate, and gentle behaviors) are gone. I often tell people, "Of course your teenager is acting like they don't have any sense—the cortisol ate it." This is the stage in which peers and friends seem to "know everything" and parents seem to know almost nothing. While alarming to parents, in reality this is a sign of brain growth and a crucial developmental stage.

Fortunately, pruning and parcellation don't last forever. A brain trained consistently with grace tends to retain this essential foundation, adding to it the ability to form strong, deep, and lasting adult-level connections with others. Adolescence is always rocky but tends to be less damaging when grace is in place. Those trained with inconsistent grace (and those around them) inevitably find this stage more destructive. Eventually, the new "herd" becomes more important than individual survival. When my grace-based group identity becomes more important than me, I am well on my way to the process of falling in love, marrying, parenting, and taking my place as a leader in God's family.

EXERCISES

DAILY AFFIRMATION 6: I AM GROWING INCREASINGLY INTO THE PERSON GOD DESIGNED ME TO BE.

This is your daily affirmation for the week. Read it aloud as an affirmation of God's work in your life each day while you are working with this chapter. If you are part of a group study, repeat this out loud together each time you meet. (For a complete list of Daily Affirmations, see Appendix A at the back of the book.)

SCRIPTURE REFLECTION: 2 CORINTHIANS 5:13-21

1. Pray and ask Jesus to guide you as you reflect on this passage of Scripture.

2. Take a moment to remember something you appreciate, or a time you have felt deeply connected to God. Reflect on that moment and remember how you felt.

3. Read the following passage of Scripture slowly. As you read, pay attention to any words or phrases that seem to stand out. Then stop and ask Jesus what He wants you to know about the word or phrase. After you ask, consider any thoughts, feelings, impressions, pictures, memories, or other scriptures that come to mind. Write these in your journal.

2 CORINTHIANS 5:13-21

If we are "out of our mind," as some say, it is for God; if we are in our right mind, it is for you. For Christ's love compels us, because we are convinced that one died for all, and therefore all died. And he died for all, that those who live should no longer live for themselves but for him who died for them and was raised again.

So from now on we regard no one from a worldly point of view. Though we once regarded Christ in this way, we do so no longer. Therefore, if anyone is in Christ, the new creation has come: The old has gone, the new is here! All this is from God, who reconciled us to himself through Christ and gave us the ministry of reconciliation: that God was reconciling the world to himself in Christ, not counting people's sins against them. And he has committed to us the message of reconciliation. We are therefore Christ's ambassadors, as though God were making his appeal through us. We implore you on Christ's behalf: Be reconciled to God. God made him who had no sin to be sin for us, so that in him we might become the righteousness of God.

4. After you've finished journaling your observations, pray over them. Ask Jesus to show you anything more that He may want you to know about what you've written. Add these to your journal entry.

5. If you have the time, continue by rereading the passage of Scripture, journaling, and interacting with Jesus.

6. After you have finished journaling, read through what you've written. Think about what you have learned from this Scripture that applies to your life right now. Is there a theme or key lesson that speaks to your heart? Or is God calling you to action or further reflection perhaps?

7. Which of your impressions, if any, might be thoughts God shared with you? Remember, thoughts and impressions we journal do not carry the authority of Scripture. It's always a good idea to share your thoughts and impressions with others you trust to help discern what God might want you to know. (If you need help distinguishing what God's thoughts may be, see "Is the Shepherd Speaking?" provided in Appendix B.)

REFLECTION/DISCUSSION QUESTIONS

These questions will help you apply this chapter's themes and your Scripture Reflection exercise in your life. They can also help you prayerfully reflect on your life and connection with Jesus so you can ask Him for help. Set aside time during the week to reflect on these questions and write the answers in your journal. If you are studying this book with a group, share your answers with other group members next time you meet.

1. Who was the face of grace you saw this week? How did they communicate "special and favorite" to you or someone else? How did you feel when you experienced this grace?

2. What does it mean to you to be a "new creation" in Christ? Do you really see yourself as someone new? Are there times when it's

hard for you to see yourself as special and favorite? What makes it hard for you to see yourself that way?

3. How often are you able to see other followers of Jesus as God sees them? Are there people and situations in which this is easier? Which make this harder?

4. How often are you able to see people who are not followers of Jesus as God sees them? Are there times when this is harder and times when it's easier? Think about people you read about regularly in the news, see on TV, encounter personally, or hear about being embroiled in controversy or evil behavior. Why is it often so difficult to see them as God does?

5. Imagine that you have one minute to tell another person who you are and how you see yourself. What would you say to them? Is this the same way God sees you? Does what you would say about yourself feel "true" to you, or does it feel fake or phony? Why?

6. Imagine that you have one minute to tell another person about your "herd." What would you say? Do you think this is the way that God sees your herd? Does what you would say about your herd feel "true" to you, or does it feel fake or phony? Why?

7. If you are in a group, how would you like them to pray for you?

HOMEWORK

Homework helps you continue to apply this week's lesson, engage with God, and prepare for the next chapter.

1. Go "grace watching" again this week. Can you find a face of grace anywhere around you? This person might be interacting with you or with someone else. How does watching another face of grace affect you, and how do you feel?

2. Continue reflecting on 2 Corinthians 5:13–21 and journal your observations. Is there someone with whom you can share your insights—or who is willing to reflect on the Scripture with you?

3. Spend some time this week asking God to help you see yourself and others as He does. Start with any situations or people you identified in questions 2, 3, and 4 in the Reflection/Discussion section above. Write any insights you learn this week in your journal.

7 Dead-end Streets: The Debate

Heaven and Hell are God's provisions for who we choose to be. It is a natural extension of the way we live. I tell people that what they get out of this life—after this life— is the person that they become now.

—DALLAS WILLARD

You have your heads in your Bibles constantly because you think you'll find eternal life there. But you miss the forest for the trees. These Scriptures are all about me! And here I am, standing right before you, and you aren't willing to receive from me the life you say you want.

—JOHN 5:39–40 MSG

There is a great gulf between the understanding that God accepts us because of our efforts and the understanding that God accepts us because of what Jesus has done. Religion operates on the principle, "I obey—therefore I am accepted by God." But the operating principle of the gospel is "I am accepted by God through what Christ has done—therefore I obey."

—TIM KELLER

Years ago my mother-in-law, Sol, bought a piece of acreage in rural North Carolina. It was in an area rich with history and full of legend, so when she came upon a jumbled ring of long-ago-charred rocks during a tour of the property, she was ecstatic; Sol was sure it was the spot where Native Americans must have once built their campfires. However, quicker than Smokey Bear on a blaze, her excitement was doused. Because the firepit was located so close to a freshwater spring, the previous owner explained, it was more likely the spot where some good ole boys had set up their moonshine still.

Isn't that just the way it is? Anytime there's a freshwater source, people want to distill it. That appears to be how it is with the topic of grace as well. People seem inclined to want to dilute it with conditions and compromise.

According to Scripture, the clear source of grace is a relationship with God. Through that Spirit-led relationship, God intends our attachment with Him to govern and inspire our behavior—reflecting Him in all things. Empowered by the context of relationship, you and I learn from Him and from His people how to do what Jesus does, see what Jesus sees, and say what Jesus says. From this source of authentic connection with God and others flows life in His kingdom—the thirst of our souls quenched as we experience that we are uniquely valuable, worthwhile, welcome, and loved. Through grace-based attachment with God, the cup of our identity is filled and, with each sip, our interior and exterior world is changed. By no work of our own doing, you and I are thus infused with the power to become world changers.

Ephesians 2:4–5 confirms it: "But because of his great love for us, God, who is rich in mercy, made us alive with Christ even when we were dead in transgressions—it is by grace you have been saved." Does this sound too good to be true, or does it resonate as what you've always longed for? Just as every cell in your body requires water to live, only grace can slake your spiritual thirst. We simply cannot live without either. So what do you think? Is God's grace enough, or do we need to top off His work? Does it seem reckless or naïve to invite the people of Christ to wade in such streams? Clearly, some think so. There is an ongoing debate on grace and license, dating back to the apostle Paul. Listen to his appeal in verses 3–4 of Jude: "Dear friends, although I was very eager to write to you about the salvation we share, I felt compelled to write and urge you to contend for the faith that was once for all entrusted to God's holy people. For certain individuals whose condemnation was written about long ago have secretly slipped in among you. They are ungodly people, who pervert the grace of our God into a license for immorality and deny Jesus Christ our only Sovereign and Lord."

As you can see, almost from the get-go Paul got pushback from critics, and that criticism continues in religious circles today. With what I believe are good intentions, many people seem inclined to add to grace in its purest form—that is, grace by faith in Jesus. Trying to add anything to grace is like trying to mix oil into a refreshing cup of drinking water— the two just don't mix. But even if they did, who in their right mind would want to drink it? Grace alone is all we need, and grace isn't slick. God's grace is . . .

- Clean and straightforward—not gunked up with conditions or grime from its intentional abuse
- Meant to soak into our souls—not slide off
- Refreshingly joyful

These are the qualities of grace by faith—also known as pure grace. As straightforward as it seems, there are other opinions out there. To keep the water clear, it seems constructive to look at two common stances people live by. They are hyper-grace and "greasy law."

HYPER-GRACE: ATTACHED TO FREEDOM

Have you ever heard the term *hyper-grace* before? It's a thing. In light of the Lord's deep love for us, it's a way of thinking that I find saddening. Anyone who tries to teach pure grace (read: people like me) will get accused of being part of the hyper-grace movement from time to time. Grace be a slippery topic, so I want to be articulate on this point: the grease of hyper-grace is the notion that because you and I are forgiven based on the finished work of the cross, we can do anything we want—right, wrong, or indifferent.

Sounds pretty good, huh? There's just enough truth mixed in to make it believable, but here's the problem: in essence, the hyper-grace movement emphasizes the importance of uncompromised grace while at the same time dismissing guilt, repentance, and confession as irrelevant to the Christian life. *Who needs to be bothered? We are Christians—sin slides right off us!* Nothing could be further from the truth; whether it's our relationship with God or another person, we *should* feel contrite whenever we betray a relationship. Under the auspices of hyper-grace, sin isn't seen for what it is: broken relational attachment with God (God's heart is broken for us when we sin—shouldn't ours be too?)

You see, long before we deliberately pursue sin under the guise that grace will cover its consequences, we have left our grace-based attachment with God. The idea that grace covers sin is not wrong, but our attachment is malformed. In this instance, we have already fallen from grace and alienated ourselves from Christ. Our sin is simply a logical, inevitable result of our plunge into murky boundary waters.

Grace does not give you and me a "get-out-of-jail-free card." Though I am still His special and favorite, if I get a DUI driving drunk, there are going to be consequences; because of my actions, I will quickly find myself handcuffed in the back of a patrol car on my way to a jail cell, regardless of how God may feel about me. Grace does not prevent me from reaping the consequences of negative behaviors. Instead, grace is what helps me sow good seeds that leads to a harvest of life.

When you or I find ourselves drifting into the oncoming traffic of sin, it would be smart to ask, Who is driving? Is it Jesus? Those who fall for the concept of hyper-grace need their keys taken away until they can soberly reconsider the ramifications of what they are believing. Out of love, I hope you would hold mine for me—that is, at least until you can help me remember how special I am to Jesus. The Word of God couldn't be clearer on this: "For the grace of God that brings salvation has appeared to all men, teaching us that, denying ungodliness and worldly lusts, we should live soberly, righteously, and godly in the present age" (Titus 2:11–12 NKJV).

In addition to the reality that sin breaks God's heart for us, whether we realize it or not, sin breaks *our* hearts too. Hyper-grace is a soul-killing setup for sin; in short, it is misguided nonsense. Remember, behavior and identity flow from whomever or whatever we are most attached to. The ideology behind hyper-grace reveals an attachment to sin.

To downplay sin is to treat the reality of pure grace with contempt; it pollutes everything good about the real thing. I don't believe in the tenants of hyper-grace any more than I believe in beating the literal hell out of people with the law. But in both cases the problem is not grace— it is the person or group misusing it.

GREASY LAW: ATTACHED TO LAW

Another common stance in the ongoing debate of grace and license is what I call "greasy law." Greasy law centers on the idea that if you give people the unbridled freedom of pure grace without a sense of punishment or consequence, then they will run amok. With this justification, those arguing in favor of greasy law slide rules and regulations subtly into

God's pure grace—unnecessarily adding to (or subtracting from) Jesus' work on our behalf. When it all boils down, a greasy law point of view shifts the focus to earning God's favor.

Without compromising the message of grace or how amazing it truly is, Paul and other New Testament writers addressed it head-on. The problem isn't grace. It's the way legalism dilutes it. Precisely, this kind of "thinning down" is referred to as antinomianism. Pure grace scares legalists, and it brings up a lot of big theological words as a result. Antinomianism is one of them; this vocab juggernaut literally means "against the Law." Welsh pastor David Martyn Lloyd-Jones embraced the term as a compliment. "If your preaching of the gospel of God's free grace in Jesus Christ does not provoke the charge from some of antinomianism, you're not preaching the gospel of the free grace of God in Jesus Christ."[1] Amen and close the Book! Paul must have embraced the term as well. In Romans 5:20–21, he explains, "The law was brought in so that the trespass might increase. But where sin increased, grace increased all the more, so that, just as sin reigned in death, so also grace might reign through righteousness to bring eternal life through Jesus Christ our Lord."

Plainly, the free grace of God opposes the law. But somewhere along the line, too many of us got the impression that the primary goal of the Christian life is making sure that everyone "behaves." It is as if God were some pursed-lipped law librarian filing our misdeeds and offenses so that papers may later be drawn up when our case is called. In the words of Dallas Willard, this reduces the good news to nothing more than "gospels of sin management."[2] Whenever behaving becomes the most essential thing for followers of Jesus, the message of grace has already been compromised. The notion that behavior—and not loving attachment with God—is the most crucial aspect of discipleship is nothing more than religious legalism.

Attachment came first. The Law came later. Knowing the end from the beginning, God put the Law in place to demonstrate our obvious need for His Savior Son. And according to Galatians 3:23–26 (NASB), now we are sons and daughters too: "But before faith came, we were kept in custody under the law, being confined for the faith that was destined to be revealed. Therefore the Law has become our guardian to lead us to Christ, so that we may be justified by faith. But now that faith has come, we are no longer under a guardian. For you are all sons and daughters of God through faith in Christ Jesus."

Relationally speaking, Old Testament Law could not force attachment—it only pointed out the ever-widening separation between God and man. Today the Law can still help serve to alert us at times when we are tempted to move away from *our own* secure grace-based attachment with Him and into sin. Of important note here is that I said "our own." You and I are not free to judge others' behavior when it comes to their actions or attitudes. Anytime we sin, it is like an indicator on our spiritual dashboard; it signals a spiritual disconnect with the Lord and His grace.

As both a human tendency and a temptation motivated by control, greasy law demonstrates a strong undercurrent of fear. The Pharisees of Jesus' day were masters at this sort of thing—and it has afflicted the Christian church ever since as well. The Pharisees criticized Jesus for healing on the Sabbath and complained that His followers did not wash their hands correctly. The Galatian church was plagued by those who demanded that followers of Jesus be circumcised to be pleasing to God. Some false teachers in the Colossian church told Jesus' followers that in order to be acceptable to God, they had to maintain special Old Testament diets and observe feast days. These tendencies to make behavior more critical than life-giving relationship with Jesus challenged the good news of God's grace back then. Neither Jesus nor Paul gave in to this temptation for an instant. Today we shouldn't either.

In modern Christian culture, nobody is talking about the need for

Jesus' followers to be circumcised or observe the strict dietary laws found in the Pentateuch. Our propensity to compromise grace is subtler, yet it is just as absurd as two thousand years ago.

UNCOMPROMISED ATTACHMENT TO JESUS

Thankfully, grace never was and never will be based on a knowledge of "the rules" or being on our best behavior at all times. Instead, it is a real and loving relationship, and that relationship is what makes faithful obedience possible. Miss this and—along with the hyper-grace and greasy law crowds—you will miss the whole point! As our attachment with the Lord grows, our behavior changes in ongoing freedom—a response to His loving-kindness. God's grace is attractive! History is our witness: attempts to use rules and regulations to make people behave have never worked.

Aside from not being part of God's character makeup, condemnation brought on by a set of man-made rules won't change who I am on the inside. External rules can never transform my identity or behaviors— attachment with the Maker of my soul will. Straight up: if my identity is rooted in Him, it changes what I want.

Take lust, for instance. If you tell the average Christian Joe not to look at a beautiful woman because he's not supposed to lust, his immediate reaction will probably be something like, "Yeah, I know . . . but she's *beautiful,* and I have these *hormones.* What's the problem with a little looking as long as I don't act on it?" God created the beauty of women, so is it wrong to admire it? No. But lust goes further than admiring to taint what is good through a lack of self-control.

The truth is, it doesn't matter whether a guy's licentious, predatory thoughts are confined only to his mind. It's still bad behavior! In and of itself, no external rule, principle, or guideline—no matter how wise it might sound—is going to keep anyone from lust. Only when our moment-by-moment relationship with God grows stronger and more important than temporary gratification will lust bow its craggy knees in submission. Then Joe can discover the true beauty of a woman through Jesus' eyes of grace. Instead of visualizing her as a sex object, he will learn to see her as God's favorite. His behavior toward women will change because he loves the Lord more; the idea of damaging his relationship with God is unthinkable. Do you see the difference here? Who Joe is on the inside is transformed. The godly heart and behavior now flowing from his life sincerely represent his desire to treat women with honor, dignity, and abundant respect.

And so it is with each of us: as you and I love Jesus more, we love others better. Recognizing our own unique forms of temptation, we all have a question to ask: *Is my relationship with God important enough to cause me to pay attention to my sin and—when necessary—to wrestle with it for the sake of my spiritual transformation?* A secure, grace-based attachment with God—not the imposition of someone else's rules—will both inspire and necessitate a resounding "yes!" Led by the Spirit within, we are attracted to life in His way. Read what Romans 8:12–14 has to say: "Therefore, brothers and sisters, we have an obligation—but it is not to the flesh, to live according to it. For if you live according to the flesh, you will die; but if by the Spirit you put to death the misdeeds of the body, you will live. For those who are led by the Spirit of God are the children of God."

As you and I learn to love God, others, and ourselves through His Spirit, we will reap a life-giving harvest (Galatians 6:8–9). So let's *really* live! Contending that pure grace should not be compromised is not the same as permitting people to sin—by license *or* by legalism. Of those mentioned, both stances in the grace and license debate lose. But as believers, we win as we count ourselves dead to sin but alive to God.

If you're chained to sinful behaviors, thinking you've got it covered by the cross, or you're shackled by the notion that the law can help you behave your way into God's good grace, then you may as well be dragging around a stinky, rotting corpse. Neither perspective represents who you and I are meant to be in Christ! Let that wash over you to clean out any gunk that may be stuck in your heart, soul, and mind. As a partaker in the pure water of God's grace through grace-based relationship with Jesus, may every unadulterated ounce of it soak into the fiber of your spiritual being.

MAKING IT STICK

A FACE OF GRACE: GEOFF

I was about eighteen when I met my friend Geoff. It was just after I had given my life to Jesus, and I had begun attending a small church. Geoff was a few years older than I, but I soon discovered how much we had in common. We both had been raised Catholic, grew up in the Washington, D.C., area, loved sports, and cheered for the same sports teams. Each of us was recovering from a wild season of alcohol and drug use and more than ready to get serious about learning to grow as followers of Jesus.

One of the first times I attended that little church, I found out that a large group of guys met to play football after services on Sunday afternoon. The routine: they would celebrate at church in the morning, go to lunch, and then meet again for an afternoon football game. Because our church met in a school, the building's athletic field made it the perfect place for such extracurricular sports.

One Sunday, soon after we met, my new friend Geoff invited me to be part of their afternoon football game. Eagerly, I accepted the invitation—that is, until I realized that I didn't have the clothes or shoes that I would need to play. I lived a long way from the church and figured I'd have to wait until next time. Sensing my disappointment, Geoff didn't miss a beat. Right away, he offered to loan me his car so that I could go home and change. Somewhat dazed that he was willing to trust a person he barely knew with his car, I jumped on the offer. The chance to play and connect with some new friends was just what I needed. Gratefully, I climbed into Geoff's old green station wagon and headed home. On the way, I noticed that Geoff left his wallet in the car. My amazement at his trusting nature grew even more. Once I got home, I changed clothes as quickly as possible and headed back for the game. When I pulled in, Geoff and some of the guys greeted me with a smile (while they were warm and glad to see me, I suspect Geoff's expression must have been partially because his wallet had made it back untouched).

Throughout the fall, football and hanging out with Geoff became a regular part of my life. Eventually, when the ground became too painfully frozen to play football, we found a gym to play basketball through the winter. When spring rolled around, we switched to playing softball together.

After a while, Geoff, some other friends from church, and I rented a house together. It was an older Cape Cod–style home, with only two bedrooms and a small landing upstairs. Geoff and I claimed the top floor. It ended up being the perfect spot for many late-night conversations, Nerf ball games, and music-listening sessions, as both our relationship with one another and our faith grew. Neither of us was perfect, and we made a lot of mistakes in our walk with Jesus, but our journey together didn't falter. Anytime things got too serious, a practical joke was sure to break the tension. We played and took turns pranking one another— including an infamous pickle juice coffee incident. (You know someone is your friend when he still speaks to you after brewing his coffee with a mixture of water and pickle juice!)

In my new relationship with Jesus, Geoff was foundational. I was new to the whole notion of Bible study, fellowship, and learning to listen to the Lord. Geoff's smile, kindness, warmth, humility, and eagerness to share his life with me were great encouragements. He also planted the possibility of something that became very important to my spiritual growth: if Geoff and I could share life like this, I began to recognize that maybe it was possible to connect with Jesus and His followers in the same way. Today, even though Geoff and I live far apart geographically, we still stay connected. No matter the distance, grace-based relationships like ours stand the test of time!

THE INTERSECTION OF GRACE, SCRIPTURE, AND NEUROSCIENCE: RELATIONSHIPS OVER REASON

In this section you'll discover how neuroscience intersects with grace and Scripture. The reality of God's grace offers solutions and benefits to all aspects of who we are made to be—body, mind, spirit, and relationship!

> "Do not merely listen to the word, and so deceive yourselves.
> Do what it says. Anyone who listens to the word but does not
> do what it says is like someone who looks at his face in a mirror
> and, after looking at himself, goes away and immediately
> forgets what he looks like" (James 1:22–24).

Recent advances in neuroscience, especially the work of Dr. Allan Schore and Dr. Daniel Siegel, confirm what Scripture teaches: the relational centers of the brain play the primary role in its ability to regulate behavior.[3] Want a couple of examples? Romans 2:4 points out that it is God's loving-kindness that leads us to repentance—not a bunch of rules and "law keeping." Likewise, 1 Corinthians 13 outlines the relational fruit we can expect to see flourishing in our grace-based relationships with God and others. You and I can only harvest these in the context of relationships. Good information and lots of biblical knowledge about things we "should" do clearly take a back seat to relationships. A quick look at some of the complexities of neuroscience offers clues as to why this is the case.

Relationships, emotions, and identity
Every second, a constant flow of information bombards our senses with a steady stream of stimuli from our ever-changing environment, people, relationships, weather, pets, traffic, and life's other random

circumstances. Quicker than we are aware (in just one-sixth of a second, to be exact), you and I receive new information and start processing. It begins in the areas that handle relational, emotional, and identity functions—our brain's control center. Faster than conscious thought, the new information first reaches the part of our brain that focuses on attachment *before* continuing on to our emotional and identity centers. This means that who—or what—you and I are most closely attached to at any given moment influences how we process and respond to sensory information. If my attachment to Jesus is strong and secure, my brain processes sensory input in light of my connection with Him. Because attachments rooted in grace remind me that I am not alone, I am less likely to be alarmed and more likely to be calm and unafraid. Again, keep in mind, all this is happening far below—and faster than—conscious thought.

After leaving our attachment center, the sensory information passes to our alarm and emotional centers. The alarm center helps us react to incoming danger to keep you and me safe (if needed), and the emotional centers generate feelings about the incoming data. Because the information is moving so fast, we may begin to have feelings about what's happening well before noticing why we are feeling them.

Finally, the information passes on to our identity center, which helps you and me figure out how to respond and behave. Our identity center is designed to help us find solutions consistent with who we understand ourselves to be (personal identity) and who we understand others who are close to us to be (group identity). To find these solutions, our identity center looks for examples of how we—or others close to us—have behaved in similar circumstances. Once our identity center finds a solution, you and I act. Remember, this trip from our attachment center to the identity center and subsequent behavior takes only one-sixth of a second. In a flash, you and I respond to the sensory information about our situation before we can consciously "think" about it.

Logic and reason

Only after our relational and emotional center has processed and reacted to a situation does the sensory input travel to the region of our brain that is responsible for logic and reason. This region of the brain functions as a giant file cabinet—allowing you and me to access stored information, rules, and regulations about how to behave. These centers operate at only one-fifth of a second, which is the speed of conscious thought. Here, we can logically consider our behavior in light of our situation and figure out if we have "met the rules"—or not. This neurological region's slower speed means that rules and regulations can only help us evaluate decisions *after*—not before—we've acted! It can never keep up with incoming stimuli—or the relational, emotional, identity centers that determine our behavior. This area of our brain is valuable because it helps us become aware of our need to repent, deal with sin, and talk with Jesus about our behaviors.

This doesn't mean that the left hemisphere is unimportant. My point is that, for too long and to our detriment, the left brain's processes have been overemphasized. See the problem? We've been taught to approach things in a neurologically backwards manner. In reality, a dynamic interplay between the control center of the right hemisphere and logic and reason of the left hemisphere is required. When you and I have a healthy control center, it enables our logic and reasoning center to do things like make plans, study, and more deeply understand things—including the Bible. As you may imagine, when you and I are relationally connected with Jesus, it makes for exceptionally good Scripture reflection. When we only try to use our logic reasoning center to do life, we get stuck. With that being said, our brain's slower region (responsible for logic and reason) is not the optimal guidance system for life. Only faster, moment-by-moment, grace-based attachment with Jesus is!

*For further information on the processing speed of our left and right hemispheres, see *Rare Leadership* by E. James Wilder and Marcus Warner.

EXERCISES

DAILY AFFIRMATION 7: JUST AS I RECEIVED JESUS, I AM LEARNING TO WALK WITH HIM.

This is your daily affirmation for the week. Read it aloud as an affirmation of God's work in your life each day while you are working with this chapter. If you are part of a group study, repeat this out loud together each time you meet. (For a complete list of Daily Affirmations, see Appendix A at the back of the book.)

SCRIPTURE REFLECTION: COLOSSIANS 2:6-15

1. Pray and ask Jesus to guide you as you reflect on this passage of Scripture.

2. Take a moment to remember something you appreciate, or a time you have felt deeply connected to God. Reflect on that moment and remember how you felt.

3. Read the following passage of Scripture slowly. As you read, pay attention to any words or phrases that seem to stand out. Then stop and ask Jesus what He wants you to know about the word or phrase. After you ask, consider any thoughts, feelings, impressions, pictures, memories, or other scriptures that come to mind. Write these in your journal.

COLOSSIANS 2:6-15 (NASB)

Therefore, as you have received Christ Jesus the Lord, so walk in Him, having been firmly rooted and now being built up in Him and established in your faith, just as you were instructed, and overflowing with gratitude.

See to it that no one takes you captive through philosophy and empty deception in accordance with human tradition, in accordance with the elementary principles of the world, rather than according to Christ. For in Him all the fullness of Deity dwells in bodily form, and in Him you have been made complete, and He is the head over every ruler and authority; and in Him you were also circumcised with a circumcision performed without hands, in the removal of the body of the flesh by the circumcision of Christ; having been buried with Him in baptism, in which you were also raised up with Him through faith in the working of God, who raised Him from the dead. And when you were dead in your wrongdoings and the uncircumcision of your flesh, He made you alive together with Him, having forgiven us all our wrongdoings, having canceled the certificate of debt consisting of decrees against us, which was hostile to us; and He has taken it out of the way, having nailed it to the cross. When He had disarmed the rulers and authorities, He made a public display of them, having triumphed over them through Him.

4. After you've finished journaling your observations, pray over them. Ask Jesus to show you if there is anything more that He may want you to know about what you've written. Enter these in your journal.

5. If you have the time, continue by rereading the passage of Scripture, journaling, and interacting with Jesus.

6. After you have finished journaling, read through what you've written. Think about what you have learned from this Scripture that applies to your life right now. Is there a theme or key lesson that speaks to your heart? Or is God calling you to action or further reflection perhaps?

7. Which of your impressions, if any, might be thoughts God shared with you? Remember, thoughts and impressions we journal do not carry the authority of Scripture. It's always a good idea to share your thoughts and impressions with others you trust to help discern what God might want you to know. (If you need help distinguishing what God's thoughts may be, see "Is the Shepherd Speaking?" provided in Appendix B.)

REFLECTION/DISCUSSION QUESTIONS

These questions will help you apply this chapter's themes and your Scripture Reflection exercise in your life. They can also help you prayerfully reflect on your life and your connection with Jesus and ask Him for help. Set aside time during the week to reflect on these questions and write the answers in your journal. If you are studying this book with a group, share your answers with other group members next time you meet.

1. Who was the face of grace you saw this week? How did they communicate "special and favorite" to you or someone else? How did you feel when you experienced this grace?

2. What does it mean to you to "continue to live your life in Jesus, just as you received Him"? What do you think God might want you to know about the secret to living as a follower of Jesus?

3. Paul mentions things like human tradition, philosophy, and basic principles of the world when he talks about the kinds of things that can lead us away from Christ. How can these things hurt us as followers of Jesus? How have they hurt you in your walk with Jesus?

4. Are there times or places in your life when you've relied on other things besides Jesus to live as His follower? Describe them. Have you ever thought that you could improve your behavior and walk with Jesus by trying harder to live up to Scripture? What happened? Did your extra effort help?

5. Why is the cross of Jesus so essential for followers of Jesus?

6. Have you fallen into the hyper-grace or greasy law traps? What happened? How did you become untangled from hyper-grace? What kind of rules and regulations did you add as a part of greasy law? How did you untangle yourself from either? Or are you still stuck in hyper-grace or greasy law?

7. If you are in a group, how would you like them to pray for you?

HOMEWORK

Homework helps you continue to apply this week's lesson, engage with God, and prepare for the next chapter.

1. Go "grace watching" again this week. Can you find a face of grace anywhere around you? This person might be interacting with you or with someone else. How does watching another face of grace affect you, and how do you feel?

2. Continue reflecting on Colossians 2:6–15 and journal your observations. Is there someone with whom you can share your insights—or who is willing to reflect on the Scripture with you?

3. Spend some time this week asking God to help you look at any areas of life in which you are stuck in hyper-grace or greasy law. If you discover you are entangled in either one—or both—ask God how you can begin walking in the freedom of His grace.

8 The Deadly Motivations of Fear

A man that flies from his fear may find that he has only taken a short cut to meet it.

—J. R. R. TOLKIEN

Yea, though I walk through the valley of
the shadow of death,
I will fear no evil;
For You are with me;
Your rod and Your staff, they comfort me.
You prepare a table before me in the
presence of my enemies;
You anoint my head with oil;
My cup runs over.

—PSALM 23:4–5 NKJV

Everybody loves a good life hack. Just check the Internet, and you'll find thousands of them. For instance, did you know . . .

- Doritos make great campfire kindling?
- toilet paper rolls can make a decent speaker for your mobile phone?
- you can chill a beverage icy cold by wrapping it in a wet paper towel and placing it in the freezer for fifteen minutes?

Life hacks are cleverly practical ideas and creative methods designed to speed productivity, solve problems, and otherwise help us manage life. They are shortcuts—sometimes best described as "cheats." Frankly, I wish I'd invented a few to wow people at parties. However, grace-based attachment is my soapbox, and—when it comes to attachment with God—that is something you and I cannot afford to shortcut. But oh, how we try!

In our defense, most of us don't even know what we are doing when we're trying out a shortcut or when we are doing it. Most likely, up until now the importance of our position as God's favorite hasn't been part of the scope and sequence of the Bible studies we've attended. It's no wonder that you and I are oblivious to our lack of divine attachment. In a million little ways, we are taught to "manage" the Christian life with efficiency—to learn the right things, do the right things, be around the right people in order to grow in a tidy, linear fashion. (Ever noticed something? Relationships are neither *tidy* nor *linear*.)

Over and over, each of us is given one grand invitation: will we respond to God's grace and live in attachment with Him—or not? RSVP. To reject or ignore His invitation is to accept a life of fear instead. And fear is the ultimate misguided life hack. Quite literally, it cuts off real life with God and others. Although most of us are not conscious of its activity in our lives, fear simply doesn't leave room for grace-based attachment with the One who loves us most. I'd venture to say, this lack of awareness has already cost most of us dearly. Both spiritually and physically, our ongoing ignorance can even be deadly. But it's not too late.

Now that you and I *are* aware, let's pay attention to the dynamics at play in our soul. Consider your relationship with God: is it grace-based, or does your life abide a lot of fear-based behaviors and attitudes?

THE REALITY OF FEAR

Apart from grace, fear is our spiritual, relational, and neurological reality. Terror and slavery were never part of God's design for us in the garden, but fear has been our fixed state ever since we left. "Inasmuch then as the children have partaken of flesh and blood, He Himself likewise shared in the same, that through death He might destroy him who had the power of death, that is, the devil, and release those who through fear of death were all their lifetime subject to bondage" (Hebrews 2:14–15).

In this passage Paul uses the Greek word *phobos.* Translated, it can refer to awe and reverential respect for God, *or* it can be used to express exceeding fear and terror. Here Paul is referencing the latter in such a way that it should make us run for the hills, horrified. The Passion Translation makes this even clearer: "Since all his 'children' have flesh and blood, so Jesus became human to fully identify with us. He did this, so that he could experience death and annihilate the effects of the intimidating accuser who holds against us the power of death. By embracing death Jesus sets free those who live their entire lives in bondage to the tormenting dread of death" (Hebrews 2:14–15 TPT).

Both scripturally and as a brain-based truth, this is our state apart from grace. Who wants to be attached to *that?* Death is the very real spiritual effect of fear in our lives.

Walk through these words in your mind. Picture the evil one suffocating you and those you love under the crushing darkness of fear. Really. Stop and imagine it in your mind's eye. Now, envision Truth's triumph in the passage: Jesus, once and for all, thrashing our adversary and any manipulative power Satan thought he had over you.

The horror of the reality is why God makes it clear that He wants us to live differently. So why don't we? For clues about how we got here, let's back up to take a look at fear's impact on our early development.

OUR DEFAULT SYSTEM

You and I come into the world profoundly dependent on caregivers to meet our emotional and physical needs. These essential relationships lay the groundwork for the development of the brain's structure, function, and chemistry. Before a brain cell is ever derived from a human blastomere, fear is our default system.

Think of it like this: when you buy a computer, it comes out of the box with a default system that automatically governs how it runs. You don't have to do anything but turn it on. It is preset to store information, work with other devices, and accomplish everyday tasks. Fear works much the same way. Deep below our level of consciousness, it runs on its own. While it can't be controlled by conscious thought at its most basic level, it is the central organizing force—the default system—for our developing mind. Just like a computer, fear will expand to meet our needs. Capable of growing on its own, it can help us determine what we have to deal with and the most efficient ways to respond. It regulates how well the rest of our brain will work, interpret, react to information, organize memory, interact with people, and accomplish everyday tasks.

If you are like me, the thought of fear actively controlling my brain at a level deep beyond my conscious control is terrifying. But before we plunge into despair together, here is the good news: consistent grace-filled interactions with parents and caregivers early in life can override and change our brain's default system. Grace—and not fear—can become our *new* default system. Each welcoming smile, a twinkle in the eye of someone who sees us as special and favorite, and every gesture of caring attention to our needs can transform us from a fear-driven to a grace-filled, joy-empowered state of relational living. And there's more good news! (This can happen at any age.)

The violence of Satan's vengeful ways, the harshness of life's trauma, and the horror of the cross Jesus endured are all worthy of fear. God knew each of us needed a way out. Whether it is a fear of perishing (see John 3:16) or His loving-kindness that motivates you and me, we must address the reality of fear in our lives. This fear is what God earnestly desires to lay to rest.

Early in life, weak, inconsistent, overwhelming, unpredictable connections or an absence of joyful interactions (which are characteristic of non-secure attachments) will cause our brain's fear, anxiety, and stress systems to become overactive. That means that fear—not grace-based attachments—will shape the reality of our spiritual, relational, and neurological world. Imagine this phase of life as the development of your relational "home." A lack of grace and joy will manifest in an incomplete and malformed foundation. Who you and I are—and understand ourselves to be—will shift depending on people and situations. This holds true for both our individual and group identities. (Remember the Jenga game?) Apart from grace, our body, brain, spiritual life, and relationships quickly become organized around our fears.

If fear abides in our relational home, it opens the front door wide—inviting identity distortions to come on in. These distortions barge into our entryway with unwanted guests in tow—all with a whole lot of baggage too! Some have packed lingering feelings that cause us to believe we are somehow fatally flawed, unworthy, unlovable, or worthless. Still other distortions unpack fantasy lives for us or an overly exaggerated sense of our self-importance. Whatever the case, if you and I don't address the unwanted visitors (i.e., fears), we will quickly find that they have become our lousy long-term roommates—the kind that never pay rent and make a perpetual mess of our lives.

FEAR AS NORMAL?

What is it like to live with an overactive fear and stress system? It is not overstating to say it does brain damage—(and much more.)Many of us find it hard to answer this question because we've lived with fear so long, it has become our spiritual, relational, neurological, and physiological "norm." Once fear has become familiar, we just don't notice it anymore.

Our passive oblivion can have unintentional relational consequences. I vividly remember a conference my wife, Maritza, and I attended in Calgary, Canada, years ago. Men and women were each accommodated in separate, basic cabins. It was late spring, but that far north, the weather was still quite chilly to us. The first to arrive in the women's bunkhouse, Maritza cranked up the heat. Shivering, she waited for the cabin to warm.

All of a sudden, a group of women from the Canadian Yukon arrived in T-shirts and shorts. Stomping their way into the bunkhouse, they frowned and immediately complained, "Who turned on that heat?" Without waiting for an answer, they proceeded to turn it *way down*. Cold temperatures had become the norm for these hardy "Canuck" ladies to the point that they were unable to notice what everyone else not from that region knew: it was stinkin' *cold* outside! They had adjusted to their environment to the detriment of Maritza and others.

Like living in a cold climate, our brain gets used to fear and all the feelings associated with it. We may find ourselves becoming indifferent to the environment—as if it is just a fact of life. That's when it easily slips in the back door. When you hear yourself or others saying things like, "I'm just stressed," "I've got anxiety issues," or "There is just so much on my mind," it's a dead giveaway. Because most of us don't want to run the risk of sounding like wimps, we prefer phrases like these or describe fear with "feeling words" like *uneasy, unsettled, upset,* or *worried.* These are all code for *fearful* or *afraid.* Christians in particular have a hard time saying, "I'm afraid!" But if our brain gets set this way early in life, it will become "normal" for us. Assuming everyone must feel the same, we never dream there is another way to live.

See how subtly it happens? You and I get numb to the environment and the language of fear, despite its active threat to our lives. Sometimes when I say this to people, they just look at me blankly and blink—as if *I'm* the one with the issues. But I promise, it's not just me! We can all live without this undertone in our souls.

To keep living this way is kind of like growing up in a home where the smoke detector is steadily blaring. If there is consistently no peace, we may learn to adapt to the noise, but it's still there. Other people living in our house may have learned not to notice it either. However, when someone else comes through the door, the outsider will probably wonder how we live with the piercing tone. It is such a part of our relational reality that we have totally lost the ability to notice it. In fact, we are likely to get offended by anyone who dares to point out that the smoke alarm is shrieking.

No matter our development and life experience, we all have a lasting need for grace and grace-based attachments. This is true whether or not we recognize fear and its devastation in our lives and family. Its active presence only amplifies our need for grace because of our relational design. From our core, you and I are called to experience life as special and favorite. The call can be at times loud or sometimes as gentle as a whisper, but it never goes away. Our need for grace has been placed there by God to draw us to Him. As long as we have breath, our spirit, soul, and body will need it.

Let's not kid ourselves, though. Our problem is that apart from grace, you and I will always end up attempting to figure out how to feel special and favorite in all the wrong ways. The apostle John was keenly mindful of our tendency to try to meet our needs apart from our relationship with Jesus. In 1 John 2:15–16 (NKJV) he warns: "Do not love the world or the things in the world. If anyone loves the world, the love of the Father is not in him. For all that is in the world—the lust of the flesh, the lust of the eyes, and the pride of life—is not of the Father but is of the world."

I especially wish the Lord had left that last part out. It's pretty sobering, don't you think? When you and I try to use worldly ways to fill heavenly holes, we will quickly find our substitutes inadequate. Specifically, John mentions misplaced cravings that include the following:

- what we see, externally, that looks desirable and catches our attention
- what our flesh wants, internally, to make us feel good
- what makes us look better by prideful comparison to others
- anything of the world that is under the influence of the demonic realm (not of the Father).

THE 4 DEADLY PS

These are the worldly warning signs of souls, both believers and others, searching for some place to connect with grace and life-giving relationships. Whenever we move away from God and His guidance system, this is where we are heading. From John's list, "the things in the world" are what I call the 4 Deadly Ps (from now on, let's refer to them as the 4 Ps). When we find ourselves from time to time living apart from grace-based attachment with God, each of us will find ourselves leaning on one or more of the following:

- **Pleasing**: how much others approve of me
- **Performance**: how well I do things
- **Pain**: what feels bad to me
- **Pleasure**: what feels good to me.

Why are they deadly? you wonder. Well, they may look innocent on the surface, but left in place, they will create fear-based soul attachments and shape our identity in toxic ways. They are deadly to our growth—spiritual, relational, and every other kind of development you can imagine. As you may have guessed, pleasing and performing are about people (how we can please and perform for them). Pain and pleasure revolve around the reactions we get from others. An identity that is more shaped by these than by grace will become lethal to us and those around us. Such toxicity is like carbon monoxide in close quarters; it quietly creeps in and builds up, creating an unstable and volatile identity for the individual and group in residence.

The 4 Ps are all things we unconsciously do when we are afraid. But again we cannot live simultaneously attached to God and fear; to think otherwise only confirms that the lethal gas has made it under the door. Whoever we are performing for or whatever pleasure we seek will suck the air right out of our spiritual lungs.

For many of us, this begins at a very young age. Dizzy without grace, we become weak—our vision of self and others, malformed. Here's what the 4 Ps may look like in action.

- Neither his mom nor his dad know what to do with crying baby Jerome. Frustrated by their seeming inability to make his crying stop, they put baby Jerome in his crib, shut the door, and stay out until he is quiet. What does Jerome learn? *Comfort comes when I am quiet and express no needs.* Jerome learns that he is more special and favorite when he doesn't upset Mom and Dad. In effect, he learns that **pleasing** and **performing** will get him what he wants.
- Matthew's father is an alcoholic who is easily angered with a hair-trigger fuse when he's been drinking. Although baby Matthew doesn't understand what Mom and Dad

are saying when they yell or fight over his dad's drinking, the loud shouts are terrifying. With no way to filter or protect himself from the rage, he discovers that anger is terrifying. As he grows, Matthew finds that it's best to remain as invisible as possible when people are angry and never do anything that upsets others. He discovers early never to talk about Dad's drinking. The **pain** of anger and conflict is intolerable. These are things Matthew will work hard to avoid his whole life.

- Soon after her baby Brittney is born, Mom is stressed trying to work from home. Her boss has been kind and lets her virtually commute but is insistent that she keep up with her workflow and team. When it is time for Mom to feed the baby, she is caught between the devil and the deep blue sea. On the one hand, she wants to feed and nurture her daughter. On the other hand, she's trying to stay on top of the digital updates being exchanged by her team members. Distracted, she hurriedly feeds Brittney while anxiously watching her computer screen. What is more pleasurable to the baby—her mom's anxious presence or the taste of milk? Which do you think baby Brittney is more likely to prefer for comfort? The **pleasure** of food.

Because perfect parents are like unicorns, everyone on the planet has something to wrestle with in this regard. You and I have each unwittingly attached to things we shouldn't have. In Christian circles, behaviors spawned here may appear as good things on the surface. Let's look again at Matthew, Jerome, and Brittney for some grown-up examples:

- Matthew never wants to do anything to make anyone mad. He prefers to avoid conflict at all costs. Is this a virtue or a vice? A look at the life of Jesus reveals that he willingly stood His ground and responded readily to religious leaders who aggressively challenged His message. Jesus was not afraid of conflict.

- As an adult, Jerome doesn't ask for much. He prefers independence and working alone. He doesn't like to ask people for help. While appearing to be a self-starting servant, Jerome is afraid to have his own needs and doesn't know how to work well with others. Virtue or vice? Imagine where we'd be if the early church worked this way!

- Once Brittney leaves home, she gets an exciting job as the sous chef of a trendy new restaurant in town. From time to time, long and intense hours in the kitchen leave her feeling "chained to the stove." She's especially happy that the owner has let her take the initiative to start a food share program, feeding the homeless with the restaurant's daily leftovers. A hard worker like her mom, Brittney earns her off time. Tired out in front of the TV most evenings (and several times on the weekend), Brittney rewards herself with a big bowl of ice cream and lots of other sweet treats. Virtue or vice? As he modeled when nourishing the five thousand, Jesus placed a high value on feeding people's needs, but for comfort he went to His Father.

See the fuzzy lines? Maybe it's time that you and I ask the Lord to show us where ours are blurred.

ASKING THE WRONG QUESTIONS

The 4 Deadly Ps are almost intuitive. *Almost.* We start doing them before we even know we are doing them. In order to feel special, you and I adopt behaviors and ways of being. See the tracks? There is a parallel between the 4 Ps and our identity. Our life hacks (or should we call them "grace hacks"?) slide in and begin to steer who we are in a direction far from grace. Instead of dealing with underlying anxiety, they become our clever way of "handling things." Often without our awareness, these behaviors and attitudes help us effectively manage and deflect whatever may bother us.

When we do this stuff, it's so transparent that it's practically funny (if it weren't so sad). In no way are you and I capable of thinking or behaving our way into God's good graces, but that's not what He's after. In response to His gracious invitation, God simply desires that we order our affections and direction around the relationship we have with Him. He longs for us to follow *His* lead. Anytime we don't, we can be sure that our life is arranged around the 4 Ps. Under their influence, instead of remembering that you and I are God's special and favorite, we will find ourselves asking questions like these:

- Who do I need to like me so I feel good about myself?
- Who do I need to please?
- How well do I have to do so I don't feel worthless?
- What can I do to make it stop?

Striving to answer these questions will leave even the best of us unnecessarily exhausted. Going down this road as a way of life, you and I will end up working very hard to earn for ourselves what God has already provided for us. Adam and Eve started it, and the religious leaders of Jesus' day followed up with a plethora of examples. You'd think we would know better by now! Unquestionably, God's not interested in being co-opted so we can prove ourselves significant. He has no intention of helping us boost our law system so that we feel more approval, higher performance, less pain, and more pleasure. He's already taken care of all that.

My friend and mentor, John Glenn, has seen this a lot over the years. He was my supervisor in one of the rehab facilities I worked in years ago. When I ran into him recently, he reminded me of something he had pointed out in my years of training. In his experience, John has noticed that to one degree or another most Christians live a variation on the theme, "I will be worthwhile if _____." In fact, anytime we tell ourselves, "I will be more worthy, special, or favorite if _____," we are back to operating out of the 4 Ps.

I hate to break it to you, but if you're asking God to help you do something to make you feel more secure, most of the time He will flat out resist you. His love cannot bear your independent effort. So what that means is any of your self-improvement programs are much akin to putting lipstick on a pig. God sees you as special and favorite *before* the lipstick. I have nothing against pigs. I have nothing against you or me. But who is the lipstick for anyway? Are we afraid we are not pretty enough in our faith?

Either way, when our identity drifts into these kinds of behaviors, we are in trouble. Just like Matthew, Jerome, and Brittney, our solutions cause damage to our individual identity. We have yet to consider how it damages the way you and I see *others*—especially in Christian circles. Even though we may model "good things," there is a natural tendency in each of us to project our standards onto others (for instance, if we perform, they should; if we don't like conflict, they shouldn't be so confrontational). Pay attention! This is never grace-based. When you and I leave grace behind, we run the risk of imposing the weight and struggle of our standards on others. All too easily from there, our group identity will slide into the 4 Ps, causing it to become malformed as well.

THE FRUIT OF THE 4 DEADLY PS

Remember: fear is the soil in which the 4 Deadly Ps—Pleasing, Performing, Pain, and Pleasure—take root. In the absence of grace, these fears will become our guidance system and strongly influence the development of our body, soul, and spirit. If fear is allowed, it will spread its branches in our lives until ultimately the bitter fruit of addiction springs forth. To help explore the ugly forms of its harvest, I use the term BEEPS:

- Behaviors
- Events
- Experiences
- People
- Substances

Some of these may even look good on the outside, but inside they are rotten. While the 4 Ps are behaviors we discover that help us mask fear and compensate for missing grace, BEEPS are what happen when we become *strongly attached* to one or more of the 4 Ps. We will explore these more in depth in the next chapter, but suffice it to say, when grace is missing and fear is the motivating factor, BEEPS can disfigure our lives—soul and all.

Before we wrap our discussion of fear and the 4 Deadly Ps, here's one more key point for review: our strongest attachments (who or what we love the most) have the most significant impact on our behavior. The experience of being seen, known, and treated as special and favorite by caregivers early in life—and by God later in life—allows you and me to form powerful attachments with these sources of grace. In turn, these relationships promise the yield of a stable individual and group identity, and the grace-based behaviors that go with it. All fear aside, we are provided with a positive, grace-based guidance system for life. Thankfully, there's just no life hack for that.

MAKING IT STICK

A FACE OF GRACE: JOHN

This face of grace story is a bit different because it describes my relationship with someone that began during a very painful season of my life. When I first met John, I was angry and upset, had no real desire to connect with him. I *definitely* didn't want to be trained by him. How can grace grow in such conditions, and how could a person I wanted to avoid have become a face of grace to me? Well, faces of grace can sometimes emerge in unlikely places, especially in relationships with people we don't initially appreciate.

When we met, I lived in Florida, serving on a Christian residential treatment program staff for men with addictions. The program was unique because it offered a rehabilitation program and a separate intensive ministry training program for those wanting to serve the addicted community. I had graduated from their ministry training program several years earlier. Then I went on to work as a pastoral counselor at a church and as an addiction counselor at a transitional housing program for homeless people in the Washington, D.C., area. When a staff member from the Florida program visited me and offered me a job working in the rehab portion of the treatment program, I eagerly said, "Yes!" and moved back to Florida. I arrived enthusiastic to begin doing what I loved—working with people in recovery.

Upon my return, I realized there had been a significant misunderstanding. Instead of working with guys in the program, I found out that what they actually hired me to help with was systematizing the rehab curriculum and producing new materials. When I met John, my displeasure was obvious. In addition to the miscommunication about my job description, I learned that I would be required to repeat a training program I'd already completed. In response, I told him that I had no intention of doing homework, writing papers, or completing reading assignments for a program from which I'd already graduated. I directly let my new boss (John) know that I would be there and take notes for the project—but that was it. John did not react. He merely smiled and, with a twinkle in his eye, said that my plan was okay with him.

As a matter of unfortunate timing, this occurred while our family was struggling with past trauma, and I was becoming aware of some agonizing issues in my own history. Both professionally and personally, I was not in a good place and felt like a failure. And since staff all lived on the rehab/training program grounds and ate meals together in the dining hall with the men receiving treatment, there was nowhere for me to "get away" from the stressful environment. With no other place to go, the internal pressure from the leaders and community to conform felt unbearable.

I showed up for class braced for a lot of information I already knew about how to do ministry. Armed with my legal pad and pen, I plopped into a chair. To avoid losing the job I disliked, I was present but seething with frustration and disappointment. However, after only a few days in class something astounding happened: I realized John had something new to teach me.

From past study, I understood the theoretical models of Freud, Rogers, Maslow, and others. Still, I'd never heard such a coherent overview of these diverse approaches to human needs as I did in John's comprehensive, straightforward delivery. His elegant presentation piqued my curiosity, but it was his explanation of the gospel of grace as it applies to (and meets) human needs that blew my mind! I'd never heard such a thing before. Though I recognized that grace applied to my spiritual needs, until John's class I never knew that grace related directly to my soul's deepest needs. To my shock, it became clear that although I'd been a Christian for years, practical, relational grace played a minimal role in my daily life. Obviously, the implications on my relationship with the Lord were huge! Worse, I was so caught up in trying to perform for leaders and program staff to gain their approval that I did not even know how to begin applying God's grace—or the gospel—in my daily life. I quickly and eagerly started completing homework, reading, and written assignments. I couldn't wait to go to class!

What became even more important to me than classroom instruction was the time I spent with John outside of class. He opened his whole world to me—home and life. He and his wife, Sandy, were the epitome of hospitality. Loving and patient with my many questions, John seemed always to answer with joy and wisdom. It didn't take long for me to realize that he was no poser; John lived the grace he taught in the classroom.

His example taught me something else I'd never seen. John was the first person I ever knew who handled anger in a manner consistent with grace. Living and working in a rehab/training community alongside a multitude of recovering addicts provided the huge potential for daily chaos. The sometimes rigid, unyielding demands for perfection and production I sometimes felt from others within the community added to the tension. To my amazement, John navigated through each crisis and adverse reaction with grace. While angered at how these difficult situations affected others, John never stopped seeing everyone involved through eyes of grace. His example stays with me always.

As I mentioned earlier, it was during this training program that I became aware of some severe personal trauma that had unconsciously plagued me for years. When it came to my attention, I went to John for help. He prayed through these painful issues with me and, more importantly, helped me start seeing myself as Jesus did. Although my understanding of grace, attachment, and neuroscience had grown over the years, the introduction to grace I received from John laid an essential foundation I needed for life—and for the future. John's face of grace remains with me today!

THE INTERSECTION OF GRACE, SCRIPTURE, AND NEUROSCIENCE: FIGHT, FLIGHT, OR FREEZE

In this section you'll discover how neuroscience intersects with grace and Scripture. The reality of God's grace offers solutions and benefits to all aspects of who we are made to be—body, mind, spirit, and relationship!

"So do not fear, for I am with you; do not be dismayed, for I am your God. I will strengthen you and help you; I will uphold you with my righteous right hand" (Isaiah 41:10).

Far below our consciousness level, the amygdala lies in the emotional and relational control center of the brain's right hemisphere. Although it is small (about the size of an almond), it packs a powerful and influential punch. If you've ever felt alarmed, afraid, or ready to fight, that is your amygdala on the job.

The amygdala is the control center's alarm system. It functions as a guard—ensuring our survival and protecting us from danger. It is always watchful and ready to sound an alarm. More quickly than the blink of an eye and faster than our mind can form words, the amygdala scans all incoming sensory stimuli for danger. In one-sixth of a second, it evaluates the incoming data and sorts our situation into one of only three categories; either the situation is good, the situation is bad, or the situation is scary.

If the amygdala thinks incoming data about our situation or circumstance is good, it takes no action. We remain at rest. But if the alarm center thinks a situation is bad or scary, it activates our body's stress and fight/flight system. In milliseconds, adrenaline and other hormones flood our system and ready us to run away, fight danger, or take any action needed to survive. When faced with an imminent threat such as a charging lion, a burglar in the house, or a shadowy figure waiting for us in a dark alley, our amygdala does its job by readying us to survive. We all want our amygdala in good working order, but two potential problems keep it from correctly evaluating our circumstances.

First, the control center's amygdala has a very long memory. Once it evaluates specific situations, people, or stimuli as bad or scary, it retains that opinion over time. The difficulty here can be obvious. If we are afraid of the dark as children, our amygdala may have concluded that dark rooms, the outdoors at night, or dimly lit spaces are bad or scary.

As adults, you and I may now consciously recognize that not all dark spaces are bad. We may have gone camping in the woods at night and enjoyed the majesty of the star-covered sky. Even though our conscious thoughts about dark spaces may have changed, the amygdala's evaluation of dark places remains the same. It still finds them bad or scary. As a result, our body is still likely to experience a brief and sudden surge of alarm when entering a darkened room or looking out the window after midnight. The more strongly the amygdala reacts to dark places, the more extreme our body's fearful reaction will be. And since the amygdala operates far outside our conscious control, we can't tell it to stop. We need strong grace-based attachments with others who are not afraid of the dark and the examples of people who are not scared of darkness to help regulate our amygdala's reactions.

The second problem we can have with our amygdala occurs when it is poorly trained to determine if situations are good, bad, or scary. If our early childhood relationships are full of large amounts of grace, joy, and peace, the amygdala is trained to view everyday life as good, especially when we are kept safe from harm. Even if traumatic experiences occur, the presence of strong, secure grace-based attachments can help mitigate its effects.

Without significant grace-based attachments, our amygdala tends to form an opinion that most of life and other people are bad or scary. In these cases, the amygdala tends to become persistently overactive. We may end up living with a chronically overactive alarm center, flooding our body with unhealthy and toxic hormones. We live in a state of ongoing stress in which our amygdala overreacts to stressful situations or becomes alarmed when things are not truly bad or scary.

Even worse, a very poorly trained amygdala tends to filter out things in life that might be good or neutral, focusing exclusively on what it considers scary, bad, or threatening. As a result, our conscious mind continuously focuses on threats and doesn't even notice when good things are happening. In the absence of the strong grace-based attachments that could guide us, our amygdala's fear-based responses to life and relationships become our brain's rapid default system for life and decision-making.

Is there hope for a poorly trained amygdala? Absolutely! As the face of grace story about John in this chapter illustrates, the amygdala's overreactions to bad/scary situations do not have to rule life. How did this occur?

As my attachment with John grew, we began to form a grace-based bond. In the context of that attachment, my brain started to pay very close attention to how John handled issues in life—especially the life-giving ways in which he held anger. His example gave my brain believable new models of how people I cared about could respond when angry. Instead of relying upon the old, unhelpful images of how my family handled anger, my brain now had fresh, life-giving pictures of healthy interactions. As my relationship with John and others in my class deepened, my group identity changed, as did my conduct. I became part of a new "herd."

Despite an irate amygdala, grace-based attachments can powerfully change our group identity and lead to new behaviors.

EXERCISES

DAILY AFFIRMATION 8: I AM A PERSON WHO IS OVERCOMING FEAR.

This is your daily affirmation for the week. Read it aloud as an affirmation of God's work in your life each day while you are working with this chapter. If you are part of a group study, repeat this out loud together each time you meet. (For a complete list of Daily Affirmations, see Appendix A at the back of the book.)

SCRIPTURE REFLECTION: PSALM 23

1. Pray and ask Jesus to guide you as you reflect on this passage of Scripture.

2. Take a moment to remember something you appreciate, or a time you have felt deeply connected to God. Reflect on that moment and remember how you felt.

3. Read the following passage of Scripture slowly. As you read, pay attention to any words or phrases that seem to stand out. Then stop and ask Jesus what He wants you to know about the word or phrase. After you ask, consider any thoughts, feelings, impressions, pictures, memories, or other scriptures that come to mind. Write these in your journal.

PSALM 23 (NASB)

The LORD is my shepherd, I will not be in need. He lets me lie down in green pastures; He leads me beside quiet waters. He restores my soul; He guides me in the paths of righteousness For the sake of His name. Even though I walk through the valley of the shadow of death, I fear no evil, for You are with me; Your rod and Your staff, they comfort me.

You prepare a table before me in the presence of my enemies; You have anointed my head with oil; My cup overflows. Certainly goodness and faithfulness will follow me all the days of my life, And my dwelling will be in the house of the LORD forever.

4. After you've finished journaling your observations, pray over them. Ask Jesus to show you if there is anything more that He may want you to know about what you've written. Enter these in your journal.

5. If you have the time, continue by rereading the passage of Scripture, journaling, and interacting with Jesus.

6. After you have finished journaling, read through what you've written. Think about what you have learned from this Scripture that applies to your life right now. Is there a theme or key lesson that it speaks to your heart? Or is God calling you to action or further reflection perhaps?

7. Which of your impressions, if any, might be thoughts God shared with you? Remember, thoughts and impressions we journal do not carry the authority of Scripture. It's always a good idea to share your thoughts and impressions with others you trust to

help discern what God might want you to know. (If you need help distinguishing what God's thoughts may be, see the "Is the Shepherd Speaking?" list provided in Appendix B.)

REFLECTION/DISCUSSION QUESTIONS

These questions will help you apply this chapter's themes and your Scripture Reflection exercise in your life. They can also help you prayerfully reflect on your life and your connection with Jesus and ask Him for help. Set aside time during the week to reflect on these questions and write the answers in your journal. If you are studying this book with a group, share your answers with other group members next time you meet.

1. Who was the face of grace you saw this week? How did they communicate "special and favorite" to you or someone else? How did you feel when you experienced this grace?

2. Why does David not feel afraid, even when enemies are around him? Who is with him, and what difference does God's presence make?

3. Can you remember a time when you felt afraid but were comforted by someone else who was with you? What happened? Why were you scared? How did they comfort you? Why did you feel less afraid? How did they help you feel less fear? Be as specific as you can be. (It will be helpful if you describe a time when you felt a mild or very moderate level of fear. Sharing fear that is too intense may feel overwhelming to you or others.)

4. If you would like to, close your eyes and imagine being present in the scene of Psalm 23. The Lord is preparing a celebration banquet for David to enjoy in safety as his enemies watch. Can you imagine feeling that safe as you enjoyed the feast? What does that feel like? Did David have to run away from his enemies to find peace and enjoy God's favor? —or did He experience being God's favorite amid his problems and enemies? What would be different about your life if you could learn to enjoy being God's favorite when things are going wrong and you feel afraid?

5. Have you ever watched another person who felt fear but responded peacefully to his or her situation? What did they do? Why were they afraid, and what helped them to feel peace?

6. If you are in a group, how would you like them to pray for you?

HOMEWORK

Homework helps you continue to apply this week's lesson, engage with God, and prepare for the next chapter.

1. Go "grace watching" again this week. Can you find a face of grace anywhere around you? This person might be interacting with you or with someone else. How does watching another face of grace affect you, and how do you feel?

2. Continue reflecting on Psalm 23 and journal your observations. Is there someone with whom you can share your insights—or who is willing to reflect on the Scripture with you?

3. Who would you like to pray for this week? Do you know someone who feels fear and needs to experience God's peace?

9 Addiction and the Weight of Codependency

There is no fear in love; but perfect love casts out fear, because fear involves torment. But he who fears has not been made perfect in love.

—1 JOHN 4:18 NKJV

Duunnn dunnn . . . duuuunnnn duun . . . duuunnnnnnnn dun dun dun dun dun dun dun dun dun dun dunnnnnnnnnnn dunnnn!

That is my attempt at the musical theme from the movie *Jaws*. (Google it. I think it's a fair representation.) If fear had a theme song, I'm pretty sure it would sound something like this. With teeth and tension, fear lurks in our lives, sometimes remaining deep below, while other times we feel it powerfully breaking through the surface, coming for us. Way too often, it is the water in which you and I swim. When we fail to face our fears and deal with the negative guidance system they provide, we are no better than chum in the sea.

Apart from grace-based attachment, if you and I allow ourselves to settle down, we can feel it. The existential angst that we are each alone, un-special, un-favorite doesn't just go away. So, where grace is meant to abide, we attempt to fill in our spiritual holes by pleasing, performing, avoiding pain, or pursuing pleasure (i.e., the 4 Deadly Ps we explored in the last chapter). And then, up from the depths swim BEEPS:

- Behaviors
- Events
- Experiences
- People
- Substances.

No matter what form they may take in our lives, the more we use BEEPS to regulate fear, the more powerfully they will affect our mood, emotions, thinking, and level of pain. Subsequently, our attachment to them will grow stronger until they take on a formidable life of their own. Though they effectively keep our anxious feelings at bay, BEEPS are no substitute for genuine, healthy relationships. All they can provide is a nonrelational, false sense of being special and favorite—or they can numb the pain of *not* feeling that way. Sometimes their influence is subtle. Other times, it is obvious. At all times, BEEPS represent our addictions. To be clear, comfort and pleasure are not inherently wrong, but where you and I find each *can* be—that's when we stray into BEEPS. With this in mind, let's explore new waters.

THE NEUROCHEMISTRY OF OUR DEVELOPING MIND

Grace, joy, and secure attachments (or the lack thereof) manifest themselves in all parts of our brain:

- structure
- chemistry
- growth
- identity center
- ability to regulate fear and negative emotions
- capacity to handle trauma.

A RHYTHM OF GRACE

Our developing mind has two essential needs that genuine grace-based attachments with God and others fulfill: joy and quiet. Regarding our nervous system, joy is a high-energy, exciting, and pleasurable state. Quiet is a low-energy state that helps us rest, calm, and recover from joy and other exciting experiences. Caregivers who see us as special and favorite tune into our needs for both joy and quiet—providing opportunities to share these experiences with us hundreds of times each day.

Joy

To my brain joy means "someone is glad to be with me."[1] The face of a grace-based caregiver lights up when they see me; their eyes sparkle and their smile is full. Before they even say a word, the message beams from their face, "I'm glad to be with you." Faster than conscious thought—in forty milliseconds, to be exact—my brain responds by releasing a sudden surge of the neurotransmitter dopamine. Dopamine stimulates the brain's reward/pleasure center, helping me feel a sudden sense of pleasure. This is the neurochemistry of grace-driven joy. The more we interact with people who see us through eyes of grace, the more we experience joy and, consequently, the more our brain releases dopamine. Repeated, consistent, ongoing joyful interactions train our brain to regulate dopamine effectively. Dopamine also helps us attach strongly to those who are glad to be with us and see us through eyes of grace.

Quiet

Following a period of high-intensity, joyful interaction, our brain needs to rest. For that it needs quiet. Those who see us through eyes of grace tune in to our need to rest. Their face becomes restful and peaceful.

and they stop trying to stimulate us with joy. Instead, they rest with us quietly while our brain recharges and prepares for another series of joyful interactions. This resting state is called "Quiet Together." As my friend Jim Wilder says, Quiet Together means

- I am not alone.
- I can rest.
- I can still and quiet myself.
- I am undisturbed because even in the presence of my enemies, I know that someone is with me.

Attachment

During such quiet times, our brain experiences the release of serotonin—a neurotransmitter that helps our brain and nervous system relax and calm back down. Repeated Quiet Together experiences help our brain learn to regulate serotonin effectively. As you and I share quieting experiences with others, our attachments with them are strengthened. Repeated interactions like this help our brain learn to regulate serotonin so well that we can eventually quiet our nervous system by ourselves.

We're so hungry for grace-driven joy and quieting interactions that by the time we're nine months old, we'll want to spend up to eight hours a day sharing them with others. Our brain is literally learning to dance in rhythms of joy (dopamine) and quiet (serotonin). This dance teaches our brain to regulate these neurotransmitters effectively and efficiently throughout our lifetime. Learning to alternate between the experiences of grace expressed in both joy and calming rhythms of deep peace will keep us in step.

These grace-driven rhythms also lead to the formation of very powerful attachments with our caregivers. When people are sincerely attuned with us and our needs, grace-driven rhythms of joy and quiet forge the most powerful, healthy attachments that can be found. The combined neurochemistry of genuine grace, joy (dopamine), quiet (serotonin), and attachment are critical to developing a robust and stable individual and group identity as well as grace-driven behaviors.

PSEUDO SOLUTIONS

Grace naturally leads to the experience of genuine joy and quiet; pseudo-grace leads to an artificial sense of joy and quiet. You've probably figured out by now that BEEPS are a primary source of pseudo-grace. If we lack the "real thing," we are pre-wired for addictions. That being the case, engaging with any on the BEEPS list will neurologically and subconsciously lead us to either pseudo-joy or pseudo-quiet.

Pseudo-joy is what we feel when the pleasure center of the brain is artificially stimulated by one of the 4 Ps in a way that mimics the feeling of real joy. Like genuine joy, pseudo-joy triggers a dopamine release in our brain, stimulating our pleasure/reward center. Pseudo-joy mimics the genuine feelings of joy that God designed us to experience in grace-based relationships with Him and others.

Pseudo-quiet is the opposite of high-energy pseudo-joy. It artificially quiets the brain, shuts off the "noise" inside, or just helps us to feel calmer and more at peace. Sources of pseudo-quiet mimic the effects of serotonin. In fact, pseudo-quiet mimics the kind of genuine shalom that the Lord intends us to get from secure relationships.

To a brain starving for grace, joy, and quiet, BEEPS are like a drink of cold water on a hot desert afternoon. But the more we use BEEPS to quench our thirst, the more our neurotransmitters and nervous system adapt to rely upon BEEPS to regulate our levels of pain and pleasure. They also mimic the effects of genuine grace. In response to these forms of pseudo-joy and pseudo-quiet, our brain, nervous system, and spirit begin to attach increasingly to BEEPS as a source of pseudo-grace and a primary form of either pseudo-joy or pseudo-quiet or both.

Healthy attachments bond us to God and others through consistent and repeated experiences. (Unhealthy attachments are forged with BEEPS in much the same way.) They are cheap knockoffs for the real thing, but make no mistake: they're dangerous to your spiritual health. Consistent and repeated encounters with sources of pseudo-joy and/or pseudo-quiet will inevitably result in bondage. Both forms of pseudo-grace attachments can be just as powerful—and often become *more* powerful—than the genuine grace-based connections and interactions you and I have with God and others. What's more, the unhealthy attachments of BEEPS can alter our individual and group identity and behaviors—and not for the better.)

HIJACKING ATTACHMENTS

(By mimicking the effects of true grace, BEEPS can hijack our entire attachment system, identity, and behaviors.) We can become more attached to them than to God and other people. To make matters worse, attachments to BEEPS take on a life of their own, making us less responsive—and more resistant to—authentic grace. Turning us away from real grace (BEEPS prove themselves to be very jealous lovers, controlling our brain, nervous system, and spirit.)

Remember, God designed grace-based attachment to Him and others as the greatest source of our pleasure and peace in all of life. If we aren't careful, pseudo-joy and pseudo-quiet will stealthily replace either one. I'll put it as plainly as I can: when you or I play with things that affect our neurotransmitters, we are playing with fire—these change the way our brain works and how we form attachments. The longer and stronger our attachment with BEEPS lasts, the more our neurochemistry is altered. After a while, the other things in life God designed to feel good just can't compete anymore.

When you and I consider the many forms of addiction, it is easy to think about drugs, sex, and alcohol and miss the other ways it can manifest in our lives. The reality is how subtle the differences can be. For instance, (the only difference between an alcoholic and a workaholic is that the workaholic's breath smells better.) Likewise, the only difference between a heroin addict and someone in ministry who desperately performs for God's approval is that the ministry addict doesn't have holes in their arm. The cravings aren't any different—at the core, all are longing the same things: genuine grace, joy, and peace.

SLEUTHING FOR SELF-DISCOVERY

Whether our arms are track-marked or not, we all have attachments to BEEPS, you know? What I believe, however, is just how few followers of Christ realize the nature of their own unhealthy, non-grace-based habits. If you and I want to enjoy a thriving life with God and others, we simply cannot afford to ignore what ours may be. Some questions to help your self-discovery:

- What repetitive behaviors do you have in place to make you feel better about yourself, but that make you embarrassed or ashamed?
- When you feel alone or hurt by others, what do you do to comfort yourself?
- Do you find yourself organizing your day around specific, nonrelational BEEPS?
- Are people close to you concerned about any specific BEEPS in your life?

Food, screen time, sex, ministry, drugs, alcohol, work, exercise, television, money, power, greed—what do you use? If it keeps you from connecting with God and others, you have an unhealthy attachment that is worth rethinking. Anytime one or more of the BEEPS take the place of our primary attachment to God, it is an unhealthy attachment.[2]

Toying with things like these is like playing with a python. It may hug you for a bit, but you will soon find yourself strangled in the grip of addiction.

UNHEALTHY COMPARISONS

A good number of us have lived long enough to know that comparison is our enemy in most areas of life. Along the same line, there's another thing to be aware of: we have an innate tendency to "rank" our unhealthy attachments (aka sin). I discovered this to be very accurate when I worked in rehab facilities. There, I commonly observed that alcoholics tended to look down on drug addicts. Drug addicts looked down on other drug addicts who use intravenous needles. Further down the recovery culture ladder were drug addicts who turn tricks to get money for their drugs. Why is it that we are strangely comforted to think, "Well, at least I'm not as bad as him!"? Comparison with others limits our capacity to see our own unhealthy attachments. I daresay, it has something to do with our misunderstanding about our grace-starved selves.

Something else is true of addiction: often, when you and I can manage to kick one, a secondary (and equally destructive) addiction may surface to take its place. During my years working with men and women who were actively involved in drug or alcohol recovery, I saw it all the time. My friend Wally is a good example. As a workaholic, he was driven and perfectionistic. Aside from the negative toll it took on his wife and kids, Wally's problem was significant enough to compromise his health. Ultimately, he suffered so many stress-related illnesses that he was forced to retire early.

His medical condition kept him from doing what he loved. Miserable and lonely, Wally tried distracting himself with hobbies like gardening and coin collecting. Still, his brain craved the pseudo-joy that work had once provided—his neurotransmitters told him so. Eventually, he found a new "fix." Under the guise of helping neighborhood women with repairs, the volunteer handyman began meeting them for sex. He switched his addiction from work to sex—promptly blowing up his entire family. Just like Wally, when grace-based attachment is lacking in our lives, you and I will strive to fill the space.

As with these examples, it's easy to see how using substances like cocaine or heroin can change our neurochemistry. But don't kid yourself, you and I can use people in much the same way. When we grow fear-based attachments with others, they have the same neurological effect on us. People can become sources of pseudo-joy or pseudo-quiet that are just as disruptive to our central nervous system and neurotransmitters as any drug imaginable. And when they do, we become half of a codependent whole.

It's simple, really. Whenever we give too much weight to our fears regarding other people's feelings, opinions, or behaviors and not enough to God, we are acting out of codependency. Our BEEPS is simply a person (or group of people).

THE DYNAMICS OF CODEPENDENCY

One clear biblical example exists in the life of Eli, the high priest, and his two sons. Eli was not just any priest but *the* high priest of God. At that time in Israel's history, Eli served as the spiritual, moral, judicial, and de facto political leader of an entire nation. Clearly, a man like Eli must have known a strong attachment with God at one point. But apparently "life happened," and this religious leader's attachment, identity, judgment, and behaviors changed course. What happened? How did Eli's attachment with God slide into the shark-infested waters of codependency?

In 1 Samuel 2, we discover Eli's sons, Hophni and Phinehas, are up to no good; they were "scoundrels," according to one translation. Pilfering the Lord's offering, blaspheming God, abusing worshippers, and sleeping with women who served at the tent of meeting,(Hophni and Phinehas treated the Lord and His house with contempt.)

Imagine what it would be like today if your pastor stole your stuff, slept with all the women in your family, and threatened to beat you if you dared to protest! Appalling, right? To his minor credit, Eli approached the two about their wicked deeds, but they chose not to heed his rebuke and returned to their evil ways. That was the end of his halfhearted attempt to intervene, but as always it was(God who would have the last word.) Not long after the father-and-sons' conversation, a prophet arrived with a word for Eli from the God of Israel. Because he "failed to restrain them," (1 Samuel 3:13) the once great leader and his sons would reap what they had sown. The prophet continued, "'Why do you *kick* at My sacrifice and My offering which I have commanded in My dwelling place, and honor your sons more than Me, to make yourselves *fat* with the best of all the offerings of Israel My people?' Therefore the LORD God of Israel says: 'I said indeed that your house and the house of your father would walk before Me forever.' But now the LORD says: 'Far be it from Me; for those who *honor* Me I will honor, and those who despise Me shall be lightly esteemed'" (1 Samuel 2:29–30, italics mine).

From this passage, (three words highlight how codependency worked in the lives of Eli and his sons: kick, fat, and honor.)

First on the list is *kick*. <u>Bâ'aṭ</u> is a word used to refer to an ox that at one point had been strong, healthy, and productive—until it got overfed and lazy. As a result of being spoiled, the animal would no longer respond to its master and would try kicking at him in an attempt to violently shake off his yoke (Deuteronomy 32:15). Like the ox, Eli and his sons took their position as special and favorite to God and used it for their own gain. They twisted their once holy and vibrant relationship with the Lord, using their station for their evil purposes.

Next, the term *fat*, which is translated from the Hebrew word *bârâ*', requires some attention. Typically, its definition is "to create" and is used to describe God's creative activity starting in Genesis 1:1. The word is also often used to describe clearing timber to make a new place to live or plant crops. Interestingly, the only place in the Old Testament where this word, *bârâ'*, is translated to mean "fat" is in this story. Eli and his sons went far beyond the sacred leadership boundaries God had put in place to protect His people. Instead, the priests used their authority and power to create an artificial space where they could continue to justify and cover up their bad behavior. They insulated themselves from criticism and thought they were above correction. In the end, their dishonor set each of them up for ruin. Clearly, Eli enabled it all.

Finally, let's consider the definition of *honor*. Taken from the Hebrew word *kâbad*, it means "to be heavy, numerous, or weighty." Quite literally, Eli gave more weight to his fears about his boys' feelings—how they may react to correction or how a break in their relationship might affect him—than he did to his attachment with God. These fears seemed to count more in his mind than what God said about things. Despite all God had done to demonstrate His favor in the high priest's life up to this point, it is hard to believe Eli chose to let his rogue sons' influence outweigh that of the Lord's. In a massive misplacement of his relational priorities, Eli chose their way, not God's. Though he had been God's man at one point, as happens with all BEEPS, Eli's sense of self and others became distorted and dictated profoundly destructive behaviors. He wandered from his attachment with God. Now, let me ask you: if pseudo-joy and pseudo-quiet can mislead a high priest, do you think you and I can handle their misleading, addictive influence any better?

This is the nature of codependency. We give too much weight to our fears and the feelings and possible reactions of others. Quite frankly, we give them too much space in our head. Often, we hope that by protecting the people we love from the consequences of their behavior or use of BEEPS, things will turn out all right in the end. When we do that, we are kicking against His grace—giving more weight to pseudo-grace in our attempts to gain others' approval or avoid rejection.

THE RIGHT QUESTIONS

The 4Ps and BEEPS may seem to help us cheat fear, but in reality they make us work extra hard to maintain the high . . . at least until we throw ourselves, exhausted, at the feet of God's waiting grace. Once we get there, it seems logical to ask, *How do I stop?* And while that's a good question, it is also the *wrong* question. You and I will never find the answer in what we should or should not do. Instead, we will discover the detox for our addiction by reflecting on the following:

- Who am I connected to?
- Where do I belong?
- Who do I understand myself and others to be?

Each of these questions can be rightly answered in conjunction with grace and attachment with God and others. No fierce individual effort will be sufficient to deal with fear and its behaviors otherwise. The only way you and I can deal with these is to find our full acceptance by God and people who see us through eyes of grace. The roles of both God and others who see us as He does are essential in this process. "The mature children of God are those who are moved by the impulses of the Holy Spirit. And you did not receive the 'spirit of religious duty,' leading you back into the fear of never being good enough. But you have received the 'Spirit of full acceptance,' enfolding you into the family of God" (Romans 8:14–15 TPT).

Really, it all boils down to relationship. Grace-based relationship, that is. Our garden walk away from grace-based attachment with God left us fumbling in our fear. It is what got us into this mess, and according to 1 John 4:18–19 (NKJV), a return to His love will cast it out, helping us to grow—and to grow up: "There is no fear in love; but perfect [*telios*: mature] love casts out fear, because fear involves torment [*kólasis*: torment, punishment]. But he who fears has not been made perfect [*telios*: mature] in love. We love Him because He first loved us.")

If fear is at the heart of every wrong attachment and worldly compulsion, we can look at this as our first plunge toward sobriety. Indeed, God's grace is the divine intervention we all need—an invitation to more profound attachment with Him and others, a snout punch releasing us from every fear that swims in our head or heart. This has been His idea from the start, and it is the most essential part of our discipleship.

Since we have been rescued, when we spot the fins of fear surface in the life of another, it is equally vital that we help clear the water—assisting those who may otherwise be pulled under by their own terror. On such a primal level, you and I need grace—and lifeguards. Long before we come to know the fullness of *God's* grace, we experience it through the eyes of others. There is something about seeing it in action—embodied in the lives of those around us—that makes the invitation clear. To be seen, known, and to belong—to be received as special and favorite, regardless of our "issues"—this is what we all long for and what each of us wants to believe about ourselves. No fear—instead, a warm and welcoming chaise awaits on the shore of grace.

MAKING IT STICK

A FACE OF GRACE: MARITZA

Without a doubt, my favorite face of grace is my wife, Maritza. Like every married couple, we have our "moments" when things don't go right. Sometimes, we don't voice our strong opinions with kindness. This is especially true given our very different cultural backgrounds. But I love being able to take a trip behind Maritza's eyes to see myself through her eyes of grace.

When I first met Maritza, I was still disabled and having a terrible day. I only saw her for about five minutes and was in too much pain to remember much about our encounter. Unbeknownst to me, she spent an hour later that afternoon praying for me on her drive home. The next time I saw her was at an international conference for addiction workers in Spain. Maritza greeted our group as we arrived. I quickly noticed that her fluent Spanish made her an invaluable (and favorite) volunteer. She had the heart of a very joyful servant. Little did I suspect that God would heal me at that conference and that six months later Maritza and I would be married! I had no idea that God was getting ready to launch us as missionaries to the global community of hurting men and women whose lives are wracked with addictions and trauma.

Among many other attractive qualities, Maritza's joy is contagious, and she loves exploring the world with me. Never afraid to laugh at herself, she thrives on the adventures—and frequent misadventures—we experience when we travel to new locations for ministry. She appreciates opportunities to share her joy and has an incredible gift of talking with strangers about things that matter. People in airports, trains, planes, and taxis open their hearts to her as she exchanges compassion and love with them. Those who attend our training sessions love her smile, joy, prayers, and kindness. She tends to see everyone as Jesus does.

Even under pressure, Maritza's grace and joy arise. Once, we ministered at a Christian conference in a nation unfriendly to the gospel. The secret police were all over the conference site, listening to ensure that nobody was ministering to non-Christians. In that nation, Christians suffer persecution, conversions are officially forbidden, and sharing the gospel with non-Christians is illegal. When the conference was over, we gave our seats on the bus returning to the capital city to attendees from developing nations who could not afford the fare. We were shocked to discover that the police would not let us use the alternative transportation we had worked out. They forbade us to leave, but the conference venue would not allow us to stay. To make matters worse, the conference organizers were already gone. We were on our own.

To make a very long story short, we jumped into a tourist minivan that agreed to make a completely unscheduled (and officially government-unapproved) rendezvous with another car in the desert. That car was set to drive us to the capital city. I thought we'd left without being noticed, but a glance out the back window corrected my illusion. To my shock, an entire truckload of soldiers armed with automatic weapons was following us. I did not know how they would react when we met the other vehicle, but I was sure they would be unhappy. We were traveling on a two-lane highway with minefields on each side of the road, and there was no place to hide. Quickly, I began to have an earnest conversation with Jesus about our safety. I was busy asking God to make us invisible or turn the soldiers around. In a moment, I looked back, and the soldiers were gone.

Meanwhile, Maritza sat back and enjoyed the ride. Later, Maritza explained that earlier in the morning, she asked God to allow her to see a very historic site in that nation, and she was thrilled that our unexpected route was taking her right by it! While I prayed, Maritza was joyfully basking in God's surprising answer to her prayer and had every confidence that the One who was answering would also protect us. God's brilliant grace and Maritza's unabashed joy and unwavering trust all shone on her face.

THE INTERSECTION OF GRACE, SCRIPTURE, AND NEUROSCIENCE: HIJACKED BY DENIAL AND ADDICTION

In this section you'll discover how neuroscience intersects with grace and Scripture. The reality of God's grace offers solutions and benefits to all aspects of who we are made to be—body, mind, spirit, and relationship!

"But I'll take the hand of those who don't know the way, who can't see where they're going. I'll be a personal guide to them, directing them through unknown country. I'll be right there to show them what roads to take, make sure they don't fall into the ditch. These are the things I'll be doing for them—sticking with them, not leaving them for a minute" (Isaiah 42:16 MSG).

It's hard to have a conversation about how addictions and BEEPS develop without discussing denial. Denial is the mistaken belief that a real problem does not exist or that it is not as severe as it truly is. Denial often minimizes the full extent of a problem, comes up with excuses to justify attachments to BEEPS, or blames the problem's existence on something or someone else. It effectively blinds us to issues that destroy relationships and hijack our attachment with God. A quick look at how the BEEPS seize the brain's neurochemistry and attachment center helps explain this baffling problem.

As we learned in this chapter, the brain's attachment center forms strong bonds with grace-based people who bring us joy or help our nervous system become quiet and peaceful. Interactions with people who bring us joy trigger the release of the neurotransmitter dopamine, which causes us to feel pleasure. Connections with people who quiet us stimulate the neurotransmitter serotonin's release, which allows us to feel calm and restful. Our attachment center responds to these powerful and consistent neurochemical changes by forming enduring bonds with the people who help us experience joy and quiet together.

BEEPS are insidious because they mimic the neurochemistry of both genuine joy and genuine quiet. Some BEEPS provide reliable sources of pseudo-joy because they stimulate the release of dopamine, causing us to feel pleasure. Some BEEPS offer reliable sources of pseudo-quiet and mimic serotonin's quieting effects on the brain. Some BEEPS do both—generating feelings of both pleasure and a reduction in distress. Because they can mimic the neurochemistry of true joyful and quieting experiences, BEEPS can fool the attachment center into forming strong, close, and potent bonds with our BEEPS. Far below our level of consciousness, they hijack our attachment circuitry and—sooner or later—become our brain's strongest attachment. Our brain becomes so "wired" to artificial sources of joy and quiet that it actually begins to prefer BEEPS over genuine grace-based connections with God and others. Soon, BEEPS become our brain's primary source of pleasure, peace, and guidance—quickly turning into a very jealous lover!

So, how does denial begin? Denial has its roots in the brain's response to the neurochemical changes caused by pseudo-joy and pseudo-quiet sources. Through repeated experiences, the brain learns that BEEPS produce feelings of joy or quiet (and sometimes both) and are a reliable source of pleasure and comfort. If we don't feel authentically happy or joyful, BEEPS artificially elevate our mood. If we feel alone or down, BEEPS make us feel better. If we feel stressed or anxious, BEEPS seemingly bring calm, confidence, and rest—these pleasant feelings are what suck us in. When interactions with our spouse, children, parents, friends, relatives, neighbors, boss, or people at church are unpleasant, BEEPS calm our distress and make us feel better. When life's circumstances leave us feeling sad, angry, ashamed, disgusted, fearful, or hopeless, BEEPS provide reliable emotional pain relief. Subconsciously, our brain is burning new neuro-connections between stress and what brings relief. Eventually, this creates well-worn neuropathways—connecting stress-relief and BEEPS. These dysfunctional neuropathways lead to the development of denial.

As BEEPS reliably continue to change our mood for the better, our conscious thoughts about them begin to reflect this new neurochemical wiring. (We start to think that BEEPS are helpful and relatively harmless—instead of seeing them as a monster waiting to destroy our lives and relationships through repeated cycles of self-destructive, self-defeating patterns of behavior) Over time, BEEPS repeatedly cause our attachment center to form steely bonds with them on levels far below consciousness. Once that happens, (it becomes extraordinarily difficult—sometimes impossible—to convince us that BEEPS are the problem.) (Our brain is especially inclined to view BEEPS as solutions when we lack consistent joy and quiet in grace-based attachments with God and others early in life.)

Later, even as attachments with BEEPS damage, devastate, and destroy our lives, (our attachment center clings stubbornly to its opinion that BEEPS are a solution to our problems—rather than the problem itself.) Instead of recognizing the need to deal with BEEPS, we typically start trying to change other people, places, things, and circumstances that we blame for our problems. "You'd drink, too, if you had my spouse," or "Don't you know how much stress I'm under? Of course I overeat!" or "Yes, I know my husband is too hungover to go to work today, but I didn't want his boss to be upset, so I called and said he had the flu. After all, I didn't want to get him in trouble!" These are only a few examples; there aren't enough pages in a book to write every form of denial!

Sadly, denial only seems to loosen its grip on life when pain brought about by the use of BEEPS becomes so intense that we are open to the possibility that we have an unhealthy attachment to sources of pseudo-joy or pseudo-quiet. In recovery communities, we call this experience "hitting bottom." Only in this place of pain do people with attachments to BEEPS find themselves open to the notion that BEEPS are the problem—not the solution. It's also the place in which they will be hungry for genuine grace, joy, and peace, and it's an incredible opportunity for you and me to be faces of grace to them.

EXERCISES

DAILY AFFIRMATION 9: I AM LEAVING OLD THINGS BEHIND AND REACHING FOR EVERYTHING GOD HAS FOR ME IN JESUS.

This is your daily affirmation for the week. Read it aloud as an affirmation of God's work in your life each day while you are working with this chapter. If you are part of a group study, repeat this out loud together each time you meet. (For a complete list of Daily Affirmations, see Appendix A at the back of the book.)

SCRIPTURE REFLECTION: PHILIPPIANS 3:12-21

1. Pray and ask Jesus to guide you as you reflect on this passage of Scripture.

2. Take a moment to remember something you appreciate, or a time you have felt deeply connected to God. Reflect on that moment and remember how you felt.

3. Read the following passage of Scripture slowly. As you read, pay attention to any words or phrases that seem to stand out. Then stop and ask Jesus what He wants you to know about the word or phrase. After you ask, consider any thoughts, feelings, impressions, pictures, memories, or other scriptures that come to mind. Write these in your journal.

PHILIPPIANS 3:12-21

Not that I have already obtained all this, or have already arrived at my goal, but I press on to take hold of that for which Christ Jesus took hold of me. Brothers and sisters, I do not consider myself yet to have taken hold of it. But one thing I do: Forgetting what is behind and straining toward what is ahead, I press on toward the goal to win the prize for which God has called me heavenward in Christ Jesus.

All of us, then, who are mature should take such a view of things. And if on some point you think differently, that too God will make clear to you. Only let us live up to what we have already attained.

Join together in following my example, brothers and sisters, and just as you have us as a model, keep your eyes on those who live as we do. For, as I have often told you before and now tell you again even with tears, many live as enemies of the cross of Christ. Their destiny is destruction, their god is their stomach, and their glory is in their shame. Their mind is set on earthly things. But our citizenship is in heaven. And we eagerly await a Savior from there, the Lord Jesus Christ, who, by the power that enables him to bring everything under his control, will transform our lowly bodies so that they will be like his glorious body.

4. After you've finished journaling your observations, pray over them. Ask Jesus to show you if there is anything more that He may want you to know about what you've written. Enter these in your journal.

5. If you have the time, continue by rereading the passage of Scripture, journaling, and interacting with Jesus.

6. After you have finished journaling, read through what you've written. Think about what you have learned from this Scripture that applies to your life right now. Is there a theme or key lesson that it speaks to your heart? Or is God calling you to action or further reflection perhaps?

7. Which of your impressions, if any, might be thoughts God shared with you? Remember, thoughts and impressions we journal do not carry the authority of Scripture. It's always a good idea to share your thoughts and impressions with others you trust to help discern what God might want you to know. (If you need help distinguishing what God's thoughts may be, see "Is the Shepherd Speaking?" provided in Appendix B.)

REFLECTION/DISCUSSION QUESTIONS

These questions will help you apply this chapter's themes and your Scripture Reflection exercise in your life. They can also help you prayerfully reflect on your life and your connection with Jesus and ask Him for help. Set aside time during the week to reflect on these questions and write the answers in your journal. If you are studying this book with a group, share your answers with other group members next time you meet.

1. Who was the face of grace you saw this week? How did they communicate "special and favorite" to you or someone else? How did you feel when you experienced this grace?

2. Reread the daily affirmation. How are you leaving old things behind? How are you reaching forward for everything Jesus has for you? What does this process look like? How does it feel as you leave old things behind and reach forward for all that God has for you now?

3. Have you ever seen anyone else leaving old things behind as they reach for new life? What did that person do? What did it look like?

4. Who are your mentors or positive role models? What drew you to them? What qualities do they have that you would like in your own life? How do they model grace to you and others? Be very specific.

5. Are there moments in your life when you give too much weight to other people's opinions or feelings? Can you describe these moments? What happens, and why do their opinions and feelings matter so much? What is it that you need in these moments?

6. Who are the people or groups that you feel most connected to? Where do you feel like you belong? Are these people or groups helping you experience and share God's grace at more profound levels? Do they help affirm your grace-based identity? If these people and groups are not helping you connect with grace, ask God what He wants you to do.

7. If you are in a group, how would you like them to pray for you?

HOMEWORK

Homework helps you continue to apply this week's lesson, engage with God, and prepare for the next chapter.

1. Go "grace watching" again this week. Can you find a face of grace anywhere around you? This person might be interacting with you or with someone else. How does watching another face of grace affect you, and how do you feel?

2. Continue reflecting on Philippians 3:12–21 and journal your reflections. Is there someone with whom you can share your insights—or who is willing to reflect on the Scripture with you?

3. Who would you like to pray for this week? Do you know someone who feels fear and needs to experience God's grace?

10 *An Invitation to Recalculate*

The eternal life of which Jesus speaks is not knowledge about God but an intimately interactive relationship with him.

—DALLAS WILLARD

The grace of God means something like: Here is your life. You might never have been, but you are because the party wouldn't have been complete without you.

—FREDERICK BUECHNER

At the time of the banquet he sent his servant to tell those who had been invited, "Come, for everything is now ready."

—LUKE 14:17

In 1891 astronomer Seth Carlo Chandler made a remarkable discovery: the earth wobbles as it rotates. The magnetic fluid deep inside the core of our planet moves—not smoothly but rather irregularly. Because of that, the magnetic field shifts a bit as it spins.

That means that "true north" (where the earth's rotational axis meets the surface) moves around.[1]

After the last couple of chapters, you may be feeling a little disoriented—like your compass can't find its true north. A little wobbly? My guess is you didn't anticipate the twists of each page turn. Grace-based attachment? The 4 Deadly Ps? BEEPS? Concerning grace, who has ever heard of these?

What you thought was neatly nailed down about the topic of grace (specifically, grace-based attachment with God and others) is more of a moving target than you may have heard. That is because, for all the certainties of Scripture, (our individual relationship with God is ever changing) God never changes—but the path we walk with Jesus is not a straight line. It is full of all the unexpected twists and turns that make our journey indescribably unique. Staying the course requires that we live in constant dependence on the gift of connection with Jesus—and others. Since He is our trail guide, our only reliable GPS is Him!

This lifelong journey is the grand invitation of grace—and it is entirely relational. The Lord never meant for us to travel alone. As Christ followers, our charge isn't to figure out how to keep ourselves on the path. Instead, we are to take care to maintain a keen attachment to the One who longs to guide our days. In this chapter, we'll explore three essential navigational aids that can help us recognize when we're on the path—and when we've wandered from our journey with Jesus. We'll start by describing God's invitation to join Him and journey together. Next, we'll discover God's repair plan to help us stay the relational course. Finally, we'll examine the markers on the trail so that we don't wander off the path.

AN INVITATION TO THE JOURNEY

Have you ever said yes to an invitation that you hoped to find an excuse *not* to attend? I have.

I will admit it: I'm a golf-shirt-and-jeans kind of guy, so I feel a creeping dread overtake me anytime I'm invited to something fancy. Nine times out of ten, in the end I'm glad I went to whatever it was. Still, in the lag time between my RSVP and the actual event, I play out a good number of excuses to get out of whatever the commitment may be (think: possible radiation exposure, the flu, unexpected company, frog plague, etc.). So why do I do that? Why do we *all* do that at one time or another? When someone appreciates our company enough to include us, why don't you and I respond graciously to their invitation for the honor that it is?

As it so happens, you've got an invitation in the mail. So do I . . . and, it's a standing one. You can read all about it in Jesus' parable of the wedding banquet (Matthew 22:2–14):

> "The kingdom of heaven is like a king who prepared a wedding banquet for his son. He sent his servants to those who had been invited to the banquet to tell them to come, but they refused to come.

> "Then he sent some more servants and said, 'Tell those who have been invited that I have prepared my dinner: My oxen and fattened cattle have been butchered, and everything is ready. Come to the wedding banquet.'

> "But they paid no attention and went off—one to his field, another to his business. The rest seized his servants, mistreated them and killed them. The king was enraged. He sent his army and destroyed those murderers and burned their city.

> "Then he said to his servants, 'The wedding banquet is ready, but those I invited did not deserve to come. So go to the street

corners and invite to the banquet anyone you find.' So the servants went out into the streets and gathered all the people they could find, the bad as well as the good, and the wedding hall was filled with guests.

"But when the king came in to see the guests, he noticed a man there who was not wearing wedding clothes. He asked, 'How did you get in here without wedding clothes, friend?' The man was speechless.

"Then the king told the attendants, 'Tie him hand and foot, and throw him outside, into the darkness, where there will be weeping and gnashing of teeth.'

"For many are invited, but few are chosen."

This is quite an invitation from the King. Why would anyone treat such a glorious banquet with rudeness and contempt? Taking a look at the culture of Jesus' day, we discover exactly why the king was so upset.

RSVP Required

Before his death in 2016, theologian and author Kenneth Bailey grew up in Egypt and spent more than forty years teaching and studying in the Middle East. From a peasant's perspective, he knew the culture firsthand. Referring to the customs associated with banquets and village culture, Bailey explained that this king would have had an "A-list" when thinking of who he would like in attendance. These were the guests far and wide who were his close and preferred attendees. The king hoped to magnify the celebration with these friends—adding to their relationship. Besides, Bailey points out, the king would have sent two invitations.[2]

In the first invitation, the king announced the banquet and sent messengers to the guests he wanted to invite. The messengers would then carry back an RSVP from each person invited. This first invitation and RSVP were not a matter of polite social custom; there was a much more practical issue. In the days before refrigeration, a host would use the RSVP list to determine how much meat was needed to feed guests. Based on the "Yes, I will come to your banquet" responses, the king would determine which animal—or how many animals—would be needed to provide meat for his guests. On banquet day, an animal (or animals) would be slaughtered, and the meat would be cooked to prepare for the feast. Since there was no refrigeration, the meat would have to be prepared, cooked, and consumed all on the same day. No leftovers! The RSVPs helped the king avoid wasting meat (which was scarce) and kept him from needlessly butchering livestock.

Once the meat was cooked and all the food prepared, the king would then send his messenger back with the second invitation, "All is ready, come to my banquet." Social custom required that all who RSVPed to the first invitation respond to the second one. These invitations carried the message of grace: "You are special and favorite to me. Please come and share my meal and grow our relationship." This social contract was relational, honoring, and understood by everyone. Unless there was an actual emergency, failure to respond to the second invitation after accepting the first was a calculated, deliberate insult to the host. In that culture few things would have been more dishonoring.

In a parallel parable in Luke 14:16–24, Jesus makes the point again, this time that the invitees' excuses were paper thin. According to Bailey, all of these excuses were outright lies and open insults to the king and his son. None of their justifications for not attending would have been acceptable. Clearly, they didn't value their relationship with the host.

In our culture, it's hard to find a comparable event. Perhaps the closest might be the most recent royal wedding, which took place on

May 19, 2018, in the United Kingdom. You may have heard about it? Coveted invitations were sent, and onlookers left outside Windsor Castle's gates lined the streets for days to catch a fleeting glimpse of the happy couple. There was a media frenzy covering every detail leading up to the big day. Whether dignitaries, family members, friends, or celebrities, you can bet anyone lucky enough to receive an invitation was quick to confirm their seat!

Now it's our turn; we've received an even greater invitation. The King has requested our company at His wedding banquet. Despite our status as commoners, His grace has been extended. And it is not merely a lavish meal He is serving. Plated up, an eternal relationship is generously being offered to us, His most cherished. The question is, will you and I respond less than enthusiastically, or worse, will we snub responding all together? When we send excuses or respond with a less-than-wholehearted commitment to His request, do we understand what we are missing? It is not only bad form, but it's also a mind-bending misjudgment on our part. If you've ever had a kid get married, you know there is nothing more frustrating than the guest list. So, come on! The Bridegroom awaits! His Father (*THE* King!) is our Host, and He has prepared a table and a place for us.

In his Christian discipleship classic, *Divine Conspiracy*, Dallas Willard writes,

> I know that, as far as forgiveness alone is concerned, the tenderness of God is far greater than we will ever understand on earth or perhaps elsewhere. That is surely what it means to say that he gave his unique Son to die on our behalf. I am thoroughly convinced that God will let everyone into heaven who, in his considered opinion, can stand it. But "standing it" may prove to be a more difficult matter than those who take their view of heaven from popular movies or popular

preaching may think. The fires in heaven may be hotter than those in the other place.[3]

The King has been tender to extend a gracious invitation to you and me. Is our life here really that hot? The point I want to press—and what Willard seems to recognize here—is that we *must* take His invitation seriously.

God doesn't want anyone left outside the gates . . . but do we really want in? With bated breath, do you and I press our noses to the glass, watching for the mailman in hopeful anticipation of the invitations each day holds? As God's special and favorite, you and I should look forward to living in God's presence here and now—not just then and there! That is one of the privileges we enjoy. If we don't honestly want to be in His company every day, why would we aspire to it for eternity?! If we spend our life on Earth scrupulously avoiding God's graceful invitation, heaven feels more like a dreadfully awkward family reunion—the kind where we pretend to enjoy spending time with the relatives we otherwise avoid! Surely, that is not the roll-out-the-red-carpet, dance-'til-eternal-dawn wedding bash that Scripture describes.

Pack Your Wedding Clothes

So you don't miss it, look at the last part of Matthew 22 again. Verses 11–14 mention something worth further note: "But when the king came in to see the guests, he noticed a man there who was not wearing wedding clothes. He asked, 'How did you get in here without wedding clothes, friend?' The man was speechless. Then the king told the attendants, 'Tie him hand and foot, and throw him outside, into the darkness, where there will be weeping and gnashing of teeth.' For many are invited, but few are chosen."

In Jesus' parable, the king had long since moved on from his original guest list, instructing his servants to fill the wedding hall. His grace moved forward, extending the once-in-a-lifetime invitation to any and all. Keeping in mind what an unequaled honor it was to be chosen by the king to attend this gala, wouldn't you dress for the occasion? Yet one man had the chutzpah to blatantly insult the gracious host by refusing to wear his wedding clothes. Violating the dress code was an intentional insult and a calculated effort to dishonor the king and the occasion. Can you imagine?

Commentaries differ about the significance of the wedding clothes. Some say the host traditionally provided the clothes (or fabric for them). Others think that culturally the people had clothes set aside for such an occasion. Two thousand years later, no one is entirely sure who provided the clothes or what they even looked like. The important thing is that this individual showed up to enjoy the benefits of the invitation, good food, fine wine, and the opportunity to mingle with important people but had no intention of honoring the host and his desire for relationship. It is the equivalent of saying, "I don't care about you—I'm just here for the party."

To make matters even worse, as the king moved about the room greeting his guests, the man clammed up and refused to talk to his host. Addressing the underdressed guest as "friend" (which is *hetairos* in Greek), the king asks the man to explain himself. This Greek word means more than a friend; it is a relational term, which also means "kinsman" or "clansman." Literally, the king reminds the guest of their relationship as kinsmen—part of the same tribe or clan. In response, the Greek text reports, the man "muzzled." In other words, he muzzled himself, shut his mouth, and refused to talk with the king at all.[4] Seeing this, the king ordered the guest bound and thrown out into the dark. Now please understand: the king did not reject the guest! Rather, his highness recognized that the man had no intention of respecting the inherent relationship that came with the invitation. Even when reminded, the guest refused to engage with the host. His heart wasn't in the room but far away in a dark place. By ordering the ungracious guest bound and thrown out, the king was simply reuniting the man's physical body with the brain (and good manners) that he had evidently left outside the banquet hall.

I hate to say it, but far too many in our current faith culture show up similarly "underdressed" these days. We all want our name on the list, yet when it comes to honoring the King's gracious gesture, some of us exert little, if any, effort. We want to set our own terms, thank you very much. But really, who is serving Whom? It seems many of us want all the "bennies" of being chosen without any relational obligation. We are like the fabled emperor with no clothes, believing that our transparent excuses actually cover the naked truth: we have no intention of taking our invitation seriously. Others may show up in the right clothes but then act like they get to pick the menu or think no one will notice if they eat and run. It's like chewing without swallowing—it will never nourish us. And as a result, we don't grow in grace.

The King's grace-based invitation to attachment with Jesus offers us access to the GPS we need for our journey. In the context of our ongoing interactions with Him, we discover direction for all of life and the circumstances we face each day. God's invitation to the path is an honor—and joy—that He wants to share with all of us.

PERSONAL DETOURS

I know how easily you and I get detoured, though. We all have a stunning tendency to overestimate our ability to navigate the path and remain on it as we follow Jesus. We don't intend to leave the path but wander off anyway when we attempt to figure out "God's will" on our own apart from grace. The drift is subtle but sure when we replace attachment to God with our understanding of Scripture, good teaching, helpful principles, rousing sermons, or others' advice and opinions. None of these are evil, but they aren't a substitute for grace-based attachment.

Do the Math

Let's consider the challenge of figuring out how to stay on the path apart from a moment-by-moment grace-based attachment with Jesus. We'll put aside sound principles we've heard in books and sermons and just concentrate on figuring out which Old or New Testament commands apply to us in the minute-by-minute changing circumstances we encounter daily. What are the odds that we can determine which Old Testament or New Testament commands should guide us at any given moment?

We'll start with Old Testament commands first. In his book *The Pandora Problem,* my friend Dr. Jim Wilder explains that there are 613 laws in the Old Testament that govern what is right and biblically correct (or true) at the same time. Based on Old Testament Law, Wilder calculates the odds of finding the right course of action as follows: "Multiplying the 613 Jewish laws of the Old Testament (creates) 2^{613} possible combinations of sacred laws that must be considered for every situation. Assuming that all commands are of equal importance, the odds of calculating the right course of action based on Old Testament commands is approximately 33,992,831,540,273,094,316,133,645,21 9,358,000,000,000,000,000,000,000,000,000,000,000,000,000,000, 000,000,000,000,000,000,000,000,000,000,000,000,000,000,000,00 0,000,000,000,000,000,000,000,000,000,000,000,000,000,000,000, 000,000,000,000,000,000.[5]

In other words, the odds of successfully calculating the right course of action based on Old Testament Law is approximately 10^{184}. That's 10 with 184 zeros behind it! Can we agree that trying to calculate which Old Testament command might apply to our situation is practically impossible?

Yet knowing how many of us think, I can hear some of you saying, "But we aren't under the Old Covenant anymore. We're under the New Testament in the age of grace—redeemed from the curse of the law, we're only interested in doing the things Jesus says in the New Testament. Surely, it's easier to figure out what the New Testament wants us to do at any given moment." Okay then. Let's do that math!

Anticipating some potential pushback here, I pursued the idea with Dr. Wilder by email. There are approximately 1,050 commands given in the New Testament (a number considerably greater than the 613 Old Testament commands, you'll notice). He helped me understand the odds of using those 1,050 commands as a moment-by-moment guidance system for every event or experience we encounter. He responded, "Assuming that all commands are of equal importance, and much higher if they are not," the abbreviated number is "1.2×10^{316}. That is 10 with 132 zeros times larger than the number for the 613 laws of the [Old Testament]."[6]

Let's put this in perspective: there are 7.5×10^{18} grains of sand in all the deserts and beaches on earth.[7] Do we realize that it is easier to count the number of grains of sand covering the entire world than to try to figure out how to apply the Old and New Testament commands correctly every moment? If we think we can figure out how to stay on the path with Jesus in this manner, we're kidding ourselves! Each time we try to live this way, we are exchanging Jesus' invitation to live in grace-based attachment with Him for nothing more than a form of self-defeating legalism. Whether we recognize it or not, our legalism becomes an excuse to avoid relationship. In essence, we forfeit the invitation.

Don't get me wrong. I'm not suggesting that Scripture is unimportant. As Paul says, "But you must continue in the things which you have learned and been assured of, knowing from whom you have learned them, and that from childhood you have known the Holy Scriptures, which are able to make you wise for salvation through faith which is in Christ Jesus. All Scripture is given by inspiration of God, and is profitable for doctrine, for reproof, for correction, for instruction in righteousness, that the man of God may be complete, thoroughly equipped for every good work" (2 Timothy 3:14–17 NKJV).

I contend that apart from an interactive, grace-based attachment with God—one in which His Spirit guides and leads us into all truth— we'll never figure out how to apply Scripture effectively. It's easier to count sand than it is to try to judge accurately on our own which passage, precept, or proposition of Scripture communicates God's will for us in every situation. Our human spirit is not the Holy Spirit!

Calibrating Our GPS

To be led by the Spirit to live in grace-based attachment with God, we must engage with Him, moment by moment, in order to discover the next right thing that He is inviting us to. In Scripture and life, we learn to recognize God's voice by spending time listening to Him speak to us each day and responding to His invitation. The GPS of grace-based attachment offers this to us: the invitation is to a life of connection— interactively abiding close to God's heart, guided by Him through a reciprocal relationship.

God issues the invitation, ladies and gentlemen. It's *His* party. He will faithfully direct us. If you've received a digital invite lately, you know they come with a map. Click and you're on your way to the party! So, commit already! If you want to follow your own path—your own system of qualifiers and laws—you need to know that you're not heading toward the Master's banquet.

Years ago I had an experience that shaped the way I view God's invitation. After I finished training for ministry, I was excited to go to work at a church with a very high-profile senior pastor. Building his success on the gifts God had given him, this leader established a dedicated, growing church following and a large regional platform for himself. I felt honored to become part of the pastoral counseling team at that church.

To everyone's shock, that pastor eventually confessed to having a series of affairs with multiple young women over twenty years. To make matters worse, I learned later that some leaders close to the pastor knew about his behavior but chose to cover it up to protect the reputations of the church and pastor. From the outside, this gifted man was a Christian A-lister. Unfortunately, looks can be deceiving. In reality, this pastor only *appeared* to be honoring God's invitation. Although he expressed love for God and seemed to care for other people genuinely, he slickly enjoyed the honor and praise he received from others more than he honored God's gracious invitation to attachment with integrity. Sadly, this man couldn't see himself or others through eyes of grace. Despite his many strengths, the pastor didn't engage his Host (God) to the degree needed. When he finally did go to treatment for his sexual issues, this talented man continued to "minister" to everyone else, but he just couldn't seem to deal with his own stuff.

Blaring from far too many recent headlines is news of pastors, priests, and leaders sexually manipulating vulnerable men, women, boys, and girls. In part, this has conditioned us to condemn this preacher's behavior easily and quickly. But he's not alone . . . is he? Outwardly too many of us check "Yes" on the RSVP but continue to go our own way. We build our own little kingdoms when we do that—constructing good Christian reputations and efforts through our gifts, personality, charisma, and intellectual pursuits. It's so subtle that we hardly know we are doing it. (While God gives us good things to enjoy and to share, He never intends these to take the place of grace-based attachment.)

At the risk of shocking some: just like this pastor, we all share deep and not so dissimilar capacities for self-deception. (Coupled with our drive for self-dependence, many of us wander from the path by substituting God-given talents for actual engagement with Him.) Like this pastor, little by little, seduced by our gifts, you and I can become tone-deaf to Jesus' call to attach. As my friend Alan observes, we often judge ourselves by our good intentions and others by their actions. How easily we wander away from friendship with our Father!

For each of us who sets out on this journey with Christ, grace-based attachment locates an essential pin on the spiritual map. Then, at last, you and I can be sure where we are! With GPS now properly calibrated, it is time to set out on the course before us! All it takes is one look at the life of Jesus to know: becoming His disciple is a relational road—one best traveled with the reliable compass of grace-based attachment. Like traveling by jet versus car, this is what can *really* get us going!

STAYING THE RELATIONAL COURSE

If you've ever enjoyed a long trip, you know how many stressful events can happen along the way. Best laid plans notwithstanding, these can happen to us all. Whether it's a blister, jet lag, Montezuma's revenge (aka Delhi belly), confusion caused by a language barrier, a dangerous encounter with local wildlife, or a mugging as you unknowingly end up in "a bad part of town," when we take a blow from something like one of these, our bodies will need repair. Countless logistics can threaten our way as well. Misbooked tickets, lost luggage, transportation cancellations, an oversold hotel all have the potential to leave us stranded. With what seems like every last nerve frayed, staying the course requires assistance.

Roadside Relational Repairs

The same things are true of our journey with Jesus. Like AAA for our spiritual life, God knows that we need ongoing relational repair to keep following Jesus' itinerary. Before we even set out, He has put a team in place to help prepare us, restore us when we are unwell or wounded, and otherwise provide the necessary roadside assistance required. More often than not, God's assistance and repair come in the form of the grace-based attachments we share with others around us. Although many of us would rather travel alone, God intends that we journey with others if we are going to stay on the path He has invited us to travel.

With no illusions, He—the Author of all relationships—recognizes that these relationships are sometimes hard work! Still, in His wisdom God knew that you and I need them for our trip to get us where He has planned. Relationships with other people (and how we respond to relational challenges) help us navigate home.

God gives you and me other people to help us learn to see them through the eyes of grace as part of *their* relational recovery too. Again, *yes!* He knows how hard relationships are! To put it mildly, some individuals and groups can be a pain. That being the case, doesn't it just make sense that they are the best possible context for our growth in grace? Through ongoing interaction with other people, you and I have an opportunity to taste and experience more of its relational flavor. On so many levels, we need grace with—and through—one another for our spiritual growth and survival!

In isolation, lasting spiritual growth cannot happen. Even as I write this, I can already hear people moaning. To keep you from blowing this off as merely *my* theory, plenty of research strengthens the statement. In his latest book, *MORE*, pastor and researcher Greg Hawkins explains that in their survey of over 500,000 churchgoers, only one in eight people (only 12 percent) in any given church are living a life of more love, more peace, more purpose—one of overall intimacy with God and others. Of those few, only 58 percent said they were "satisfied" with how their church helped them grow. From this research, two key factors correlate with people who experience deep, spiritual transformation: 1) engaging with Scripture; and 2) close relationships with God and others.[8] In their findings, the thing that stands out most to me is the relational significance of both. Remember: apart from attachment and healthy identity (individual and group), our behavior will not change. Transformation becomes a myth. Neuroscience supports Greg's research: our behavior reflects our attachments and identity.

Ephesians 4:11–16 offers more inescapable evidence. Please pay particular attention to what I've emphasized in the passage, and then, if you can't shake your skepticism, take it up with the Author:

> So Christ himself gave the apostles, the prophets, the evangelists, the pastors and teachers, *to equip his people for works of service*, so that the body of Christ may be built up until we all reach unity in the faith and in the knowledge of the Son of God and become mature, attaining to the whole measure of the fullness of Christ.

> Then *we will no longer be infants*, tossed back and forth by the waves, and blown here and there by every wind of teaching and by the cunning and craftiness of people in their deceitful scheming. Instead, *speaking the truth in love*, we will grow to become in every respect the mature body of him who is the head, that is, Christ. From him the whole body, joined and *held together* by every supporting ligament, grows and builds itself up in love, as each part does its work. (Ephesians 4:11–16, italics mine)

This passage describes the perfecting, repairing, and equipping that happens between us. The word "equip" in the first verse is the Greek word *katartismos*, derived from a root word meaning "mend." The word also encompasses the idea of being restored—repaired and *prepared*. Although I know that relationships are painful, this kind of work is done person to person—it's not just part of the pastor's job. The intention is clear: you and I—the laity—are distinctly empowered for action. Our spiritual growth is contingent upon it, and others are essential in the process.

We will never be able to stay on the path to Christlikeness without God *and* other people. God intentionally designed relationships with Him, and especially with others, to be the place of repair, restoration, and healing. Only together can you and I be edified—built up and not stuck in our immature ways. If you and I expect to grow in life with God, we need one another . . . otherwise, the world will "eat our lunch."

Speaking the Truth

In a healthy Christ-centered community, each of us has a chance to grow up as we learn what it means to "speak the truth in love." For too long those five little words have been loaded as ammunition to shoot the Christian wounded among us by scores of misguided followers of Jesus. Incorrectly applied, this verse is twisted—forcing the weak and vulnerable to stare down the barrels of correction wielded by too many misguided and sometimes spiritually abusive followers. To help prevent more casualties, let's be 100 percent clear: at best, this demonstrates misguided and immature thinking and, at its worst, sheer religious abuse.

Without question, the basis for bonding *does not* mean we are free to tell others what's wrong with them—especially in the name of Jesus. No one learns to be authentic with others by having their failures constantly blasted. Continually pointing out the faults of another person does not spread grace or cause grace-based attachments to grow. On the contrary, this practice causes fear, the 4 Deadly Ps, and BEEPS to grow, and teaches community members to hide their weaknesses to avoid shameful exposure.

What telling the truth in love *does* mean is that we can be trusted to *remind* one another lovingly of the best of who we are—especially when we fail to live out of our identity as God's special and favorite. We need others to remind us of how God sees us continually. Our "truth-tellers" will most likely be people who share the vision and practice in their own lives. Trusting the motive and means of these close others, we can be ourselves.

I am not suggesting that you and I wholly ignore flaws, character defects, and violent behavior in others. (Sticking our heads in the sand simply provides abusive people with a much more inviting target!) I *am* saying that we *all* have blind spots and need the help of others to see them. These malfunctions and faults exist in our lives as proof that we each have room to grow in grace (When you and I are not functioning according to God's design,) we need reminding of who we *really are* through compassionate, grace-centered correction—that is, to be told the truth with a strong emphasis on grace and our God-given identity. Without these holy hallmarks, we are "telling the truth" in something more akin to hate. Input like this does not help anyone grow to become who the Lord created them to be! Quite the opposite, it will leave the best among us spinning in self-condemnation—less like His image than ever.

You and I can't be what we don't see, and we can't do what we don't know. That's just part of why relationships are *so* essential. Guaranteed, all of us miss grace from time to time. By connecting with God and others, we help one another to:

- see what grace looks like (Because most of us have been wounded by other people, Christian or not, both sides of this relational equation must be learned. Offering and receiving grace are equally important.)
- commit to practice and find healing as we learn from our mistakes and those of others
- share in the suffering of Jesus as we discover what it means to struggle well, side by side.

Practicing Love

If we want to be like Jesus, staying in grace-based relationships is not an option. Like none other, God—the Author of all relationships—recognizes that relationships are hard work! Have you ever noticed that each of the "fruit of the Spirit" described in Galatians 5 isn't useful for much without the presence of others in our life? Love, joy, peace, patience, kindness, goodness, gentleness, faithfulness, and self-control are practiced and experienced *with* other people—not in a vacuum. Notice I used the word "practiced." It is practice that perfects these in each of us. That practice tends to be the most effective in the presence of those Luke describes as our "enemies":

> If you love those who love you, what credit is that to you? Even sinners love those who love them. And if you do good to those who are good to you, what credit is that to you? Even sinners do that. And if you lend to those from whom you expect repayment, what credit is that to you? Even sinners lend to sinners, expecting to be repaid in full. But love your enemies, do good to them, and lend to them without expecting to get anything back. Then your reward will be great, and you will be children of the Most High, because he is kind to the ungrateful and wicked. Be merciful, just as your Father is merciful. (Luke 6:32–36)

More than anyone ever, Jesus Christ experienced enemies—religious, cultural, governmental, and tribal. He understands. He bumped up against all sorts of adversaries. No doubt the Messiah stood in the way for a lot of people. But that is not how He experienced them—or how he experiences us. In fact, His love afforded Jesus the strength to give His earthly life for those who hated Him.

Like Jesus, God allows people in each of our lives who don't treat us with grace. Not only do they *not* see us as special and favorite, often these lovelies seem to make it their mission to let us know how small and insignificant they believe us to be. But can you see it? In reality, God uses them to draw us more deeply into grace. *His* grace. At times like these, you and I have the opportunity to become more dependent on how God sees us than anything else! (*Take that, mean people!*)

God's heart of grace longed for us well before we were ready to respond. In effect, we were the Lord's opponents then. (Without being intentional about it, you and I can make God and anyone into an enemy even now.) But if loving our enemies is the goal, I'm confident that just as Jesus modeled for us, we can find numerous opportunities to die to ourselves each day as temptations to judge and compare the actions of other people arise. By remembering ourselves as who God says we are and reminding close others of their own identity, we extend the kingdom of God. This strengthens the image of Christ in us. And this will rock the world!

For the greater good, here's a helpful measure. Frequently and often, you and I would do well to ask ourselves, *How well am I loving others when it is of no benefit to me?* An honest answer will consider how we love our friends . . *and* our (overt) enemies. God's grace is foundational for both.

Because of the differences of each and every unique soul, is it any wonder Scripture exhorts us to "speak the truth in love" as we go about life? In my experience working with many rehab programs over the years, I've seen many attempts at this—good, bad, and train wreck interventions. The idea of speaking the truth in love is a central part of many therapeutic community models (Christian or not). For some people, loving confrontation can help them come out of denial. For others, listening to people give input in an organized group or during community activities does the trick. Either can be powerfully productive on an individual's path to recovery.

But sometimes people exploit the concept in horribly damaging ways. They use "speaking the truth in love" as an opportunity to vent. In those instances, everyone in the area can tell by the confronter's voice tone and posture that they don't like the person they are confronting. It may be the truth, but nothing is loving about their approach. "I'm just telling you this 'cause I love you" is code for whatever ax someone has to grind. More than they will help the one being spoken to, the words that come next are bound to highlight the dysfunction of the one speaking. In either case, both people likely miss the point entirely.

Done well, the real intent that must drive a grace-filled exhortation is the desire to call someone back to who they really are. Remember the splendor of each person's true identity? We must *appeal* to them in light of that. Whether the confronted individual has circumstantially forgotten or never really known it before, such intervention will help them discover more of their true identity. Generally, telling people how they are wrong will not. It definitely does not inspire an awakening of positive growth. Whenever you and I speak the truth in love, we aren't calling a person to die to something—we are calling them back to life. As Jesus said to the girl he had resurrected, "Talitha cumi!" which means "Little girl, I say to you, arise" (Mark 5:41 NKJV). Anytime that happens, the Lord's grace shines!

For relational repair—not to mention God's glory—such loving-kindness is required. As you and I learn to deal graciously with difficult people, we have the opportunity to experience God's heart—extending the sphere of grace in which we operate. That is how grace is grown and shared. However subtle, it is a major heart shift.

MARKERS TO GUIDE US

Before I damaged my back and neck, Maritza and I used to love hiking backcountry trails. We especially rejoiced at the opportunity to snowshoe in the wilderness. There was nothing quite like walking in the woods with snow falling around us as we tracked the animals who had left footprints behind.

Over the years, I've noticed that mountain trails have markers along the way so hikers know which way to turn when the path bends. These markers are easily visible in the summer since they are attached low on trees or on stakes driven into the ground. But everything changes in heavy snow. Then the markers tend to disappear. That's why certain trails have bright orange tags tacked high in the trees or on long poles extending from the ground. Some of these aren't very noticeable in the summer because they are too high. But when four to six feet of snow is on the ground, these markers are suddenly at eye level to guide us on the trail.

In the same way, you and I need some biblical trail markers to ensure that we're staying on the path. Given our propensity for self-deception, these guideposts are essential! How can we be sure that we're on the path and haven't strayed off course? Here are some key signs to help us know we are moving in the right direction. In the context of a growing spiritual life of grace-based connection with God and other people, you and I will

1. **Share grace.** Grace received is grace to be shared. God has given us status as His special and favorite so that we will share it. If we aren't, you and I can be reasonably confident that we aren't growing. (Luke 6:32–36)

2. **Bless those who curse you.** We have already looked at what Luke has to say about this. Another teaching from Jesus in Matthew 5:43–48 underscores its significance:

    "You have heard that it was said, 'Love your neighbor and hate your enemy.' But I tell you, love your enemies and pray for those who persecute you, that you may be children of your

Father in heaven. He causes his sun to rise on the evil and the good, and sends rain on the righteous and the unrighteous. If you love those who love you, what reward will you get? Are not even the tax collectors doing that? And if you greet only your own people, what are you doing more than others? Do not even pagans do that? Be perfect, therefore, as your heavenly Father is perfect."

(As Christ followers, being able to love our enemy is one of the most significant indicators that we are heading in the right direction.)

3. **Develop increasing "God sight."** God sight is the increasing ability to see ourselves and others the way God does. As 2 Corinthians 5:16–17 says, "So from now on we regard no one from a worldly point of view. Though we once regarded Christ in this way, we do so no longer. Therefore, if anyone is in Christ, the new creation has come: The old has gone, the new is here!" This kind of vision enables us to see someone. Whenever we look in the mirror or directly into another pair of eyes, God loves looking back. The better you and I get at this, the less we will catch ourselves defining people by their outward behavior, problems, or mistakes. How's your vision?

4. **Consider the plank in your own eye.** Speaking of vision, most of us can admit that it's easier to notice flaws in someone else than in ourselves. Without judging or comparing, grace looks in the mirror of its motivation before offering correction or an opinion. (Matthew 7:3–5)

5. **Got love? Joy? Peace? Patience? Kindness? Goodness? Faithfulness? Gentleness? Self-control?** Whichever of these fruits seem to call for growth, pay attention. God is inviting you to more grace. (Galatians 5:22)

6. **Even when it's hard, love others**. Love needs to be an increasing priority for us all if we want to grow in grace. Especially if you find yourself lacking motivation, read and digest 1 John 4:19–21: "We love because he first loved us. Whoever claims to love God yet hates a brother or sister is a liar. For whoever does not love their brother and sister, whom they have seen, cannot love God, whom they have not seen. And he has given us this command: Anyone who loves God must also love their brother and sister."

7. **Follow directions**. Jesus made it pretty clear: grace doesn't exclude obedience. "If you love me, keep my commands. And I will ask the Father, and he will give you another advocate to help you and be with you forever—the Spirit of truth" (John 14:15–17). If you and I are going God's way, the Holy Spirit will be our guide—helping get us to the Lord's desired destination. Love and keep on loving Him (and others) through your faithfulness to these words.

8. **Stay spiritually hungry**. Understanding that God sets the banquet before us, are we hungry for the nourishment He wants to provide? If not, there is a chance you and I may be ruining the feast by filling ourselves up on the world's junk food. Matthew 6:33 invites each of us to "seek first his kingdom and his righteousness, and all these things will be given to you as well." God knows our *real* needs. If you and I stay connected and engaged in grace-based attachment with Him, the rest will follow.

9. **Embrace humility**. Part of maintaining humility is to remain teachable. When you and I approach our relationships with God and other people as learners, we can readily avoid presumption and build connection at the same time. James 3:17 (NKJV) encourages us: "But the wisdom that is from above is first pure,

then peaceable, gentle, willing to yield, full of mercy and good fruits, without partiality and without hypocrisy." The sign that you and I are connecting with *what true grace looks like* is the fruit of a humbly curious heart.

With guaranteed adventure, these markers will keep you and me steadily moving ahead on a joyful, grace-based journey with God—one surrounded by faithful companions and a cloud of witnesses. If we forget them, however, none of us will get far from our own front door. With Jesus as the impetus behind each, these ways make our load lighter—not heavier. By taking His invitation seriously enough to practice what's here, our attachment with Him will be strengthened—helping us to stay on track. And let's be honest, these are attributes that the world longs to see from the church . . . and so do I!

SAFELY HOME

Though many of us have maps, most of us aren't very good at reading them anymore. Grace is like that; it's still out there but seldom referred to as we go about our lives. We keep it in the glove compartment these days. It's there if we need it, we tell ourselves. That is why I've sought to reframe things for you and me. If we stop short, limiting the capacity of grace to merely "saving us from our sins," we miss the fullness of this global relational force. Understood for all its meaning, grace speaks to a deep and reciprocal longing in each of us—a desire to abide with our Father and in the kindness of friends.

We are His *special* and *favorite* ones. *Each* one. *We* are. Assured of that, do you suppose He'd ever lose track of you or me? Never. To stay mindful of the bond we share with Him promises to point us in the right direction—calibrating our True North in Jesus, every time. No wobble.

No matter what our terrain or mode of transportation, the guidance of God's grace is the only sane route to choose. As Christians, orienting our spiritual lives around anything else would be foolish. Follow His route and new horizons will ever unfurl. Steered homeward by the GPS of grace-based attachment with God, you and I will find an adventure big enough to bring Him glory before we even get there. Along the way, our faces shine progressively brighter with God's grace until, at last, we are home again.

MAKING IT STICK

A FACE OF GRACE: JIM

In 2003 I went to a conference in Canada, eager to learn how to better serve hurting people. Dr. Jim Wilder was there, presenting groundbreaking information about the brain and trauma. That is where I first met his remarkable face of grace, and since then, he has become closer to me than a brother.

Right away, Jim's brilliant mind, intense curiosity, and honest humility stood out. As he delivered his messages, I would furiously scribble across the pages of my notepad—hoping not to miss a thing. When he described the brain's emotional and relational control center, my mind raced—the implications for addiction treatment were both astonishing and hopeful! Later that day, during a break, I sat at a table with Jim as he fielded questions and listened to the group's feedback. At one point, the two of us began talking about addictions. As he engaged with me on the topic, his eyes lit up with warmth, and by the time we finished our conversation, he validated a lot of my thinking and encouraged me to keep learning.

In the years since that conference, Jim and I have developed a prized friendship. Whenever he sees me, his face lights up. Like few others in my life, Jim affirms me, and at times when I've seemed to have forgotten "the real Ed," he is quick to help me remember who I truly am. Because he cares about me, Jim is aware of the physical limitations that back and neck surgeries have imposed on my body. More than once, I've noticed that my friend proactively guards me against situations that could aggravate my condition and cause me pain. He embodies what it means to be a gentle protector.

Presenting together at conferences in the U.S. and around the globe, Jim and I know each other so well that we can share the platform for hours using very few notes. We've done it so often that we can practically finish each other's sentences. In "real time," the two of us understand one another's body language, voice tone, and thinking.

Whenever we have an opportunity to work together, we both notice that creativity and imagination flow freely. Our individual ideas become stronger as a result. Jim and I cultivate a high-joy environment that allows us to move seamlessly between focused work and spontaneous joking, inevitably leading to uproarious laughter. Our creative process is full of God's grace, and I think He enjoys partnering with us!

Being that we are never too old to play, Jim and I have made many great memories throughout our friendship. Once, he picked me up from a conference in Modesto, California, and introduced me to General Sherman and the other giant sequoia trees in Yosemite. Another time, while we were in North Carolina to film some training videos, Jim and I tried a local favorite, deep-fried OREO cookies (which incidentally I don't recommend to anyone). On another trip, we found ourselves in a leaky raft adrift in the frigid waters of Alaska. Against our better judgment, the two of us made it an unnervingly hilarious adventure. Other escapades have included snowshoeing near Big Sky, Montana, and snowmobiling in an alpine meadow with Maritza and another good friend, Chris Coursey. Still more great memories have been made around the dinner table. Our shared fondness for green chili has led to many unresolved debates on the Scoville scale.

Probably our favorite thing to do together is to play music. Jim plays guitar, and I play bass. So, when we have the chance, it's normal for us to spend six to seven hours at it. What makes this exceedingly fun is that we enjoy being together as much as we love music. We value one another more than we expect perfection. As a result, both of us are gentle with each other's musical weaknesses. To keep us playing and improving, this is an essential quality of our friendship. The joy we share playing music makes our hours of practice well worth it!

In all these ways and more, it is easy to see that Jim and I really enjoy hanging out together. Even when we are miles apart, both of us make an effort to video chat regularly to catch up on work, life, God, and the other fun things that make life worth living.

Intentionally nurturing grace and joy in our relationship just never feels like work with this friend. And at times when I'm struggling, I know I can count on Jim—and he knows the same is true of me. This friendship has given us both a glimpse of what grace awaits us with Jesus!

Note: If you'd like to learn more about cultivating a grace-filled, joyful environment, see *Joy Starts Here: The Transformation Zone* by E. James Wilder, Ed M. Khouri, Chris M. Coursey, and Shelia D. Sutton (Pasadena, CA: Shepherd's House, Inc. 2013).

THE INTERSECTION OF GRACE, SCRIPTURE, AND NEUROSCIENCE: ATTACHMENT AS A GPS FOR LIFE

In this section you'll discover how neuroscience intersects with grace and Scripture. The reality of God's grace offers solutions and benefits to all aspects of who we are made to be—body, mind, spirit, and relationship!

> "A new commandment I give to you, that you love one another; as I have loved you, that you also love one another. By this all will know that you are My disciples, if you have love for one another" (John 13:34–35 NKJV).

Attachment as a GPS for life begins in infancy and starts our connection with Mom. Her joyous smile, sparkling eyes, and lit-up face when she sees her baby helps an attachment bond grow between them. As Mom tends carefully to the infant's need for warmth, touch, food, and diaper changing, she builds a profoundly lasting attachment with her baby. Noted UCLA psychologist and researcher in neuropsychology Dr. Allan Schore has spent years compiling the data. His work highlights that, at this point in the infant's development, "90% of maternal behavior consists of affection, play, and caregiving, while only 5% is geared toward prohibiting the child from activities."[9] Consistent, high-joy, grace-based attachments are born here. This type of secure attachment becomes a GPS for the baby.

Later as the baby begins to crawl and eventually toddle, the grace-empowered youngster is gripped by curiosity and starts exploring the environment. Moving across the floor to examine a new toy, bright light, or interesting face, the baby is intent on discovery. Careful observers notice something important: as the baby explores, he or she regularly checks to see Mom's face. The developing brain wants to continue sharing a high-joy state with Mom and looks to her face in search of a reassuring, approving smile. The smile lets the baby know that the attachment is secure, even though Mom may be across the room. Her face, voice tone, and body language tell the baby that Mom is tuned in and shares the baby's feelings of excitement. She shares the baby's joyful emotions. Reassured that distance and activity don't break their attachment, the baby happily keeps exploring. As long as Mom is smiling, nodding, or gently voicing encouragement, the baby continues the activity, securely attached with Mom.

But not all of the baby's actions are helpful or healthy. This is when we enter the "no stage." Schore's research notes that from the age of eleven to seventeen months, mothers express prohibition in response to the baby's activities once every nine minutes![10] The baby is now at the stage where the development of impulse control is essential. Where joy, play, and caregiving once dominated the relationship, Mom now has a full-time job helping the baby explore safely. At this point a large part of Mom's job is to keep the baby from self-inflicted harm or behavior that hurts other people, property, or pets. At this stage toddlers start to learn family and life rules, including things like, "No, you can't bite your sister. No, you can't throw your food. No, you can't bite the cat. No, you can't color your brother." If you've ever been around an energetic toddler, you already know that this is a challenging task.

How does the toddler learn at this stage? Guided by the expression on Mom's face, her voice tone, and her body language, the toddler learns in the context of the attachment they already share with Mom. As we already noticed, exploring toddlers check Mom's face for reassurance frequently. When a toddler engages in a prohibited activity, these same indicators say it all—"No!" The toddler, expecting to see Mom's grace-filled, joyful face smiling back at them, is stunned. Suddenly, the toddler's world turns upside down. They experience intense and immediate pain in the brain's attachment center because they suddenly feel alone and disconnected from Mom. At this tender age, it is the worst kind of distress the brain's control center experiences. In response, toddlers begin to cry and need a comforting reconnection. A problem arises when no comfort is to be found. Wise moms use this opportunity to hug, cuddle, or reassure the toddler that their bond is still intact. Soon, the baby is ready to begin the process of play or exploration all over again. What's important to note here is that in the context of shared attachment, the look on Mom's face has become the baby's GPS! These repeated interactions help the toddler discover that the best way to maintain the feelings of a close, grace-filled attachment with Mom is to follow her lead!

Eventually, the baby internalizes "No" and learns to self-regulate his or her behavior. The memory of Mom's smiling face—and the memory of Mom's unhappy, disapproving look—serve as guides to the growing child, even when Mom is not around. Later, as other relationships with peers, spouses, close friends, and God become more important, the attachments shared with them also help shape behavior. By this time, although the child has long outgrown the toddler stage of life, the same basic attachment dynamics are at work. The attachments the individual shares with the person—or people—they love the most have the most significant influence on their behavior throughout their lifetime. Attachment is the context in which we all develop our internal GPS for life.

EXERCISES

DAILY AFFIRMATION 10: GOD IS WORKING IN ME TO WILL AND DO THE THINGS THAT BRING HIM PLEASURE AND FULFILL HIS PURPOSES IN MY LIFE.

This is your daily affirmation for the week. Read it aloud as an affirmation of God's work in your life each day while you are working with this chapter. If you are part of a group study, repeat this out loud together each time you meet. (For a complete list of Daily Affirmations, see Appendix A at the back of the book.)

SCRIPTURE REFLECTION: PHILIPPIANS 2:1-13:

1. Pray and ask Jesus to guide you as you reflect on this passage of Scripture.

2. Take a moment to remember something you appreciate or a time you have felt deeply connected to God. Reflect on that moment and remember how you felt.

3. Read the following passage of Scripture slowly. As you read, pay attention to any words or phrases that seem to stand out. Then stop and ask Jesus what He wants you to know about the word or phrase. After you ask, consider any thoughts, feelings, impressions, pictures, memories, or other scriptures that come to mind. Write these in your journal.

PHILIPPIANS 2:1-13

Therefore if you have any encouragement from being united with Christ, if any comfort from his love, if any common sharing in the Spirit, if any tenderness and compassion, then make my joy complete by being like-minded, having the same love, being one in spirit and of one mind. Do nothing out of selfish ambition or vain conceit. Rather, in humility value others above yourselves, not looking to your own interests but each of you to the interests of the others.

In your relationships with one another, have the same mindset as Christ Jesus:
Who, being in very nature God,
    did not consider equality with God something to be used to his own advantage;
rather, he made himself nothing
    by taking the very nature of a servant,
    being made in human likeness.
And being found in appearance as a man,
    he humbled himself
    by becoming obedient to death—
        even death on a cross!
Therefore God exalted him to the highest place
    and gave him the name that is above every name,
that at the name of Jesus every knee should bow,
    in heaven and on earth and under the earth,
and every tongue acknowledge that Jesus Christ is Lord,
    to the glory of God the Father.

Therefore, my dear friends, as you have always obeyed—not only in my presence, but now much more in my absence—continue to work out your salvation with fear and trembling, for it is God who works in you to will and to act in order to fulfill his good purpose.

4. After you've finished journaling your observations, pray over them. Ask Jesus to show you if there is anything more that He may want you to know about what you've written. Enter these in your journal.

5. If you have the time, continue by rereading the passage of Scripture, journaling, and interacting with Jesus.

6. After you have finished journaling, read through what you've written. Think about what you have learned from this Scripture that applies to your life right now. Is there a theme or key lesson that speaks to your heart? Or is God calling you to action or further reflection perhaps?

7. Which of your impressions, if any, might be thoughts God shared with you? Remember, thoughts and impressions we journal do not carry the authority of Scripture. It's always a good idea to share your thoughts and impressions with others you trust to help discern what God might want you to know. (If you need help distinguishing what God's thoughts may be, see "Is the Shepherd Speaking?" provided in Appendix B.)

REFLECTION/DISCUSSION QUESTIONS

These questions will help you apply this chapter's themes and your Scripture Reflection exercise in your life. They can also help you prayerfully reflect on your life and your connection with Jesus and ask Him for help. Set aside time during the week to reflect on these questions and write the answers in your journal. If you are studying this book with a group, share your answers with other group members next time you meet.

1. Who was the face of grace you saw this week? How did they communicate "special and favorite" to you or someone else? How did you feel when you experienced this grace?

2. Reread the daily affirmation. Are there areas of your life where you can see God helping you change your desires and behaviors? Describe the changes and the things you're doing now that are consistent with God's wishes. Are there places where your desires have changed but you're having a hard time fulfilling them? How is God helping you move forward? Be specific.

3. What do you think is God's purpose for your life? How do you know? Have you seen others fulfill God's purposes in their lives? What did they do?

4. In this chapter, we studied God's invitation to engage with Him and grow a deeper relationship together. How are you joining with God at this point in your life? Please describe the things you are doing and how these are helping you respond to God's invitation. How is your attachment with Him growing? Be specific as you share because you may help others gather new ideas.

5. How are relationships with other people helping you grow a stronger attachment with God? Who are the supportive people in your life who help you see yourself through the eyes of grace? How do they "speak the truth in love" to help you remember how God sees you? Are there people who frequently point out your faults? Do they help you grow? In an average week, do you spend more time with people who help you grow in grace or people who are critical and unhelpful? Do you need to change the amount of time you spend with people from these two groups?

6. Of the trail markers we listed in this chapter (see list below), which are the most helpful to you? How do these guides help you stay on track as you respond to Jesus' invitation? Be specific.

   - Share grace.
   - Bless those who curse you.
   - Develop increasing "God sight."
   - Consider the plank in your own eye.
   - Got Love? Joy? Peace? Patience? Kindness? Goodness? Gentleness? Faithfulness? Self-control?
   - Even when it's hard, love others.
   - Follow directions.
   - Stay spiritually hungry.

7. If you are in a group, how would you like them to pray for you?

HOMEWORK

Homework helps you continue to apply this week's lesson, engage with God, and prepare for the next chapter.

1. Go "grace watching" again this week. Can you find a face of grace anywhere around you? This person might be interacting with you or with someone else. How does watching another face of grace affect you, and how do you feel?

2. Continue reflecting on Philippians 2:1–13 and journal your reflections. Is there someone with whom you can share your insights—or who is willing to reflect on the Scripture with you?

3. Who would you like to pray for this week? Do you know someone who feels fear and needs to experience God's grace?

Author's Note

Most of us are educated way beyond the level of our obedience.

—MARK BATTERSON

The grace of our Lord Jesus Christ be with you all. Amen.

—ROMANS 16:24 NKJV

I sat still, listening intently to Gordon Cosby as he preached one winter Sunday morning in 1988. I was visiting the Church of the Savior and was quite eager to hear Gordon, who is legendary among those who care for the poor and homeless in Washington, D.C. As Gordon spoke, I found myself nodding in deep agreement and taking copious notes. I was enthralled by his clarity, his deep love for the gospel, and his challenge to apply it.

After the service Gordon asked me, "Ed, did you hear anything radical?" "No," I responded. The message seemed right on target. I didn't hear anything out of the ordinary. What happened next, I'll never forget. "That's too bad," Gordon responded, "because the gospel must *always* be radical."

Gordon's words rocked me. Had I heard the gospel so frequently that I'd become tone-deaf to the extraordinarily radical claims of grace? Had I become so familiar with Jesus' teachings that I missed its demands for a radical response from me? Gordon was gracious—suggesting that perhaps his message hadn't been clear. But I knew the truth. He was clear. The problem was *me*. It's been over three decades since Gordon's question, and it is still ringing in my ears.

I don't think I am alone. After close to forty years in ministry, it seems to me that many of us filling pews and pulpits are so familiar with grace and the gospel that we don't believe there is anything else to learn. Acquaintance with the gospel has calloused our hearing and hardened our hearts. Seemingly passivity has replaced passion, and comfort has supplanted commitment. Certainly, we have missed the fullness of God's gracious invitation, and in so doing, we have missed the point of being part of His kingdom entirely.

So, I ask you: Did you hear anything radical in the pages of this book? If so, how will you respond? Practically speaking, what does that look like for you? How would your life be different if you began living in the truth that you are God's favorite? Going forward, who will you travel with on this journey of grace?

For all the motivation you've discovered, I also hope you find yourself empowered. Take some time to articulate what has meant the most? Spiritually and otherwise, how do you see your life and relationships differently? Has this helped you reimagine doing life and relationships without fear?

Perhaps your Scripture Reflections and Reflection/Discussion Questions have provided a launching point. I want to encourage you to continue contemplating these scriptures—or any others that God brings to mind. If you haven't already done so, gather a group and study this book together. It is remarkable how interaction with others can accelerate your growth. And spiritual growth never stops! Keep after it.

If the radical nature of grace—the reciprocal, relational message of the gospel and the power that grace-based attachment with God and others has to guide us through life—has challenged you, then you've activated your GPS. Take this blessing with you:

✳ *Blessing and summary!*

- May your walk with Jesus grow stronger as your attachment with Him deepens.
- May you become increasingly captivated by the One who calls you His favorite.
- May your identity become increasingly rooted in His grace—and the grace of His people.
- May your relationships be blessed in every way and reflect the radical nature of grace to your world.
- May the eyes of your spirit open to see the people you love—and those you dislike—through God's eyes. (They are His favorite too.)
- May your heart be open to embrace those who wander, and may your lips, hands, and feet be quick to share His amazing grace.
- May you grow to respond tenderly to your weaknesses and the weaknesses of others.
- May you increasingly give weight to what God thinks as His love displaces your fears.
- May the grip of the 4 Deadly Ps and BEEPS continually weaken.
- May your relationships be healing and keep you on track as you respond to God's invitation.
- May you always recognize the markers to help you stay hot on Jesus' trail.
- May a life-transforming, grace-based attachment with God and His people guide you safely home.

I look forward to seeing you on the road.

Daily Affirmations

Each chapter of *Becoming a Face of Grace* includes a Daily Affirmation. Each corresponds to the chapter you have just read. By reciting it, you and I acknowledge a biblical truth relating to our identity; each affirmation helps us recognize and reinforce how key truths in Scripture uniquely apply to us in our daily lives.

Whether you are studying this book alone or with a group, I encourage you to speak each daily affirmation aloud as a personal, daily practice. Doing so stakes a claim, so to speak—you are declaring with your words that in *this* way, you belong to God. You may find it helpful to copy the chapter-specific daily affirmation on a note card so you will see it as you go about your day. If you are part of a group study, repeat the entire Daily Affirmations list out loud together each time you meet. In this case, be sure to change it to group language. (For example, the daily affirmation for chapter 1 would read, "We are a people who are being transformed by grace.")

Chapter 1: I am a person who is being transformed by grace.
Chapter 2: I am becoming like Jesus because I am His apprentice (disciple).

Chapter 3: My heart is at home when I am with Jesus.

Chapter 4: I am learning to know my Shepherd and hear His voice.

Chapter 5: My weaknesses are an opportunity for God's grace to grow more deeply in me.

Chapter 6: I am growing increasingly into the person God designed me to be.

Chapter 7: Just as I received Jesus, I am learning to walk with Him.

Chapter 8: I am a person who is overcoming fear.

Chapter 9: I am leaving old things behind and reaching for everything God has for me in Jesus.

Chapter 10: God is working in me to will and do the things that bring Him pleasure and fulfill His purposes in my life.

APPENDIX B

Is the Shepherd Speaking?

Psalm 23 describes God as our Good Shepherd. A shepherd leads and guides his sheep in various ways—they know his voice and can identify his manner. As part of His flock, you and I can expect God's personal and unique direction in our lives too. So how can we know if He is speaking? By staying close to His grace, you and I will begin to recognize the characteristics of any word we receive. Any message we hear from God should do the following:

- Pass the "Shalom Test." Do you feel an abiding sense of God's peace after as you journal your scripture reflection with Him?

    And let the peace of God rule in your hearts, to which also you were called in one body; and be thankful. (Colossians 3:15 NKJV)

    Peace I leave with you, My peace I give to you; not as the world gives do I give to you. Let not your heart be troubled, neither let it be afraid. (John 14:27 NKJV)

> I, therefore, the prisoner of the Lord, beseech
> you to walk worthy of the calling with which you
> were called, with all lowliness and gentleness, with
> longsuffering, bearing with one another in love,
> endeavoring to keep the unity of the Spirit in the
> bond of peace. (Ephesians 4:1–3 NKJV)

- Be consistent with Scripture.
- Reflect the character and nature of God revealed in Scripture and His people.
- Enhance grace-based relationship and foster the growth of new ones with God and others. Generally, it will not break relationship if at all possible.
- Mirror biblical wisdom.

> Who is wise and understanding among you? Let
> them show it by their good life, by deeds done in
> the humility that comes from wisdom. But if you
> harbor bitter envy and selfish ambition in your
> hearts, do not boast about it or deny the truth.
> Such "wisdom" does not come down from heaven
> but is earthly, unspiritual, demonic. For where
> you have envy and selfish ambition, there you find
> disorder and every evil practice. But the wisdom
> that comes from heaven is first of all pure; then
> peace-loving, considerate, submissive, full of mercy
> and good fruit, impartial and sincere. Peacemakers
> who sow in peace reap a harvest of righteousness.
> (James 3:13–18)

- Encourage and comfort—not condemn.
- Not be toxic if it is a word of correction but will lead to the growth of grace-based relationship.

- Be consistent with what God has already been speaking to you.
- Respect and honor His established authority in your life.
- Mirror God's work in His people over time and not develop new doctrines.
- Feel like a spontaneous conversation with someone you love. By experience and practice listening to His voice, your sense of this will become stronger.
- Offer confirmation through circumstances. By themselves, circumstances are a bad guidance system. But God may speak in ways that are consistent with your current situation or confirm His words to you through external circumstances.
- Reveal God's perfect timing. He is not anxious; He is patient and His words lead to peace.

Note: We're talking about learning to hear and test what God says to us *personally*. In this instance, we are not learning to "hear" God for others. God never intends for you and me to take His place or put words in His mouth. Because it helps each of us grow a deeper relationship with God, the goal is to encourage one another to connect with Jesus and learn to hear from him for ourselves.

APPENDIX C

How Do Attachments Grow?

How do grace-based attachments grow to become a reliable source of guidance?

Grace-based attachments don't spontaneously fall from heaven. They are cultivated and grown through repeated interactions in which others see us as special and favorite. God's means of guidance in our lives are relationally based. As such, grace always leads to the development of relationships.

While we each travel a different course during our earthly life, God never intended that we go it alone. Psalm 68 says that He set us in families. By His design, our families are the place each of us learns to live in God's grace. Extended to us in this context, grace helps you and me to see our value and worth. Even when times are hard or we really mess up, the Lord intends family to be a "soft place to fall." Ideally, it is also where we learn to see others through those same eyes of grace—sharing the hope of salvation and transformation with those we see everywhere we go. For those of us who experienced something other than this, stay tuned. Trust me when I say God's plan for us is better than we have experienced or imagined.

Just as He looks at us, God intends the family to be the place where we learn to see ourselves as He does. It's where we see our worth and value reflected back at us through eyes of joy. From the moment you and I were born, we began to form attachments with those who cared for and provided for us. Each interaction between our parents (or primary caregivers) and us provided an opportunity for attachments to grow. When they saw us through eyes of grace-filled joy, strong, healthy, and enduring attachments took root. Each time they met our physical and emotional needs and related to us as their favorite, important bonds were forged. Neuroscientists call these grace and joy-filled interactions "Glad to be with you moments."[1]

Of course, early in life, we can't speak or understand language. Parents share grace through the sparkle in their eyes and the smile on their faces when they see us. They sing silly songs to us. Their voices rise an octave or two when making strange noises to greet or soothe us. Their healthy touch reassures and delights us. They offer care and nurture—making sure we're not too cold or too hot and making sure that our food is just the right temperature. In countless ways, repeated grace-filled and joyful interactions grow strong bonds between us and our parents, and it's not too long before we respond. By the time we are nine months old, we want to spend up to eight hours a day sharing smiles, giggling, and quiet with our mom. These nonverbal, face-to-face interactions communicate louder than words (which we couldn't understand anyway) that we are Mom or Dad's special and favorite person. These grace-filled interactions lay the foundation for connecting with God and make it easier for us to respond to Him later in life.

By sharing grace, family and other close relationships have the power to help us discover who we are. Importantly, they teach us a lot about what God is like too. Family and close relationships provide the context in which we first and consistently experience the loving-kindness of His grace. Parents who are empowered by God's grace share a priceless gift with their children. By the time we are old enough to start talking, our foundation of grace and joy must already be in place. The experience of consistent, abundant, and timely grace gives us a healthy foundation from which future learning and developmental tasks grow.

Though early attachments definitely set the table, developmental stages serve up new courses. Ask any teenager. At puberty our brains delete neuropathways in order to accommodate the growth of new ones organized around our peer group. And, Moms and Dads, you and I don't necessarily outgrow our need for strong attachments. That's why it is essential to keep in mind that who (or what) we love is more important to our spiritual growth than what we know. Our attachments form early and can grow and recalibrate throughout life in response to grace and the development of new, grace-based attachments.

The kind of grace-based bond that grows in early family life is called "secure attachment." Bonds of emotional love, touch (sexual and nonsexual), and relational intimacy are its hallmarks. Securely attached people view themselves as worthy of love and rest assured that they can obtain it from the trustworthy people in their lives. Like those in every group, securely attached people have experienced hard things. But unlike those in other groups, individuals who are securely attached are more freely able to give and receive from others.

We want to notice at this point that some kind of attachment between parents and children will grow, even if grace is not in place. Grace simply makes attachments healthy. The absence of grace in sufficient quantity or consistency tends to make attachments less healthy and less life-giving. These are called "nonsecure attachments." They include dismissive, distracted, and disorganized attachments.

Nonsecure attachment styles are *not* rooted in grace. These unhealthy bonds form in families where grace is missing, inconsistent, or unreliable. It's important to realize that people with nonsecure attachment styles still form bonds with others. They have relationships. The problem with nonsecure attachments is that they are rooted more in fear, and they experience unmet needs to be "special and favorite." Nonsecure bonds with God and others tend to break down or fail under stress. They are an unreliable GPS for life and discipleship. Here are the three other attachment styles.

Dismissive attachment. Those with dismissive attachment styles tend to dismiss the importance of relationships, people, feelings, and attachments. These things just don't seem important to them. While dismissive types may feel grace, they express it less intensely. People who hit puberty with a dismissive attachment style may lose the ability to notice emotions in themselves and others.

Distracted attachment. In contrast to those of a dismissive style, people with a distracted attachment style overvalue the importance of relationships, people, attachments, and feelings. These folks are always distracted by thoughts along the lines of "maybe 'it' will happen now." When "it" does, they react with great intensity—either too clingy and way too close or too explosive. They don't realize they're doing it. They feel all the feelings in a relationship—whether the other party wants to or not. Unconsciously, they desire to close any space that they sense exists between them and others.

Disorganized attachment. Those with disorganized attachment are a combination of the previous two (dismissive and distracted). Common in those who have suffered in families with abusive or addictive systems, those with disorganized attachment desire connection while at the same time finding it to be a source of terror.

When considering your attachment style, remember the best news of all: God designed us for secure attachment. The ways you and I connect with Him and others can change in response to grace, no matter our age. Research shows that people with a less-than-secure attachment style can grow a more secure attachment. All it takes is a joyful, consistent, ongoing relationship with someone who has a more secure attachment style. Grace works! This is true for our brain, and it's true for our spiritual life.

Endnotes

Introduction

1   William Broyles, Jr., *Cast Away*, directed by Robert Zemeckis (Los Angeles: 20th Century Fox, 2000), DVD.

2   Dallas Willard, *The Divine Conspiracy: Rediscovering Our Hidden Life in God* (New York: HarperOne, 2018), XII.

3   Lawrence Kasdan, George Lucas, and Philip Kaufman, *Indiana Jones and the Raiders of the Lost Ark*, directed by Steven Spielberg (Hollywood: Paramount Pictures, 1981).

4   Greg Hawkins, "Moving the Church Toward Transformation," (keynote lecture, Transform 2018 Conference, Coker United Methodist Church, San Antonio, TX, April 27, 2018).

Chapter 1: So You Think You Know Grace?

1   *Incredibles 2*, directed and written by Brad Bird (Emeryville, CA: Pixar, 2004).

2   John M.G. Barclay, *Paul and The Gift* (Grand Rapids, MI: Wm. B. Eerdmans, 2015), 24-32.

Chapter 2: A Relational God

1   Andrei Rublev, *The Holy Trinity*, "File:Angelsatmamre-trinity-rublev-1410.jpg," Wikimedia Commons, the free media repository, accessed February 24, 2019, https://commons.wikimedia.org/w/index.php?title=File:Angelsatmamre-tritity-rublev-1410.jpg&oldid=337752351.

2   Dallas Willard, *The Divine Conspiracy: Rediscovering Our Hidden Life in God* (New York: HarperCollins, 1998), 276.

Chapter 3: The Bad Breakup

1   David G. Benner, *Surrender to Love,* expanded ed. (Downers Grove, IL: InterVarsity Press. 2015), 27.

2   A. W. Tozer, *The Pursuit of God*, updated ed. (Harrisburg, PA: Christian Publications, Inc. 2015), 17–18.

Chapter 5: Weakness Required

1   Andrew Murray, *Humility: The Journey Toward Holiness* (Minneapolis, MN: Bethany House, 2001), 77.
2   E. James Wilder, Edward M. Khouri, Chris M. Coursey, and Shelia D. Sutton, *Joy Starts Here: The Transformation Zone* (Pasadena, CA: Shepherd's House, Inc. 2013), 15.

Chapter 6: Grace and Identity

1   Merrit Kennedy, "Equifax Says 2.4 Million More People Were Impacted by Huge 2017 Breach," National Public Radio, March 1, 2018, https://www.npr.org/sections/thetwo-way/2018/03/01/589854759/equifax-says-2-4-million-more-people-were-impacted-by-huge-2017-breach.
2   Michael J. Wilson, writer, *Ice Age,* film, directed by Chris Wedge (Los Angeles: Twentieth Century Fox, 2002).
3   C. S. Lewis, *The Weight of Glory* (San Francisco: HarperOne, 2001), 45–46.

Chapter 7: Dead-end Streets: The Debate

1   Martyn Lloyd-Jones, "The Faith of God Without Effect? A sermon on Romans 3:3," sermon, Westminster Chapel, London, n.d., https://www.mljtrust.org/sermons-online/romans-3-3/the-faith-of-god-without-effect/.
2   Dallas Willard, *The Divine Conspiracy: Rediscovering Our Hidden Life in God* (NewYork: HarperCollins Publishers, 1998), 35-59.
3   For further research, see Allan N. Shore, *Affect Regulation and the Origin of the Self: The Neurobiology of Emotional Development* (New York: Taylor and Francis Group, 1994), 71–91, or Daniel J. Siegel, *The Developing Mind: How Relationships and the Brain Interact to Shape Who We Are.* (New York: Guilford Press, 1999), 239–75.

Chapter 9: Addiction and the Weight of Codependency

1   Ed Khouri, *Restarting Workbook* (Pasadena, CA: Shepherd's House, Inc., 2010), 30.
2   E. James Wilder and Ed Khouri, "Cravings and BEEPS Assessment," *Belonging* (Pasadena, CA: Shepherd's House, Inc., 2010), 120–124.

Chapter 10: An Invitation to Recalculate

1   Anne Casselman, "The Earth Has More Than One North Pole," *Scientific American,* February 28, 2008, https://www.scientificamerican.com/article/the-earth-has-more-than-one-north-pole/.

2   Kenneth Bailey, *Through Peasant Eyes* (Grand Rapids, MI: Wm B Eerdman's Publishing Company, 1980), 95–99.

3   Dallas Willard, *The Divine Conspiracy: Rediscovering Our Hidden Life in God* (New York: HarperCollins, 1998), 301–2.

4   Joseph S. Exell and Henry Donald Maurice Spence-Jones (module created by Rick Meyers), *Pulpit Commentary*, e-Sword version, 10.0.5, 2012.

5   E. James Wilder, *The Pandora Problem: Facing Narcissism in Leaders & Ourselves* (Carmel, IN: Deeper Walk International, 2018), 43.

6   Jim Wilder, email message to author, "New Testament Commands," December 27, 2018.

7   David Blatner, *Spectrums: Our Mind-boggling Universe from Infinitesimal to Infinity* (London: A&C Black, 2013), 20.

8   Greg L. Hawkins, *More: How to Move from Activity for God to Intimacy with God* (New York: Multnomah Press), 41–45.

9   Allan Schore, *Affect Regulation and the Origin of the Self*, Hillsdale, New Jersey: Psychology Press, 1994, 199–200.

10   Schore, 200.

Appendix C: How Do Attachments Grow?

1   E. James Wilder et al., *Joy Starts Here* (Pasadena, CA: Shepherd's House Publishing), 7.

About the Author

ED KHOURI is president and co-founder of Equipping Hearts for the Harvest, a ministry empowering leaders, missionaries, churches, and ministries to serve people, locally and globally. His conference teachings, workshops, writing, and curriculum development offer training and mentoring at the intersection of grace, Scripture, and neuroscience, leading to spiritual transformation.

Ed met Christ in 1978 while attending the University of Maryland. After graduation, he attended and graduated from the police academy in Montgomery County, Maryland. He went on to serve as a police officer for police departments of Montgomery County and, later, the City of Delray Beach, Florida. Recuperating from an on-the-job injury, he sensed God's call to full-time addiction ministry, completing his training through the Servant Leadership Program at Dunklin Memorial Church in Okeechobee, Florida. Since his ordination in 1988, Ed has served as a pastoral counselor, addiction counselor, and Senior Therapist. He is an Elder and small-group coordinator at New Life Church of Taylorsville, North Carolina.

The author of *Restarting* and coauthor of *Joy Starts Here,* Ed resides in Conover, North Carolina, with his wife, Maritza.

Visit www.EquippingHearts.com for *Becoming a Face of Grace* facilitator training and free video resources.

secure attachments dev. thru joy of parents

We lend capacity to oneanother just by being attached. It helps form + complete my identity

secure attachment also grows by quieting (+ joy)

fear causes anxiety + distrust

When life is fear based I try to FIX

Joy w/ others is healing even when life is hard
└ "someone is glad to be w/ me."

The one thg that can grow in my brain is the joy center - + can change me

my brain needs pictures to process

When you isolate due to trauma, does a number on you

CPSIA information can be obtained
at www.ICGtesting.com
Printed in the USA
BVHW080401100222
628500BV00001B/50